D1274753

CAMBRIDGE STUDIES IN CRIMINOLOGY XXXI
*General Editor :* Sir Leon Radzinowicz

# Sentencing the Motoring Offender

THE HEINEMANN LIBRARY OF CRIMINOLOGY
AND PENAL REFORM

# CAMBRIDGE STUDIES IN CRIMINOLOGY

# Sentencing
# the Motoring Offender

A STUDY OF MAGISTRATES' VIEWS
AND PRACTICES

*by*
Roger Hood
*Fellow of Clare Hall*
*and Assistant Director of Research*
*in the Institute of Criminology, Cambridge*

*with the assistance of*
K. W. Elliott *and* Eryl Shirley

HEINEMANN
LONDON

Heinemann Educational Books Ltd
LONDON   EDINBURGH   MELBOURNE   TORONTO
AUCKLAND   SINGAPORE   JOHANNESBURG   KUALA LUMPUR
IBADAN   HONG KONG   NAIROBI   NEW DELHI


ISBN 0 435 82421 X

*Publishers' Note:* This series is continuous with the Cambridge
Studies in Criminology, Volumes I to XIX, published by Macmillan
& Co., London


Published by Heinemann Educational Books Ltd
48 Charles Street, London W1X 8AH

Printed in Great Britain by Butler & Tanner Ltd
Frome and London

# Foreword

## by Sir Leon Radzinowicz

In terms of death, maiming, injury and destruction, motoring offences are the most dangerous and expensive in modern society. In terms of numbers they are the most frequent. More people appear before the magistrates for such trangressions than for any other offence. Yet our attitude to them is ambiguous. The predicament is at its most acute in the courts, since it is there that decisions have to be made about the penalties imposed. Magistrates hear evidence of the appalling consequences of some of these offences, and they dare not minimize their gravity. They see before them motorists, often citizens with blameless records and guilty of more than carelessness, and they are reluctant to class them as criminals. How do they resolve such dilemmas? This is one of the basic questions Dr Hood has set out to answer.

He is eminently qualified for the venture. His well-known *Sentencing in Magistrates' Courts*, has paved the way, and the magistrates themselves have been eager for him to embark upon this further exploration. His methods have broken new ground in this country. Instead of depending upon records, never an adequate basis for such investigations, he has sounded the magistrates direct, by way of interviews and a series of sample cases, and he has evolved a research design which is both original and provocative. He has thus been able to collect information about the social and personal backgrounds of magistrates, to assess their influence upon decisions and to discover what kinds of case produce most disagreement.

Of crucial importance are the differences of attitude amongst magistrates to the relationship between motoring offences and other kinds of crime. These are a major factor in producing discrepancies in sentencing, discrepancies which are widest where the offences are nearest to 'ordinary' crime, in terms of the injury to the victim or the previous record of the motorist.

It emerges, however, that members of a Bench tend to share a common policy. Dr Hood suggests that any attempt to achieve yet further uniformity, by a system of tariffs or basic penalties, would be misguided. It would inhibit the urge to make more explicit the assumptions that underlie sentencing. That kind of questioning is vital. It is not the least of Dr Hood's achievements to have given it this further impetus. His report is remarkably succinct and makes remarkably good reading.

On behalf of the Institute of Criminology I would like to express our great appreciation to Baroness Wootton of Abinger and the other members of the Consultative Committee who have given us so much of their time and so much good advice.

*Cambridge, March* 1972

# Contents

# Membership of the Consultative Committee

The Baroness Wootton of Abinger [Chairman].

Mr T. S. Lodge, C.B.E., Director of Research and Statistics, Home Office Research and Scientific Department.

Mr R. North, J.P., Chairman, Road Traffic Committee and Member of the Council of The Magistrates' Association.

Mr B. Price Francis, O.B.E., LL.B., D.P. A., Clerk to the Justices, City of Coventry.

Mr J. B. Turner, J.P., Member, Council and Executive of The Magistrates' Association.

Dr N. D. Walker, Reader in Criminology, Nuffield College, Oxford.

Mr A. M. F. Webb., C.M.G., Deputy Secretary of Commissions of the Peace, Lord Chancellor's Office.

# Acknowledgements

THE RESEARCH which this book reports has rather a long history. After the publication of my book *Sentencing in Magistrates' Courts* (1962), the Magistrates' Association suggested that I investigate the extent of disparity in sentences imposed by magistrates' courts on motoring offenders. It appealed to me because of the opportunity to extend my previous work to other areas and to try new methods of investigation. The project was financed by the Home Office and a Consultative and Steering Committee was set up with members from the Magistrates' Association and other interested bodies. The pilot work began in 1964 and the main fieldwork, which involved interviewing over five hundred magistrates, was carried out between 1965 and 1967 when I was Lecturer in Social Administration at Durham University. The remaining work was completed in Cambridge.

Throughout the project, and since the fieldwork was completed, there have been some changes in the law, in practice and in the outlook of magistrates, notably through the great expansion of training schemes. I have been very much aware of how the scene can change, and have therefore tried to present the findings of the empirical study in the context of the ever-developing debate surrounding the problem of dealing with motoring offenders in the courts.

Over the years I have been greatly helped by many people and organizations. First I should make clear my belief that the study would not have been possible without the keen support of the Magistrates' Association, the Lord Chancellor's Department, the Justices' Clerks' Society and the Home Office, all of whom laid the foundation for our acceptance as *bona fide* researchers by the vast majority of magistrates we approached. In particular, I would like to thank the members of the Consultative and Steering Committee who advised me at all stages and provided access to the records of Magistrates' Association Committees. Nevertheless, I especially want to make it clear that none of these bodies is in any way necessarily associated with, or responsible for, the views presented in this book.

My main helpers in carrying out the survey and in dealing with the data were, as indicated on the title page, Mr Kenneth Elliott and Miss Eryl Shirley, who were employed at different stages as full-time research workers. Mr Elliott was in at the beginning, tirelessly helping with the collection of material for the pilot stage and then undertaking, at great personal sacrifice, the task of travelling round the country to interview almost all the magistrates. It was due to his tact and wisdom that so many eventually agreed to become the subjects of research—and, I venture to say, to enjoy the experience. He was also in charge of coding most of the data (before leaving in 1967) and at the end patiently read my manuscript and gave extremely helpful advice based on his exceptional experience. Miss Shirley joined me for a year at the end of 1969 as the statistician responsible for analysing the data concerned with the spread of sentences and the relationship between the social and personal backgrounds of magistrates and their sentencing decisions. She not only developed the necessary computer programmes and made the decisions on how best to handle the voluminous array of data but presented the results in a clear form as a basis for my report. At a later stage she also read the manuscript and gave valuable advice in dispelling my statistical misconceptions. The statistical appendix was drafted by Miss Shirley.

I am also grateful to Dr Terence Willett for advice and co-operation at the planning stage; to Rodney Coleman who undertook some early statistical analysis on a part-time basis and who, with his student, Richard Heagerty, helped me to analyse the 'decision-making game' which is reported in Chapter 6; to Patricia Brantingham for the substantial assistance with computer programmes; and to Dr David Darwent, who aided Mr Elliott with the interviews for a short period. I wish also to thank all those who helped with coding and secretarial work, especially Miss Margaret Guy, who carefully transcribed many drafts. My colleagues Richard Sparks and David Thomas made a number of very helpful comments on the manuscript. Naturally, I am extremely grateful to all those magistrates and clerks who gave so freely of their time and ideas. I hope that in return the study may prove to be of some interest and value to them.

I wish finally to thank Sir Leon Radzinowicz, who welcomed my continuing concern with this study when I came to Cambridge from Durham in 1967. He has not only wholeheartedly encouraged me to complete it, but at the stage when drafts were confused, messy and disordered, helped me enormously to impose a framework for the final version.

# CHAPTER 1

# The Problem

ABOUT a million persons appear each year before magistrates' courts charged with offences relating to motor vehicles. Nearly all plead or are found guilty.[1] Many still seem to feel a sense of grievance. They may blame the police for prosecuting them but their main complaints seem to be directed against the sentences imposed by the magistrates. These complaints are due partly to ignorance about the principles on which sentences are decided and partly to a genuine belief that there are gross disparities in the penalties given to offenders who have committed the same kind of offence and have similar personal circumstances.

The objects of this research are both practical and theoretical. On the practical side it sets out simply to chart the extent to which disparities exist. At the same time it attempts to expose the theoretical basis of sentencing by studying the views of magistrates about the motoring offender and his punishment and treatment; thus, it is hoped, providing a basis for explaining sentencing disparity. An entirely new method of inquiry has been used in an attempt to overcome some of the problems which have plagued earlier studies of judicial decision-making.

Motoring offenders were chosen originally because of the practical interest of the Magistrates' Association. After the publication of *Sentencing in Magistrates' Courts* in 1962 (which dealt with variations in practice in the sentencing of indictable cases, mostly theft,

---

[1] In 1964, when this research was first suggested, 839,684 persons were convicted at magistrates' courts in England and Wales. In 1967, when the field work was completed, the number was 1,043,115 and in 1969 it was 974,334. The increase over this period has been much greater for some offences than others. For example, the total number of findings of guilt (not persons) for driving while disqualified was 6,653 in 1964 and 10,968 in 1969; for driving under the influence of drink or drugs the figures rose from 5,980 to 21,742 (largely due, it seems, to the Road Safety Act 1967). The only two serious offences for which there was a decline in numbers were dangerous driving (8,459 in 1964; 6,716 in 1969) and failing to stop after an accident (19,193 in 1964 and 10,968 in 1969).

by twelve magistrates' courts)[1] the editor of *The Magistrate* pointed out that 'the field of motoring penalties offers the most promising opportunity for magisterial efforts at rationalisation since traffic offences are on the whole more of a kind and easier to "price" than indictable offences'.[2] The Association then asked me if I would be interested in carrying out an inquiry into the disparities in sentencing traffic offenders. Originally their suggestion was that it should focus on relatively minor cases 'since these do provoke the most widespread criticism',[3] but it seemed likely that this would become a routine accountancy exercise.[4] Simply to show for any offence the average fines and the range between minimum and maximum would provide no insight into why the disparities existed or what kinds of opinions were held by magistrates on the offence and its appropriate punishment. Whatever the degree of disparity eventually found, it seemed essential that the ideas lying behind sentencing practice should be open to scrutiny. There is no virtue in adopting the 'average' practice if it cannot be supported either logically, in terms of a coherent penal policy, or on the basis of the results it achieves. This inquiry concentrated therefore on the aims, assumptions and perceptions of magistrates and their relationship to sentencing practice. A parallel but independent study by Dr Terence Willett examined the effects of a sentence on the offender.[5]

The Road Traffic Acts cover an enormous range of offences. They are all concerned with the convenience and safety of the public, but clearly the 'convenience' offences, such as parking for over the prescribed limit in a restricted zone, are regarded differently from those which endanger life, such as dangerous and drunken driving, or which fail to protect persons or property, such as not insuring vehicles or reporting accidents, or which flout an order of the court, such as driving whilst disqualified. The convenience or purely regulative offences are being dealt with increasingly by fixed penalty notices so that the offender pays a standard fine (just as he pays for

---

[1] Roger Hood (1962), *Sentencing in Magistrates' Courts: a study in variations of policy*, London, Stevens. Reprinted as a Social Science Paperback, 1969.

[2] *The Magistrate*, *18* (1962), 147.

[3] Private correspondence from the Secretary, J. F. Madden.

[4] In fact, at a later date information on fines was collected by the Lord Chancellor and the Home Office and was used to calculate, for each Petty Sessional Division, the average fine and the distribution. The results were sent to all Clerks to Justices in 1968. Home Office Circular No. 249/1968. *Fines imposed for speeding offences.*

[5] This work is not yet published, but for a general review of the few studies of the effects of penalties on motoring offenders see Wolf Middendorf (1968), 'Is there a relationship between traffic offences and common crimes?' *Int. Criminal Police Review*, No. 214 (Jan. 1968), 4–13.

overdue books at the public library) without a conviction being recorded. Among the other offences, however, discussion about appropriate penalties has been bedevilled by at least three—sometimes conflicting—considerations. First, there is the question of the extent to which they can be considered in the same light as 'ordinary' crime such as larceny and assault. The normal tests of *mens rea* (or deliberate intent) are both difficult to prove and confounded by another important variable—the degree of harm caused or the potential danger involved. The point is illustrated by the lack of any clear distinction between dangerous and careless driving[1] and the tremendous difficulty in deciding whether a driver who deliberately overtakes on a bend at night and causes no accident has committed a worse offence than someone who, through lack of attention, has driven from a minor on to a major road and caused severe injuries to several people. Or, to take another example, whether a driver who deliberately goes at 40 m.p.h. in an area restricted to 30 differs in any important respect from the man who simply failed to look at his speedometer. Second, even where there is *mens rea*, there is strong public rejection of the idea that offences which are commonly committed by people from all social classes and, to some extent, tolerated and joked about can really be classed as 'crime': certainly the offenders do not wish to be considered as 'criminals'. Examples include drunken driving and exceeding the speed limits. It still seems to be considered unfortunate if one is 'breathalysed' or caught in a radar trap,[2] and it is only when the consequences are made explicit through accidental serious injury or death that the terms 'crime' and 'criminal' are likely to be used. Even then they will probably be avoided if the offender can prove 'respectability'. It is indeed enlightening that the main interest of Willett's *Criminal on the road* lay in his claim[3]

[1] See Glanville Williams (1967), 'Absolute liability in traffic offences', *Crim. L. R.*, 142–51 and (especially) 194–208.

[2] See H. Mannheim (1964). 'It is in fact the prevailing popular theory that these unfortunate victims of the motor age have been brought into the sphere of the criminal law and criminal courts only by a deplorable combination of legal tricks and social and moral judgements which should be put right without delay.' In Foreword to T. C. Willett, *Criminal on the road*, London, Tavistock. And Barbara Wootton (1963) says, 'with the possible exception of drunken driving, hardly any guilt [in its psychological sense] today attaches to motoring offences, even those of a quite deliberate nature which cannot be laughed off as due to incompetence or carelessness.' *Crime and the criminal law*, London, Stevens, 25.

[3] Later analyses of his data did, of course, indicate that those who had been convicted of driving while disqualified or failing to insure were much more likely to have previous convictions for non-indictable offences than were dangerous or drunken drivers—and Willett's sample also did not include careless drivers. See D. J. Steer and R. A. Carr-Hill (1967), 'The motoring offender—who is he?' *Crim. L. R.*, 214–24.

that a significantly large minority of those convicted of the more serious offences were 'criminals' because they had convictions for other 'real' crimes—not because of their motoring offences alone. There is, then, a resistance to being treated in court 'like a criminal', and this has implications not only for procedure but also for the kind of information that is collected, the way it is perceived and interpreted, and the sorts of penalties considered appropriate. This is the crux of the third point. In the face of rising accidents and deaths there is an understandable concern to use the law, as far as possible, as a means of prevention, for without doubt motoring offences as a whole lead to far more deaths, injuries and destruction of property than do those offences which are called 'real' crimes of violence. Yet a preventive system would undoubtedly entail an individualized approach to sentencing which would attempt to distinguish between those who are unlikely to repeat their offence and can be dealt with by a nominal penalty and those who are really dangerous either because of anti-social attitudes or because of sheer incompetence. But to find out who falls into which category involves asking precisely those questions which are asked about the ordinary criminal and ultimately leads to a complex system of penalties in which (at least to the citizen observing from outside) there is no clear correspondence between the offence actually committed and the penalty received. As far as motoring offences are concerned the public view of justice certainly seems to demand a retributive or tariff approach based on the gravity of the offence committed with (perhaps) mitigation of the fine for those with low incomes. A problem might arise in agreeing on what criteria are admissible as evidence of the gravity of the offence, but considerations of future recidivism would rarely be considered relevant. It is for this reason that criticism of variations in penalties for motoring offences is particularly strong. This criticism is taken seriously precisely because it comes from those who do not regard themselves as criminals; those, indeed, to whom the courts normally look for moral support.[1]

Magistrates obviously face a problem in deciding how to perceive the motoring offender. They have to administer a system of penalties which adequately distinguishes between offences of different gravity, appears to be effective in preventing bad driving, *and*, at the same time, 'fair'.

It is because the subject is so complex, because it is important to understand how magistrates perceive the problems facing them, and because we need to understand the principles on which they operate,

[1] This is discussed further on pages 105–8.

Case 1   1. View of road in daylight

Case 1   2. View of road in opposite direction

Case 1   3. View of vehicles at scene of accident

Case 1 4. View of vehicles from opposite direction

that this study goes much further than examining disparities in sentencing. Everyone knows that these disparities exist, and we knew at the very start of the project that they were due to some extent to the way in which different systems of 'basic penalties' were being operated[1] even in adjacent courts. At the time this inquiry was launched the view that sentences for motoring offenders should be 'rationalized' had received considerable support. Many magistrates wished to have, either at a local or national level, a commonly agreed list of basic penalties for an average case: a guide to be considered in relation to the usual aggravating and mitigating circumstances surrounding the nature of the offence and the circumstances of the offender. Whether there was in fact common agreement on what these circumstances would be, or what *weight* would be attached to particular factors such as a previous conviction for a similar offence or the defendant's financial means, or what these factors *indicated* in relation to the most appropriate penalty and disqualification, was not discussed at the time. This was probably because there was (and still is) a widespread belief, which the editor of *The Magistrate* stressed, that the 'differing opinions on morality, penology, culpability, responsibility, deterrence and reform, probation and mercy'[2] which are found in relation to indictable offences, such as theft, do not exist to the same extent so far as traffic offenders are concerned. There is obviously a great deal of truth in this when minor offences relating to parking, lighting and even speeding are considered, but it is less obviously true for drunken and dangerous driving, driving while disqualified, failing to insure and, perhaps, careless driving and failing to stop after or to report an accident. We knew nothing about the range of views on the aims of sentencing and the merits of disqualification and alternative new methods of treatment, the conception of the motoring offender and the offence he had committed. Furthermore, the amount of data available about the magistrates themselves was both limited and out of date. It was my intention therefore to try to show whether personal and social background as well as driving experience were related to different attitudes and sentencing practice or whether the basic penalty approach, so much in use for these cases, was an overriding factor.

This research, then, is part of a recent development in criminology away from a sole interest in the offender towards a concern to understand the behaviour and assumptions of those whom sociologists like to call 'agents of social control'. For it is the views of these 'agents'—here the magistracy—which may reflect, or be

---

[1] This term and variants of it are discussed on pages 66–70.
[2] *The Magistrate, 18* (1962), 147.

reflected in, the way offenders of different sorts are perceived, categorized or labelled both in court and by the community as a whole.[1]

The complexity of some cases which magistrates face is illustrated by the following three examples. Each one is a transcript of what was heard in court. They are examples of the kind of sentencing problem which was given to magistrates in this inquiry: their use in the research is fully explained in the next chapter.[2] Readers may find it an interesting exercise to decide what they would consider the appropriate penalty for each case. (See Appendix IV, Table 3.)

### Case 1 (Group A)

DEFENDANT: S.S.E., 22 years

CHARGE:
(a) Driving a motor car in a dangerous manner. Section 2 R.T.A. 1960.

PLEA:
The defendant appeared in person. He elected summary trial and pleaded not guilty to the charge. He was represented by a solicitor. A sketch plan and four photographs were available to the magistrates (copies attached).

PROSECUTION CASE:
The prosecutor said that the proceedings arose from an accident which occurred at 11 p.m. on a Friday in February. It had been raining lightly and the roads were wet. A Ford Popular motor car was being driven by a witness along a length of straight, well-lighted road in a semi-rural area. It was being followed by a Standard motor car driven by the defendant.

As both these cars were approaching the brow of the hill in the direction shown in photograph 2, the Standard car, driven by the defendant, drew out to overtake the Ford car and collided head-on with a Ford Cortina car travelling in the opposite direction.

It was the submission of the prosecution that this was an atrocious piece of driving. The Standard car had overtaken the Ford at a fast speed approaching the brow of a hill and the prosecutor said this was very dangerous driving.

The first witness was the driver of the Ford Cortina car which was travelling in the opposite direction to the defendant. He said just before

---

[1] See Note 2, page 27.
[2] These are three of the forty cases sent to a sample of magistrates for their consideration. The code number (e.g. Case 8) will be referred to later in the text. The group letter (e.g., Group B) is used to identify each case in Tables, 3, 4, 5 and 6 of Appendix IV. For each kind of offence (e.g., dangerous driving) there were five types of cases identified as A, B, C, D, E. Case 1 above is the dangerous driving case A; Case 6, the driving while disqualified case Group A; Case 8, the careless driving case Group B. The meaning of this notation is fully explained in Chapter 2.

the accident he was driving his car in the direction shown in photograph 1. His brother was a passenger with him. It was very dark. There had been slight rain. The street lamps were lit and he was driving on dipped headlights. Looking at photograph No. 1, the witness said as he was coming up to the top of the hill shown in the photograph he saw two pairs of headlights coming towards him. One set of headlights was on his side of the road and the other was on the opposite side, that is, on the near side for a car travelling in the opposite direction to him. He had no idea how fast they were travelling. He realized that an accident could not be avoided. He had either to hit one of the vehicles or run off the road. There was a lamp standard on his near side and he tried to go between the car which was on its wrong side, that is, the defendant's car, and the lamp standard. He was travelling at about 28–30 m.p.h. which may seem rather slow, but he intended to turn left a bit further on and he had begun to slow down. He was not able to get between the lamp standard and the defendant's car and there was a collision between them. Looking at photograph No. 3, that was how the cars finished up, and photograph 4 was a photograph taken from the opposite direction.

As a result of the accident he had a cut leg and two hair-line fractures. His brother, the passenger in his car, was seriously injured about the face and legs. It was a heavy impact. He, the witness, had been wearing a safety belt but his passenger had not.

Cross-examined, he said photograph 1 showed the view which he had as he approached the brow of the hill. He was about 50 yards from the crest when he first saw the headlights. The collision actually happened over the crest of the hill. He would estimate 20–30 yards, perhaps 40 over the crest when the cars actually collided. He assumed from the position of the two sets of headlights that there were two cars overtaking and, the witness said, he was quite sure the defendant's car was still on the wrong side of the road when his car collided with it. The defendant's car and the small Ford car, on its proper side, were almost abreast when the defendant's car collided with the witness's car. The witness said he did not see the other car, that is, the Ford Popular car, turning to its near side. He was watching the defendant's car and he was steering close into his own near side, moving left to try to avoid the defendant's car. He could not say at what speed the two cars coming towards him were travelling; he was travelling at 25–28 m.p.h. He knew the road was restricted at this particular point. The defendant had come out of a de-restricted area into a restricted area a little bit farther back along the road. He had had to judge by impression to some extent. It was dark at the time of the accident and he would not say that he could see entirely clearly.

Re-examined, the witness said that a driver travelling in the direction he was, could not see anything coming up the rise from the opposite direction until right on the crest of the hill.

The next witness was the brother of the driver of the Ford Cortina car. He said he was a passenger in his brother's car at the time of the accident. Looking at photograph 1, it showed the view of the road along which they were travelling. The witness himself did not drive and had not been paying a lot of attention to what was going on. He could not remember what the weather conditions or the lighting were like, but he could remember looking out from the car and seeing two sets of headlights coming towards him. They were spread out across the road. There were four lights and they all seemed to be abreast. When he first saw them he would estimate that his car was near to the first lamp-post on the left-hand side of the road shown in photograph 1.

There was a collision and the next thing he remembered was sitting outside the car.

Cross-examined, the witness said their car was not travelling fast. He could not say how many miles per hour but it was what he would call a moderate speed. They were well into the near side in the left-hand lane. He just saw the lights, then there was a bump and he went through the windscreen.

The driver of the Ford Popular car, which was travelling in the same direction as the defendant, said he was travelling along the road in the direction shown in photograph 2. His car was showing sidelights and one dipped headlight. He was 2–3 feet from the kerb and he was travelling at about 30 m.p.h. as he approached the brow of the hill. Just after the 30 m.p.h. restriction signs he realized that a car was overtaking him. It had its indicators flashing and he would estimate its speed as between 35–40 m.p.h. His impression was that this car, which subsequently turned out to be driven by the defendant, started to overtake him when he was between the first lamp-post on the right-hand side of the road shown on photograph 2 and the hut between the first and second lamp-posts.

When they got near to the brow of the hill a car came from the opposite direction. There was a collision between the overtaking car and the car travelling in the opposite direction. He heard a clatter at the side of him and then the overtaking car shot across the front of him so close that he could not avoid colliding with it. The witness said his car hit the defendant's car and then he, the witness, swerved hard to his left to try to avoid hitting it again. His impression was that the collision between the defendant's car and the car travelling in the other direction happened when the defendant's car was just behind him, that was to say, just behind the driver's seat of his car, but alongside the car.

Cross-examined, the witness said he first became aware of the defendant's car overtaking when it was coming up fast behind him. He was then 2–3 feet from the kerb. The width of his car was 4′ 6″. He could not describe the position of the overtaking car, except to say that he realized it was on his off side. He could not say how far it was from the off side of his car. He did not see the car coming in the opposite direction until they were almost on the brow of the hill. It was raining at the time and his windscreen-wipers were working. He would estimate that the defendant's car, when it was overtaking him, would be travelling 5–10 miles an hour faster than he, the witness, was travelling. He would not have considered the speed excessive had the vehicle overtaken him at a different point on the road.

He would estimate that the collision between the cars happened less than 30–40 yards from the crest of the hill. He could not say what the exact distance was. In his estimation it was near the hut shown in photograph No. 2. After the collision the defendant's car went in front of him. The witness said he was reducing speed but he could not have avoided colliding with the defendant's car in any case, because it came across the front of him, travelling diagonally towards the kerb. It stopped in the position shown in the sketch plan and in the photographs. The collision between the witness's car and the defendant's car was more of a scrape than a bump. He did not notice any marks on the road.

Re-examined, the witness said that it was his impression that the defendant, in the overtaking car, had swung the wheel away from whatever it was that the car had collided with. That was the reason the defendant's car came diagonally across the front of his. He did not think that the defendant was pulling back into the nearside lane trying to avoid the other car.

A passenger in a car following the defendant's was called and he said that they were following the Standard car, driven by the defendant, at about 30 m.p.h. He saw the flashing indicators of the Standard car indicating that it was going to overtake a Ford Popular. In his estimation, the Standard began to overtake the Ford just before the first lamp-post on the left-hand side of the road shown on photograph 2. He did not think it was a good place to overtake, because of the brow of the hill. He thought the Standard driver was cutting it rather fine to get back onto his own side before reaching the crest of the hill. The next thing he saw was the brake lights on the Popular car come on. They were about 30 yards from the Popular when the brake lights came on. His driver, a provisional licence holder, braked hard and their car skidded into the rear of the Ford Popular car.

Cross-examined, the witness said they were about 30 yards behind the Standard car, driven by the defendant, when it began to overtake the Ford Popular. The indicators were switched on and the defendant pulled into the middle of the road. It was his view that even when they were straight abreast and overtaking, the Standard car was still on the crown of the road with the Ford Popular in the nearside lane. He did not think that it was right over on the off side of the white line. He could not say how many yards from the brow of the hill the Standard car was when it began to overtake. He did not see the car coming in the opposite direction until after it had collided with the defendant's car.

A police officer gave evidence that he visited the scene and took photographs and measurements to prepare a sketch plan. The Ford Popular car had been moved before he arrived. It began to rain a short time after he arrived. Sodium street lights were on and gave a good light. As far as he was able to ascertain, the collision between the Ford Cortina car and the defendant's car took place near the second lamp-post on the right looking at photograph 2. That lamp-post was the one shown on the sketch plan. It was also near to the hut shown in photograph 2. The constable

said that he saw the defendant at the scene of the accident and asked him
to explain what had happened. The defendant was cautioned and he made
a statement which read as follows:

> Somewhere around 11 o'clock on a Friday night in February, I was
> driving my Standard Vanguard car. I was following a Ford Popular car
> as we were going up the bank. It was not travelling as fast as us. The
> road in front of us was clear and I put my right indicator on to overtake
> the Ford. I have flashing indicators and they were working. I overtook
> the Ford in second gear—it's a three-speed gear box. I had passed the
> Ford and was beginning to swing into the left in front of him when I
> saw a car approaching fast showing only side-lights. This car was
> coming down-bank straight at me. I was swinging in to go to my own
> side of the road when I was hit by this other car. He hit my right front
> wing. If I had braked the fellow behind would have rammed me. I had
> my side lights on at the time. The road is well lit.

DEFENDANT'S CASE:
The defendant in evidence agreed that he had made the statement which
had been read. He was driving his Standard car following the Ford
Popular. Photograph 2 showed the view he had of the road. He said he
remembered pulling out to overtake the Ford Popular. It was well into the
near side of the road, and the road ahead was clear. He looked in his
mirror, put on his indicators and, as there was still nothing coming from
ahead of him, he pulled on to the crown of the road and began to overtake.
His offside wheels were about two feet to the off side of the white line. He
began to overtake the Ford Popular when they were near the first lamp-
post on the left-hand side in photograph 2. He was sure it was before the
restriction sign. There was nothing coming. The road ahead was clear and
he saw no danger in overtaking. Then he saw the other car coming
towards him. It was on the crown of the road. He realized that part of the
vehicles must be in line so he started to swing into the left and accelerated
in order to get clear of the on-coming car. He had not time to do so before
the two cars collided. It was the front off sides of the vehicles which
collided. The defendant said he swung his car to the left in an effort to
miss the collision and as this was happening the Ford Popular, which he
had been overtaking, scraped against the rear near side corner of his car.
That was because he swung in trying to miss the other car. It was not
because he was cutting in. He stopped in front of the Ford Popular in the
position shown in the sketch plan and the photographs. He could not say
what lights the Ford Cortina car had on as it came towards him.

Cross-examined, the defendant said he was not in a hurry at the time of
the accident. There were four passengers, all female, in the car with him.
He did not see any headlights on the car approaching him. When he saw
any lights at all they were on the crown of the road. There was plenty of
room to pass to the off side of him had the driver of the oncoming car
moved over from the crown of the road. He knew, said the defendant,
what the Highway Code said about overtaking at the brow of a hill,
but in this case the road was clear and he was sure that he had time to

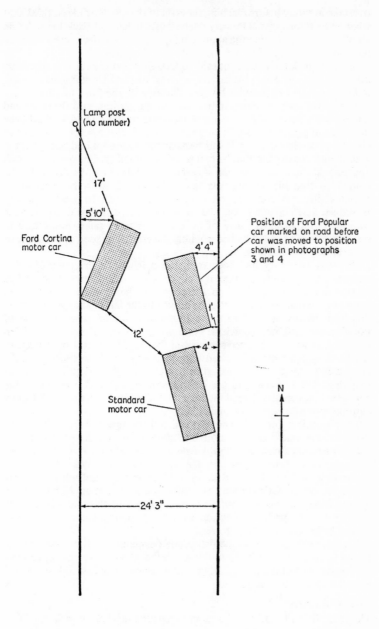

Lamp post (no number)

17'

5' 10"

Ford Cortina motor car

Position of Ford Popular car marked on road before car was moved to position shown in photographs 3 and 4

4' 4"

1'

12'

4'

Standard motor car

N

24' 3"

overtake in safety before reaching the crest of the hill. He did not think that what he had done was extremely dangerous. He had cut back to the left in an effort to avoid hitting the approaching car which had sufficient room to pass on the off side of him.

Re-examined, the defendant said he thought the other car was travelling fast. The angle at which his car came to rest resulted from it being pushed in front of the Ford Popular by the collision with the Ford Cortina car.

The defendant's solicitor, addressing the magistrates, said the court had undoubtedly heard of many similar incidents to the one which had been described in evidence. Usually these incidents appeared before the court as charges of careless driving. It was because the defendant had been charged with dangerous driving that he had pleaded not guilty. The defendant well appreciated there was a degree of carelessness in the way he drove, but he contended that his driving was not dangerous. It was the defendant's responsibility, said the solicitor, to see that it was safe to overtake before he did so. The defendant said that it was safe, that he began to overtake sufficiently far from the brow of the hill to do so in safety and return to his own side of the road before reaching the crest. The road at the scene of the accident was 24′ 3″ wide.

The way the story had been told, the defendant's driving was being made to seem much worse than it really was. The defendant had said when he saw the car approaching on the crown of the road he realized there would be a collision unless either he moved to the left or the oncoming car did. The defendant tried to move to the left but because of the Ford Popular car had not sufficient space to get clear before the collision occurred. It was the defence submission that he did not cut in in front of the Ford Popular car. What had happened was that he collided with the approaching car and was pushed in front of the Ford Popular. The fact that the Ford Popular and the defendant's car collided was due to the collision between the defendant's car and the Ford Cortina, not to any cutting in on the part of the defendant.

Leaving this point aside, said the solicitor, it appeared from the sketch plan that the road was wide enough to allow three vehicles to pass. It was the prosecution's case that the defendant was right on the off side, but there was some doubt about this. The defendant said he was on the crown of the road and the driver of the Ford Popular car could not say exactly where the defendant's car was as it was overtaking. It could be that the approaching car was well out from its near side of the road. This could account for the point of collision with the defendant's car and the way in which the two cars came to rest.

On the evidence and on the defendant's explanation, the solicitor said, he felt justified in submitting to the bench that there was a case of careless driving but not of dangerous driving, and therefore he asked them to deal with the case in that way.

ADJUDICATION:
The magistrates found the charge of dangerous driving proved.

ANTECEDENTS:
The prosecutor said that there was nothing known to the detriment of
the defendant. The prosecution costs amounted to £5 16s. 1d. and there was
an Advocate's fee of £5. 5s. 0d.

## Case 6 (Group A)

DEFENDANT: W.R., 30 years, unemployed

CHARGES:
(a) Driving a motor lorry whilst disqualified. Section 110 R.T.A. 1960.
(b) Using a motor lorry without insurance. Section 201 R.T.A. 1960.
(c) Taking motor lorry without the owner's consent. Section 217 R.T.A.
1960.

PLEA:
The defendant appeared in court in custody, having been remanded to
prison at an earlier hearing. He elected summary trial and pleaded guilty
to each of the offences; he was not legally represented. A charge of stealing
a motor lorry was dismissed before the defendant pleaded to it, the
prosecutor offering no evidence.

PROSECUTION'S STATEMENT OF FACTS:
The prosecutor said that the defendant appeared before the court as a
consequence of an unhappy chain of events which had taken place over a
period of a few days some three months before the hearing. The defendant
was a wanderer by nature and had been working away from home. On
occasions he had been employed by his brother-in-law, a scrap-metal
dealer at Leeds, who was the owner of a motor lorry. At the time of the
events leading up to the charges this lorry was based at Salford. The
scrap-metal dealer visited Salford and discovered that his lorry was missing
from where it was customarily parked. He reported this to the police.
Enquiries were made as a result of which the defendant was interviewed at
his home some 200 miles from Salford. At the time of the interview, the
defendant was not in possession of the motor lorry and denied having
taken it from Salford or knowing where it was. Police enquiries were
continued in the locality of the defendant's home and some ten days after
the defendant was first interviewed the lorry was found on a car park near
the defendant's home.

The owner of the lorry was notified that it had been found and asked to
collect it from the car park. Two days later when he came to collect the
lorry he found it was missing again, and reported this to the police. Police
enquiries failed to discover the lorry and nothing could be traced to
indicate that the defendant was responsible for its removal either from
the parking place at Salford or from the parking place near his home.

Six weeks after the lorry had been taken from the car park near the
defendant's home, the defendant went to the local police station and said

to a detective 'I have come to give myself up about the lorry, I drove it away from the car park here and I brought it here from Salford.' He said he took the lorry from the car park near his home and drove it to Liverpool, a distance of 200–250 miles. There he had left it. He had last seen the lorry when he parked it in a car park in Liverpool, on the outskirts of the city, three or four weeks earlier. He admitted that he had been driving the lorry between the time that he took it from Salford to the time when he left it at Liverpool.

It was pointed out to the defendant that he was disqualified for driving for five years, some 2½ years before these events, and consequently the vehicle was not covered by insurance during the time he was using it. He said, 'Yes, I understand I am disqualified. I took the lorry from the car park but I didn't intend to steal it.'

When he was cautioned and charged with stealing the motor lorry, taking it without the owner's consent, driving it while disqualified and using it without insurance, he made no reply. The prosecutor said that the defendant had asked that the additional offence of taking the motor lorry without the owner's consent from Salford should be taken into consideration when the magistrates dealt with him for taking the lorry from the car park in his home district.

DEFENDANT'S STATEMENT OF MITIGATION:
The defendant made a statement of mitigation to the bench in which he said that the offences were committed on the spur of the moment. As the prosecutor had said, he was of a wandering nature and frequently worked away from home. At the time he took the lorry from Salford there were domestic difficulties at home and he wanted to go home to see his wife so he took the lorry to do so. The lorry was his brother-in-law's and he did not realize when he took it that it was not insured. He asked the magistrates to consider a letter which he handed to them, and added that if the court felt able to give him a chance he could get work straight away and was hopeful of being able to avoid the separation which his wife was threatening.

The defendant called a former employer for whom he had worked in his home district. The employer said that the defendant had come to him some three years ago when he came out of prison. He had then worked for the employer for two years until he began to feel restless, and eventually left the job to work away from home. The employer said that during the time the defendant worked for him he had been very trustworthy, a good worker and timekeeper—a workman he could always rely on. The employer said he would give the defendant a job as soon as a vacancy arose, and he anticipated this would be very soon, within a few days.

ANTECEDENTS:
The police history showed that the defendant was 30 years old, married with two children, aged four and two years. He had had an elementary education. As a boy he twice appeared before a juvenile court and at the age of eleven was sent to an approved school for truanting from school.

On leaving school at the age of 15 he joined the Army as a boy soldier but was discharged on his being committed to Borstal training at the age of 18. Since his discharge from Borstal he had had frequent jobs of a labouring nature, as a furniture remover and in general dealing, but he seemed not to be able to settle to any one job and usually gave up a job to work away from home. He was unemployed at the time of his appearance and was not in receipt of any benefits from unemployment or national assistance sources. His wife was the tenant of a three-bedroomed house, the rent of which was £1 3s. 0d. a week. The attached list of convictions was made known to the bench.

A probation officer's report, a copy of which is attached, was also handed to the bench.

| Time before present hearing | Where Tried | Offence | Sentence |
|---|---|---|---|
| 12 years | Assizes | Shopbreaking (2 cases) (3 cases t.i.c.) | Borstal Training |
| 10 years | Magistrates' Court | Larceny | 14 days' imprisonment Recalled to Borstal |
| 9 years | Quarter Sessions | Larceny | 6 months' imprisonment |
| 3½ years | Quarter Sessions | Storebreaking | 12 months' imprisonment |
| 2½ years | Magistrates' Court | Taking motor vehicle without owner's consent | 2 months' imprisonment |
| | | Dangerous Driving | 3 months' imprisonment |
| | | No Insurance | 1 month's imprisonment consecutive Disqualified 5 years |
| 1½ years | Magistrates' Court | Attempted Club-house-breaking | 6 months' imprisonment |
| 1 year | Magistrates' Court | Larceny | 3 months' imprisonment |

## DEFENDANT'S LETTER

Youre Worships, I have never stood in Court before and pleaded for a chanse as I am doing now, you will see from my Record, I have been in Prison a number of times, and have been sent to Prison every time I have been brought before the Court for breaking the law.

But this time, I'm begging you to give me a chanse on probation, for I know I will take this as my final chance, Sirs and Madames, I have given a lot of thought, to the way of life I've been living in and out of Prison, and I realise life is no good that way, I am now 30 years old and have a wife and two small children to think of, and if I don't do the right things in life, I will loose everything that matters in life to me, for my wife has told me if I go to Prison, she is through with me, even tho she still loves me, for she doesn't know how I'm going to end up in life, youre Worships you must know, that at one time in a lifetime of a person, thay say a thing and really and truly mean to do it. Well I am saying it now, I mean to stay out of trouble and do only the things that are right, youre Worships, I gave myself up to the Police for this charge to get everything over, so that I could get everything over, and go out and try my hardest to get the respect back people once had for me, and to work hard for my wife and two children, and keep out of trouble, and live a good and honest life, your Worships, I Beg you to give me this once chance in life, so that I can show you and everyone els. I can and will do what is right.

Your Worships, I leave myself at youre mercy, hoping you will kindly show leaniency to my plea for this one chance of a lifetime, to show what I can do. And most of all to save my marrage from breaking up.

Youre Worships
I remain Your Humble and Obediant
Servant,
W.R.

Confidential

## PROBATION OFFICER'S REPORT

| Full Name: | W.R. | Born 5.12.34. | Age 30 |
|---|---|---|---|
| Religion: | R.C. | Occupation: Unemployed | |

Offence (or matter before the Court): Taking motor vehicle without owner's consent. Previous Orders of the Court: As given by police.

*Family*
*Defendant—30 years. Unemployed*
    *Wife—25 years. Housewife and part-time cleaner.*
    *Son— 4 years.*
*Daughter— 2 years.*

The wife resides at the above address with her children and her grandfather, who is in ill health and bedridden during the winter months.

The couple were married some seven years ago and since that time have been separated on at least twelve occasions. The wife states that at various times she has left her home in order to live with her husband and make a fresh start, but each time she has had to get in touch with her family to obtain assistance to get back home.

When the defendant appeared in Court on remand last week, he informed your Worships that he was able to return home to his wife and children should he be allowed to do so. Having interviewed his wife I find that she is, in fact, taking proceedings in order to obtain a separation from her husband and there is at this time little chance of reconciliation.

The defendant is at present unemployed but has only been so for about a month and I believe he has always been a good worker when employed. He was for some time—approximately three years—employed by a local Furniture Remover, who speaks highly of him as a worker. Nevertheless, at the present time he is unemployed and says that if free to do so he will possibly return to London where the prospects are much better than locally.

This report was prepared on the request of the defendant, and as stated previously I interviewed his wife to see if there was any way in which the Probation Service could be of assistance. Bearing in mind the matrimonial situation and the record of this man, however, it would seem that supervision along the lines which probation affords would be inappropriate in his case.

Signed:

Probation Officer

## Case 8 (Group B)

DEFENDANT: N.U.N., 28 years, Demolition Worker

CHARGES:
(a) Driving a motor car without due care and attention. Section 3 R.T.A. 1960.
(b) Failing to stop after an accident. Section 77(1) R.T.A. 1960.
(c) Failing to report an accident. Section 77(2) R.T.A. 1960.

PLEA:
The defendant did not appear in person. He was represented by a solicitor who pleaded guilty to all the charges. A sketch plan was available to the magistrates (copy attached).

PROSECUTION STATEMENT OF FACTS:
The prosecutor told the bench that the proceedings arose out of an accident which occurred in a side turning off a main thoroughfare in a built-up area close to a town centre. The accident occurred at 10.55 p.m. on a Saturday in December, in a side street, the width of which was 22 feet. The road surface was of tar macadam, in good repair. The street was lighted and visibility was moderately good at the time, although it was raining heavily.

In the side street, and some distance from its junction with the main thoroughfare, a motor car had been parked by its owner on the near side of the road outside his house. The parked car was showing a parking light. Immediately before the accident, two pedestrians were walking along the street on the footpath approaching the parked car from the front. They would have told the magistrates that they saw a motor car, driven by the defendant, coming along the road towards them and approaching the parked car from its rear. The car was travelling along the centre of the road and the two pedestrians would have said that they expected it to pass the parked car without any difficulty. However, when it was a few feet from the rear of the parked car, it suddenly swerved to its near side and ran into the back of it. It then reversed away from the parked car and drove off towards the main thoroughfare at a fast speed. Both the pedestrians took the registration number of the motor car.

Another witness would have told the magistrates that he was sitting in a stationary motor van on the opposite side of the road from the parked car and facing it. His motor van was some 20 or more yards nearer the main thoroughfare than the parked car. He would have said that he heard a loud bang and then saw a motor car driven by the defendant had collided with the rear of the parked motor car. Before he could get out to go to the accident, he saw the car reverse and drive away at a very fast speed. It went past him and he saw it turn left into the main thoroughfare. He also took the registration number of the car.

The incident was reported to the police, who made enquiries and interviewed the defendant at 12.10 a.m., an hour and a quarter after the collision. He was asked if he owned the car which had collided with the parked car earlier that night and he said he did. He was then asked if he had been driving at the time of the collision, and he said 'Yes, I have been waiting for you to come.' He was cautioned and asked if he would like to make a statement about the incident, and he said 'There is nothing I can say. I heard someone say that he had taken my number.'

The defendant's car was examined and damage was found on the front and front near side. The defendant was told that he would be reported for consideration of prosecuting him for reckless, dangerous or careless driving, for failing to stop after an accident and for failing to report an accident as soon as practicable. He did not say anything, but nodded his head.

DEFENDANT'S STATEMENT OF MITIGATION:
The defending solicitor said that his client had been unable to appear personally as he had been obliged to keep a pre-set appointment some miles away from home.

This was a case, he said, which could be briefly summed up as the case of a red-haired man and his past. Had the defendant appeared the magistrates would have seen that he had a shock of bright red hair and he, the solicitor, was bound to say immediately that the defendant's record was a clear indication that he possessed the temperament usually associated with red-haired men. He had a very serious record, but there was one important point which could be made in mitigation of it. Apart from one conviction for a minor traffic offence, which had been recorded eighteen months before, the defendant had, for over four years, kept himself out of trouble and the solicitor suggested that this was an indication of the effort the defendant had been making to make good what must inevitably appear to be a very bad record as a young man.

The circumstances which had given rise to the offences with which he was now charged, said the solicitor, would, had the defendant kept his head, have been a very simple matter of exchanging names and addresses with the owner of the parked car and of making arrangements for the repair of the damage. Instead of this, because of his previous convictions and his previous experience of road traffic offences, the defendant got into a blind panic. He was afraid of what would happen to him if the accident came to light. Consequently in the desperation of the moment he tried to run away in the hope that it would be covered up. He behaved like an

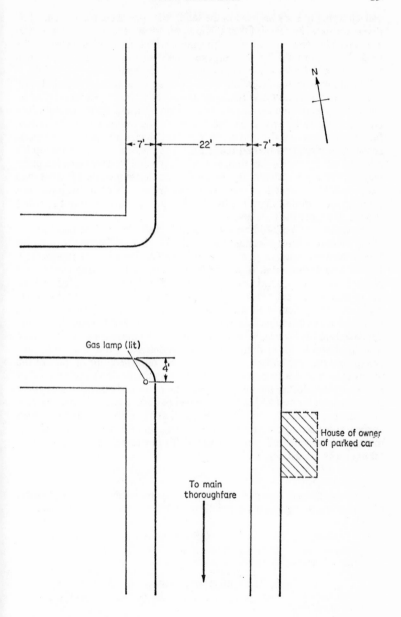

ostrich trying to bury his head in the sand. But once his panic abated, when it was too late, he realized that this was no good. It was to his credit that as soon as he realized, he tried to put things right. He saw the owner of the parked car and paid for the damage caused in the collision and he had the damage to his own car repaired at his own expense.

The statements the defendant made to the police officer indicated, said the solicitor, that he knew his number had been taken. He knew that he could not escape the consequences of running away from the collision. Again, it was to his credit that, realizing this, he waited up for the police, for he was expecting them to come. Having driven on in panic and having subsequently realized he had taken the wrong action he had made up his mind to tell the truth, and that was precisely what he did. Once his panic had subsided he did not try to avoid the consequences of what had happened. His instructions were, said the solicitor, that had the police not come to see him that night he, the defendant, intended to go to the police station to report the accident.

The defendant realized he must be punished and he realized that because of his record it must inevitably enter the magistrates' minds to take his licence away. It was for this reason that he had been legally represented. For he also realized that to a man in his position his driving licence was of vital importance. During the four years that he had struggled to keep out of trouble he had been engaged in a one-man demolition business. He was now doing very well and his business depended upon his driving licence. His business, his livelihood and, much more important, his family depended on his licence, said the solicitor. If the magistrates were to take it away it would mean destitution for the defendant and his family. He recognized that he, himself, must be severely punished, but his plea to the magistrates was not to punish his family, Despite his long early record of misbehaviour, during the last four years he had been making a real effort to rehabilitate himself and in that time had built up a business, had married and begun a family. It might very well be that his native wildness had been curbed and that he could go on doing well. Punish him the magistrates must, said the solicitor, but he asked them not to ruin the defendant by taking away his driving licence.

ANTECEDENTS:
The prosecutor said that there were no costs, and informed the magistrates of the defendant's previous convictions as set out on the attached list.

| Time | Offence | Penalty |
|---|---|---|
| 11 years before present hearing | 1. Dangerous driving | Fined £7 L.E. |
| | 2. Fail to stop for Police Constable | Fined 40/– |
| | 3. P.L.H. drive unaccompanied | Fined 20/– |
| 10 years before present hearing | Use trailer without mudguards | Absolute discharge 4/– costs. |
| 8½ years before present hearing | M/cycle no driving licence | Fined 10/– |

| Time | Offence | Penalty |
|---|---|---|
| 8 years before present hearing | 1. Fail to keep records | Fined 10/– |
| | 2. M/vehicle no warning instrument | Fined 20/– |
| | 3. Identification marks not in accordance with Regs. | Fined 20/– |
| | 4. Driving without a licence | Fined £5 |
| 7 years before present hearing | 1. Exceed speed limit | Fined £6 L.E. |
| | 2. M/vehicle inefficient brakes | Fined 40/– |
| | 3. Fail to keep records | Fined 20/– |
| | 4. Fail to produce driving licence | Fined 20/– |
| | 5. Fail to produce Insurance Certificate | Absolute discharge 4/– costs |
| 7 years before present hearing | Exceed speed limit | Fined £3 L.E. |
| 6 years before present hearing | 1. Fail to conform to traffic lights | Fined 40/– |
| | 2. Fail to illuminate rear plate | Fined 20/– |
| 5½ years before present hearing | 1. Aid and Abet failing to report an accident | Fined £5 |
| | 2. Aid and Abet failing to stop after an accident | Fined £5 |
| | 3. Aid and Abet careless driving | Fined £5 |
| 5½ years before present hearing | 1. Fail to notify change of ownership of motor vehicle | Fined £2.10.0. |
| | 2. Fail to notify change of colour of motor vehicle | Fined £2.10.0. |
| 5 years before present hearing | 1. M/lorry insecure load | Fined £5 |
| | 2. M/lorry no goods licence | Fined £2 |
| 5 years before present hearing | 1. Use M/lorry without goods licence | Fined £2 Costs 10/– |
| | 2. Permit M/lorry no insurance | Fined |
| 4¾ years before present hearing | 1. Careless driving | Fined £80 L.E. |
| | 2. Rear plate not easily distinguishable | Fined £1 |
| 4¾ years before present hearing | 1. Drive m/car when unfit through drink | Fined £20 or 2 mths. Disqualified for 3 years. Pay costs £1.1.6. |
| | 2. Drive m/car in manner dangerous to public | Fined £30 or 3 months |
| 4 years before present hearing | Permit m/lorry no insurance | Fined £20 or 2 months |
| 1½ years before present hearing | 1. Use m/lorry no warning instrument | Fined 10/– |
| | 2. Lights not maintained in efficient working order | Fined 5/– |
| | 3. Use m/lorry without a goods licence | Fined 20/– |

# CHAPTER 2

# Choosing a Strategy

## THE NEED FOR A NEW APPROACH

AT PRESENT evidence about the sentencing of motoring offenders is hard to come by. The annual statistics, *Offences relating to motor vehicles*, indicate the proportions of offenders fined, imprisoned, given a suspended sentence, discharged and disqualified. An average fine per *offence* (and any offender may have been convicted of more than one at the same time) and the various periods of disqualification can be calculated, but there is no breakdown in the amount of the penalty by police district—and so no possibility of even a rough comparison between parts of the country, let alone variations from court to court. The only study so far is Terence Willett's *Criminal on the road*, in which he analysed the penalties imposed for five serious offences in eleven magistrates' courts from 1957 to 1959. He concluded that only three of the eleven magistrates' courts appeared to follow a consistent policy—the two most severe and the most lenient—while in the rest 'the sentences cover a wide range, as is evidenced from the large standard deviations [spread] for fines and disqualifications for each class of offence (except for driving while disqualified)'.[1] Willett's study is, however, vague about the reasons for this. First, he is not able to give any detailed comparisons of offenders and offences appearing before the different courts because records are a poor basis for such comparisons.[2] He can only say that 'prolonged study of the facts in these 653 cases leaves an inescapable *impression* that sentencing is very much a matter of chance . . . no coherent policy based on definite criteria is evident' [my italics].[3] Second, his study, being concerned mainly with the offenders, provided no data about the magistrates and their opinions.

These problems in interpreting evidence from fairly crude comparisons between courts have also been encountered in all previous

---

[1] T. C. Willett (1964), *Criminal on the road*, London, Tavistock, 261.
[2] See pages 32–3 for a discussion of the value of records for research purposes.
[3] Ibid., 276.

sentencing inquiries. Every magistrate recognizes the first difficulty, for he will undoubtedly have grown to resent comparisons made between cases on the basis of brief press reports, which conceal what he may regard as gross differences in the circumstances of the offence or offender.[1] The researcher must not fall into the same trap. He must find a method which controls the variability in sentence due to differences *in the cases* actually dealt with rather than in the judge's handling of them.[2] For example, Willett compared 104 persons convicted of driving under the influence of drink or drugs (hereafter called drunken driving) at eleven courts. Obviously it is not possible to conclude that each court had similar cases, for some courts must have dealt with very few. Other studies have assumed that with large enough numbers cases will be randomly distributed among judges, but Green in particular has cast serious doubt on this assumption.[3] The alternative method of 'matching' cases (whether directly item by item or through prediction techniques) is also full of problems, not the least being the decision on which factors the cases should be matched for, and ensuring that enough factors are considered to convince everyone that the matched cases are really similar.[4] This is particularly a problem where records are inadequate.

But even if this problem had been overcome, previous studies would still have failed to provide adequate measures of the variables in judicial backgrounds or attitudes which might explain different sentencing practices. With the exception of a study of Ontario

[1] For example: 'The popular outcry that fines vary from court to court and from bench to bench is because many ignore, or are ignorant of, the varying circumstances of each case and each defendant,' *Justice of the Peace*, 127 (1963), 767. Also a letter from Mr William Higham, a Worcestershire justice, 'Thousands of magistrates, all of them different, deal with tens of thousands of cases a year, all of them different. How can we therefore work towards uniformity of sentence?' *The Magistrate*, 23 (1967), 149.

[2] See R. Hood and R. Sparks (1970), *Key issues in criminology*, London, World Univ. Library, 141–70; H. Mannheim (1958), 'Some aspects of judicial sentencing policy', *Yale Law J.*, 67, 961; (1962) Introduction to Hood, *Sentencing in magistrates' courts*, London, Stevens; E. Green (1961), *Judicial attitudes in sentencing*, London, Macmillan, 8–20; R. F. Sparks (1965), 'Sentencing by magistrates: some facts of life', in P. Halmos (ed.), *Sociological studies in the British penal services* (Sociological Review Monograph No. 9, University of Keele); H. Zeisel (1969), 'Methodological problems in studies of sentencing', *Law and Society Review*, 3, 621–31.

[3] E. Green, op. cit., 16–20.

[4] The problems of matching offenders dealt with by different courts are similar to those found in other types of criminological research. See R. Hood (1967), 'Research on the effectiveness of punishments and treatments' in, *Collected studies in criminological research*, 1, Strasbourg, Council of Europe, 73–113.

magistrates recently completed by John Hogarth,[1] no information has been provided about the judges. Their influence has been attributed to ill-defined 'personal characteristics' or simply to the 'personal equation'. For example, in a study of Israeli judges, Shoham says:

> The personal attitude of the trial judge and his individual sentencing habit have in fact a marked influence on the severity of punishment . . . in a great many cases, this *indefinable element* [my italics] may play a more important role in determining the type and severity of sentence than the nature of the offence and personality of the offender.[2]

Whether the latter part of this statement can be substantiated is doubtful, but there is certainly a need to try to pin down this 'indefinable element'.

In order to try to overcome both problems at once I chose to send to samples of magistrates taking part in the research *exactly* the same detailed cases. Thus factors about the offence and offender were held constant, the only variables being those associated with the magistrates making the decisions. Recognizing that this was a 'game' method, an attempt was made to compare decisions reached on these cases with sentences passed on similar cases in court. Also, some of the responses from magistrates were checked against observations of actual court practices.

In collecting information from magistrates there were two aims in mind. As the research was concerned originally with disparity I wanted to isolate those factors which would discriminate between (and perhaps even help explain) those who reached different decisions on identical cases. But because so little is known about magistrates, the opportunity was taken to collect as much information as possible about their backgrounds as well as their views on, and perceptions of, the motoring offender. The remainder of this chapter will therefore first review the hypotheses and assumptions underlying the choice of information collected, and then describe how it was obtained.

THE THEORETICAL BASIS

Although the methods are quite different, the areas explored in this study are very similar to those of an inquiry which was being carried

---

[1] J. Hogarth (1967), 'Sentencing research—some problems of design', *Brit. J. Criminol.*, 7, 84–93, and J. Hogarth (1971), *Sentencing as a human process*, University of Toronto Press.

[2] S. Shoham (1959), 'Sentencing policy of criminal courts in Israel', *J. Crim. Law, Criminol. & Police Sci.*, 50, 327–37.

out at the same time by Hogarth in Canada. Both investigations have assumed that there are five important 'factors' affecting the way individuals make decisions. First, there are social, personal and 'judicial' characteristics; second, attitudes towards the 'disposal' (to use a neutral word) of offenders; third, perceptions of the nature of the offence and the characteristics of offenders; fourth, the type of information considered relevant and the way in which it is interpreted; and, fifth, the controls or constraints exercised either formally by the law or by courts of appeal, or informally through local sentencing norms, the court officials, group pressures, or traditions in court practice. It is assumed that there is a strong link between these factors—the personal characteristics influencing views on principles of punishment and attitudes and perceptions, these views influencing the choice and interpretation of information, and both views and information being modified by the formal and informal controls. Thus, while there may be connections between social and personal attributes and sentencing, one would expect these to be explained through the intervening variables describing attitudes, perceptions and information use. The information sought about magistrates, their views and their use of information is described briefly below—noting in each case where constraints or controls may be influential. Each issue is taken up in detail in subsequent chapters.

## 1. *Magistrates: Their Social and Personal Backgrounds*

There are many individual attributes of magistrates which might be related to different attitudes and decisions. Some are related to their judicial role, such as length and amount of experience (those in large urban courts seeing many more cases than those in small rural divisions), seniority on the bench, experience in the juvenile court, and interest in penological and other 'professional' issues. Others are social factors such as occupation, education, political party affiliation, and involvement in community affairs. Others are personal, such as sex, age, personality, general social attitudes; and yet others, especially related to motoring, including driving experience, self-rating of driving skill, degree of enthusiasm for driving as a hobby or sport and experience of prosecution either personally or through relatives or friends.

It is also obviously extremely important to understand how decisions are modified in the group. What influence has the chairman on his deputies and the clerk? Does length of experience on the bench carry weight in the group? Are group decisions really compromises of individual extremes or do some individuals have more influence than others? To what extent do magistrates actually retire to consider sentence?

## 2. Aims and Perceptions

(a) *Aims or purposes of the penalty.* It seemed reasonable to assume that little would be gained from an exercise which tried to make fine distinctions between retribution (in its various meanings), denunciation, specific and general deterrence, reform, and removal from risk (or protection as it is sometimes called). In motoring cases 'punishment' (rather than 'treatment') is the *general* aim, and it is often difficult to disentangle the *particular* purposes of the sentence. Yet even though nearly all offenders are fined,[1] sentences may vary depending on the importance given to specific deterrence aimed at 'individualizing' the sentence, as against the need for keeping a 'just proportion' between sentences imposed for similar *offences*. Obviously this could have repercussions both on the size of the fine and the time allowed to pay it where offenders have committed the same offence but have different means or previous records. Similar differences in attitude may affect views on the use of such informal constraints as basic penalty schedules, the provisions for pleading guilty for less serious offences without a personal appearance, and the problem of whether to make an offender pay heavy prosecution costs. Again, the emphasis placed on general deterrence or on removal from risk is likely to influence attitudes towards disqualification and the power to order new driving tests, or the appropriateness of probation or other 'remedial' measures for certain types of offender. For some offences there are legal constraints, for example a court is required to disqualify for a minimum of twelve months an offender found guilty of drunken driving (for three years if it is the second offence within ten years), unless 'special reasons' can be found for not so doing. Another is the 'totting-up' procedure of the Road Traffic Act 1962, under which magistrates must disqualify for at least six months an offender who has been convicted of a third endorsable offence committed within three years, unless there are 'mitigating circumstances'. There appears to be some variation both in the use of these provisions[2] and in attitudes towards them. Similarly it is important to know to what extent sentences are affected by, or even approach, the legal maximum penalties available.

[1] With the exception of driving while disqualified, where a substantial minority are imprisoned—or since 1967 given a suspended sentence or sent to quarter sessions for sentence. See pages 63–5.

[2] See page 89.

In addition, at a more prosaic level, techniques for arriving at the sentence may be important. The importance of the basic penalty method has already been mentioned. But there are also problems in dealing with multiple charges. In reaching the total penalty two different practices may be employed. A 'global' figure may be fixed and parcelled out between the various charges, or individual penalties for each charge may be added up. The results could be quite different.

(b) *Perception of the nature of the offence.* It was necessary to examine the range of views on three aspects of magisterial perceptions of motoring offences.

First, views on the seriousness of motoring offences in general as compared to other criminal offences. Lady Wootton, for example, has suggested that the idea that motoring offences are less 'criminal' and therefore less serious is a reason for what she considers to be the comparatively lenient treatment of motorists.[1] These views, if they are held, may well reflect a general public tolerance, which could be an important constraint on magisterial policy. Now that fining has become such a widely used penalty for indictable offences, such as theft, the range of penalties imposed on these offenders may well set a limit to what magistrates and the public consider a fair penalty for a motoring offence.[2]

Secondly, views on the relative seriousness of different motoring offences. For example, Willett considers failing to stop after an accident to be a 'serious offence', but not careless driving. Looking at the national statistics as a whole, however, it can be seen that in 1964 the average fine for failing to stop was £4 15s. 0d., but for careless driving £10 2s. 0d. Furthermore, 5·6 per cent of the latter offenders were disqualified, compared with 2·5 per cent of the former.[3]

[1] Barbara Wootton (1963), *Crime and the criminal law*, London, Stevens, 25–26. For other similar views see discussion on pages 97–9.

[2] We did not investigate this aspect of the problem in detail, but as an example of the point, news of a recent recommendation from the Magistrates' Association to increase basic penalties for certain offences was greeted by the comment that heavier punishments should be imposed instead on offenders who commit 'conventional' crimes. See leading article, *Daily Express*, 18 March 1970, and comments by Lord Chesham of the R.A.C. Reported in *The Daily Telegraph*, 19 March 1970; and pages 104–105.

[3] The figures for 1968 were: careless driving £11·6, failing to stop, etc., £5·8, and the proportions disqualified 4·0 per cent and 3·4 per cent respectively. It should be noted, though, that a higher proportion of those failing to stop are imprisoned—0·3 per cent compared with 0·02 per cent (1964). This may be because this offence is sometimes included as part of a multiple charge involving more serious offences—and of course there are a few very serious cases of 'hit and run'.

Penalties for failing to stop after an accident may well vary according to whether it is regarded as serious or not when compared with
other offences.

Thirdly, sentences could also vary depending upon whether there
is or is not a common perception of what is a 'serious', 'average' or
'trivial' example of any particular kind of offence. Is there common
agreement on what is a 'very serious case' of dangerous or careless
driving or drunken driving?

(c) *Perception of the characteristics of motoring offenders.* There may
be some crucial differences in the way in which the motoring offender
is perceived. His offence may be regarded as serious, but is he considered to be a 'criminal' in the same sense as this label is applied to
those who steal, rob or commit sexual offences? And how do views
vary according to the type of offence? What is the general picture (or
stereotype) the magistrate has when confronted, for example, by a
man convicted of drunken or careless driving? Is he seen as 'anti-
social', 'emotionally unbalanced' or as 'someone who has done
something which I could do (or have done) myself'?

It should be clear that aims of magistrates and their perceptions of
the seriousness of an offence and the type of person committing it are
closely interrelated and interacting—one affecting the other. The
magistrate who is punitively oriented may classify these offences and
offenders differently from someone who basically wishes to deter or
reform individuals from repeating their acts. On the other hand,
regular exposure to cases will modify attitudes towards methods of
punishment—evoking perhaps sympathy, detachment or anger.
Certainly, these perceptions of the problem are very likely to influence the kinds of information regarded as relevant to the sentence.

3. *Information: Its Relevance and Use*

The Streatfeild Committee recommended the kind of 'comprehensive
and relevant' information which ought to be provided before sentence is passed on offenders convicted of indictable cases heard in
the Higher Courts.[1] It has been assumed that the criteria apply
equally to magistrates' courts, but it is less than clear whether they
are intended to extend to motoring offences—or if they are, to
which ones.

It is not even obvious which information about the nature of the

[1] *Report of the Interdepartmental Committee on the Business of the Criminal
Courts* (1961), H.M.S.O., Cmnd. 1289, para. 336 in particular.

*offence* is relevant to the sentence. What criteria, for example, are used in assessing the relative seriousness of dangerous, drunken or careless driving? Is the amount of harm done—which can vary from a near-miss to grave injury—important? Is the level of intoxication regarded as relevant? Obviously similar questions arise in relation to the offender—his previous convictions (and *which* ones; all, or just those for similar offences?), income and outgoings, family background, mental state, driving capabilities and attitude towards his offence, to name only a few areas of possible interest.

There is also the practical issue of how such information is to be collected. To what extent are probation pre-sentence reports thought to be of assistance? There are likely to be different views on the importance of having the offender physically before the court. Many cases of speeding are dealt with by offenders completing a form of guilty plea (under the Magistrates' Courts Act 1957) on which they *may* state facts in mitigation, but are not under any obligation to state their income. Even in cases of careless driving and failing to stop after, or report, an accident offenders may, at the courts' discretion, be dealt with in their absence on the basis of a guilty plea in a letter. Also the information magistrates possess before passing sentence may in some courts depend partly on what is fed through to them. In motoring cases, in particular, the prosecutor and the police may follow a policy of not reading out previous convictions for non-motoring offences. They may also refrain from giving any evidence about alcoholic consumption unless a charge of drunken driving is being preferred, and in careless driving cases there are different opinions about informing the bench if fatal injuries have occurred. Often, then, only the information which others (i.e., the prosecution) think is relevant to sentencing is given to the magistrates, and the bench may hesitate to question what has become an established procedure.[1]

THE METHODS OF INVESTIGATION

### 1. *The Offences Chosen for Study*

It was decided that the inquiry should concentrate on serious motoring offences, but that two offences which are normally regarded as less serious should also be included. The major reason for studying serious cases is that the penalties which can be imposed are relatively severe and there is a wide range open to the discretion of the magistrates. In most minor offences, such as parking or failing to show lights when parked, the maximum penalties are low. Even if there are

[1] This is discussed further on pages 109–12.

inconsistencies in sentences for such offences they are not likely to be of great importance.

Which are the 'serious' motoring offences? We followed Willett's argument that they were those with at least two of three characteristics present in 'ordinary' criminal offences—deliberate intent, harm to persons or property, dishonesty.[1]

Willett's list is therefore:[2]

> Driving recklessly or dangerously
> Driving under the influence of drink or drugs
> Driving while disqualified
> Failing to insure against third-party risks
> Failing to stop after, or to report, an accident

Careless driving was added to this list both because it shared with the other offences a high maximum penalty,[3] including imprisonment for a second offence, and because it is often indistinguishable from dangerous driving.[4] It was also one of the 'serious offences' for which the Magistrates' Association, the Lord Chancellor and Lord Chief Justice considered a 'basic penalty' to be inappropriate.[5] Furthermore, the national statistics and a pilot study showed that magistrates gave, in most cases, higher penalties for careless driving than one of Willett's other offences—failing to stop after, or report, an accident.

The 'less serious' offences[6] included were the very common offence

---

[1] On a similar basis, the Council of the Law Society suggested that motoring offences should be divided into two categories—'offences against' and 'breaches of' the Road Traffic Acts. The first category would include all but the last offence in Willett's list (failing to stop) and would be dealt with in the criminal courts because of their intrinsic 'criminality'. A distinction is thus drawn between those who act deliberately, or commit acts or omissions that 'show such disregard for the lives and safety of others as to amount to crimes against the State and conduct deserving of punishment' and those whose driving 'whilst improper by any reasonable standards of road usage, falls short of recklessness'. See *Motoring Offences*, Memorandum by the Council of the Law Society, June 1965. This idea is discussed in more detail on pages 105–107.

[2] Excluding causing death by dangerous driving, which is dealt with at Assize. See *Criminal on the road*, 11. The first three offences in the list can be dealt with by the Higher Courts, but the vast majority of convictions occur in magistrates' courts.

[3] £100. Statutory maximum penalties for the offences included in the study are shown in Appendix IV, Note 7 to Table 3.

[4] See *Criminal on the road*, 89–92.

[5] This is discussed further on pages 66–7.

[6] Some would probably include speeding in a list of 'serious' offences, but in general penalties are low and disqualification rarely used. See P. J. Fitzgerald's review of *Criminal on the road*, *Law Q. Rev.*, 92 (1966), 121–4.

of exceeding the speed limit and the less common offence of neglecting traffic regulations at pedestrian crossings. These two offences both carry a maximum penalty of £50 and are included in the list of offences under S. 5(3) (R.T.A. 1962) which can be 'totted up' so that compulsory disqualification follows if three such offences are committed within three years. They are therefore both 'relatively serious' offences for which magistrates have quite wide discretionary sentencing powers.

## 2. The Courts

Three areas covering sixteen counties in different parts of the country were chosen, and courts from these areas were selected. The three areas are based on a radius of 30 miles from Reading, Burton-on-Trent and Durham.[1] The advantages of concentrating the research within distinct and separate areas (rather than selecting courts from the country as a whole) were that it facilitated administration of the project and reduced research expenses. The major disadvantage was that this approach could not produce a truly representative sample of the courts or magistrates in the country as a whole. What the biases are one cannot tell, but by choosing three distinct regions, each containing large cities (or parts of outer London), medium-sized and small towns as well as rural areas, the results should reflect some of the main differences of background and views to be found among English magistrates.

There are no statistics available to show whether any variations in sentencing practice actually exist between different courts in respect of motoring offences. One cannot therefore sample courts on this basis, as was done in my study of indictable offences.[2] It seems likely, however, that variations in policy are more likely to occur between benches in different counties than between those in the same county. This is because local meetings and training sessions of Magistrates' Courts Committees and Magistrates' Association Branches are usually arranged on a county basis. Therefore, two courts from each county were chosen—making 32 courts in all. One of the courts in each county served a population of over 100,000: the other a population of under 100,000: they were selected at random. Benches of different sizes, probably dealing with different proportions of motoring offences, were chosen in order to examine whether the amount of

[1] The choice of these areas was made in consultation with Dr Willett, whose study of the effects of sentences involved interviewing offenders sentenced by the courts in the same areas.

[2] *Sentencing in magistrates' courts*, 11–13, 21–7.

contact with these cases affected the magistrates' decisions and whether differences existed between urban and rural magistrates.

## 3. *The Samples*

The total number of magistrates on the active lists at the 32 courts was about 860.[1] For reasons relating to the distribution of cases (see section 4 below) and the time available for fieldwork—approximately 18 months—we aimed to include about 500 magistrates. Because chairmen and deputy chairmen have an important role in the structure of most magistrates' courts we decided to include all of them plus a random sample of two-thirds of the other magistrates stratified so as to be representative of the age, sex, length of services and rota structure[2] of the bench. Where the total sample would drop below ten all members of the bench were included. This made it necessary to allow for this over-representation of members of small benches, where necessary, in the analysis.

Altogether 650 magistrates were approached and 538, or 83 per cent, agreed to co-operate. The vast majority of those who refused apparently did so because of illness or a heavy work schedule. Very few refusals appeared to be based on a genuine rejection of the inquiry. No doubt the backing of the Magistrates' Association, Lord Chancellor's Department and Home Office was influential in gaining such a high response rate. It led to the study being taken seriously, even though, in a few instances, the spectre of a 'Government inquiry' might have seemed daunting.[3]

## 4. *Choosing Cases*

At a pilot stage the possibility of using records was reviewed. We discarded this approach for the following reasons:

(1) in many courts it would have been impossible to get sufficient cases without going back over many years—especially in rural courts;

(2) records often do not contain all that is heard in court and, conversely, some of the information may not have been made known to the bench;

[1] Boundary changes in the Midlands made it impossible to be precise.

[2] In some courts, for example, the magistrates' rotas are worked out on a daily basis so that the 'Monday bench' may rarely meet with the 'Wednesday bench', and so it was necessary to reflect possible difference in practice between them.

[3] In general there was an immediate response rate of between 50 and 60 per cent. The remainder agreed after the fieldwork in the area had begun, when they had received good reports from their colleagues.

(3) it would have been very difficult to compare cases in terms of relative seriousness.

If cases coming before different benches are to be compared they should, ideally, be matched on a combination of factors. But to do this one needs vast numbers—and even then it might be statistically impossible.[1]

It was for this reason, then, that I chose to send magistrates transcripts of actual cases so that the factors about the offence and offender were kept constant.

When they agreed to co-operate, magistrates were sent a collection of eight printed cases—one of each offence in the study—and asked to study them in private before being interviewed.[2] A questionnaire attached to each case asked them to decide on the appropriate penalty, to give their reasons for it and to say whether they would allow time to pay, whether they wanted more information about the offender, whether they would have retired to consider the sentence, to what extent they thought their decisions reflected what their colleagues would have done, and lastly to rate how serious 'of its kind' the case was.[3] The cases were edited transcripts of real cases noted in court and included all the sketch plans, photographs, letters and reports made available to the courts. Identifying details were of course changed. Examples have already been given in Chapter 1, and others are included in Appendix II. In other words, decisions were made on the same basis as in the court except that the defendant could not be seen personally, and the decision was made alone and not in a group, in the atmosphere of a court. The research was therefore carried out in a 'game' situation.

We wanted magistrates to deal with a variety of types of each kind of offence. As we intended to interview about 500 magistrates we collected five types of each kind of offence (e.g., five different cases

---

[1] In a review of *Sentencing in magistrates' courts*, R. F. Sparks suggests that the various factors considered should have been interrelated: 'What matters is the combination of factors and the relative weights assigned to each and investigation of these factors one at a time can show nothing whatsoever about this.' But besides the difficulty of deciding *which* factors should be grouped together, and what their relative weights are, this approach was clearly impossible with a small sample of 70 offenders in each court. I presume that even if the samples had been larger and three or four characteristics combined the study would still have been open to the attack that differences in sentences were due to other factors not taken into account. The corollary of Sparks' position is (quite rightly) that sentencing research based on records will always be extremely inadequate. See R. F. Sparks, 'Sentencing by magistrates: some facts of life', op. cit., 79–82.

[2] This was to ensure that their decisions would not be contaminated by ideas raised at the interview.

[3] The questionnaire is reproduced in Appendix I.

of dangerous driving) and asked 100 magistrates to deal with each one. The easiest system was to make five packages, each containing one of the types of all eight kinds of offence, and send the packages (or groups of cases) in random order as replies were received from magistrates at each court.[1] The aim was to get 100 decisions on each of five different types of eight different kinds of offence. Thus there were 40 cases (5 × 8 kinds), each to be sentenced by 100 magistrates: 4,000 decisions altogether.

FIGURE 1

PLAN OF RESEARCH DESIGN

Number of magistrates to deal with each type and kind of case

*Type of offence*

| Kind of offence | A | B | C | D | E | Total |
|---|---|---|---|---|---|---|
| Dangerous driving | 100 | 100 | 100 | 100 | 100 | 500[2] |
| Drunken driving | 100 | 100 | 100 | 100 | 100 | 500 |
| Driving while disqualified | 100 | 100 | 100 | 100 | 100 | 500 |
| Careless driving | 100 | 100 | 100 | 100 | 100 | 500 |
| Driving without insurance | 100 | 100 | 100 | 100 | 100 | 500 |
| Failure to stop or report | 100 | 100 | 100 | 100 | 100 | 500 |
| Speeding | 100 | 100 | 100 | 100 | 100 | 500 |
| Pedestrian crossing offence | 100 | 100 | 100 | 100 | 100 | 500 |
| Grand total: | | | | | | 4,000 |

Two problems arose in using this technique. Firstly, the 40 cases had to be selected. How could one be sure that they were 'typical' and not of a kind rarely encountered? Secondly, how was the dis-

[1] This ensured that the five packages (A, B, C, D, E) were distributed evenly between the members of any one bench. Thus if there were twenty members, four would have dealt with group A, four with group B, etc. As they were sent in *random* order, if senior magistrates replied first they would not all get groups A or B. This is important in relation to later analyses (see Chapter 8, Page 143).

[2] It will be seen that eventually 538 magistrates were interviewed, but as some were unable to complete particular cases (usually because of the time involved) the numbers actually dealing with each case were very near 100. See fn. 1 to Table 3, Appendix IV.

tribution of decisions reached in the 'game' the magistrates were playing related to the distribution of decisions that would have been made if the cases had been dealt with in court?

It was clear that the cases chosen for the study had to be matched with real cases appearing before the courts in order to ensure their typicality and to compare the distribution of decisions reached.[1] Because records would not have provided sufficient information, a form was designed and sent (with the co-operation of the Home Office) to justices' clerks. They were asked to fill in the details as cases appeared before them in court. By this means clerks at 115 courts[2] in the three areas covered by the study provided (over various periods) information about court proceedings, the offence, the offender and the penalties imposed for each of the eight offences. Information was received on over 3,000 cases.

When enough cases of each offence arrived the data were analysed.[3] The three attributes (one describing the court proceedings, one the offence and one the offender) which most nearly split the sample 50 : 50 were chosen. There were rarely more than three attributes so distributed. All combinations of these three attributes produced eight groups or types of each offence (e.g., $+a +b +c$; $+a -b +c$, etc.). The 100 cases were then distributed between the groups, and the three groups with the fewest cases in them discarded, for they obviously represented types of cases which occurred infrequently in the courts.[4] For all eight kinds of offences the five remaining types between them contained 75 to 85 per cent of the cases collected from the clerks. Five offences of each kind (e.g., five dangerous driving cases) from a collection of 165 cases heard in courts over a wide area of the north-east of England were then matched with the five types

---

[1] It would not have sufficed to compare the 'game decisions' with the one 'real' decision reached when the case was before the court—for this decision may have been one that would not have been made by any of the courts in which the magistrates being interviewed sat.

[2] Forty-nine clerks refused to comply with the request to provide information. There is no reason to think that this affects the typicality of the cases received.

[3] Cases of driving while disqualified and drunken driving were slow to be returned by the clerks (perhaps because we had overestimated the likely incidence of them in a six month period). The analysis for these two offences was based on 38 and 76 cases respectively. For all other kinds of offences 100 cases were analysed.

[4] I am very much indebted to Peter MacNaughton-Smith, who first suggested that such a comparison be made and who suggested the method of matching the cases. The items used for matching were, for example, 'defendant present/not present'; 'legally represented/not legally represented'; 'guilty plea/not guilty plea'. So sparse was the information about the offenders themselves that they were difficult to match on personal characteristics and so, for example, we were forced to match through items such as 'defendant's means known/not known'.

as analysed from the information sent by the clerks. Cases which appeared to have very unusual features were excluded.

This method ensured that the cases sent to magistrates were not completely atypical and that they represented a range of circumstances fairly common in magistrates' courts. As it was only based on three attributes the matching was obviously crude, but it made possible a rough comparison between the distribution of decisions reached in the 'game' situation, alone and at home, with the distribution of well over 2,000 decisions made in the courtroom.[1] Thus the biases in the findings will be easy to spot.

One further difficulty existed. Many of the cases contained multiple charges. Was a case of careless driving and failing to stop after an accident to be counted primarily as an example of the first offence or the second? A decision was reached on the basis of an analysis of the cases obtained from the clerks. They were ranked first by their order on the charge sheet (usually an indication of seriousness) and second by the sentences imposed. The cases with multiple charges sent to magistrates were classified under the most serious charge. Thus, for example, our discussion of careless driving cases excludes those in which this has been a subsidiary charge to drunken driving or driving while disqualified.[2]

## 5. *The Interviews and Questionnaires*

After completing the case material, each magistrate was interviewed for between one and a half and three hours. They were asked about their social and personal background; the information they took into account in reaching decisions and the way in which such information (e.g., income) was used in fixing the penalty; the use made of 'basic penalties'; their policy in relation to costs; fining in multiple-charge cases; pleading guilty by letter; attitudes towards remanding for inquiries; attitudes towards motoring offenders, particularly in relation to their criminality; the aims of disqualification and ordering new driving tests; lengths of disqualification and reasons for not disqualifying; attitudes towards new proposals for dealing with offenders; the role of the chairman and clerk in formulating or influencing the policy of the bench.

These questions were, therefore, concerned with providing information relevant to the factors outlined in the first part of this

---

[1] Although over 3,000 cases were gathered altogether, we only, of course, compared those cases which were matched with the cases sent to magistrates.

[2] The effect of multiple charges on the penalties imposed for offences included in the list is discussed on pages 79–80 and 135.

chapter—personal characteristics of magistrates, their aims in sentencing; perceptions of offenders, norms of court practice, and the information they considered relevant to sentencing.

In addition to the interview two self-completion questionnaires were administered and completed with the case decisions before the interview. The first was aimed at assessing the perceptions of the relative seriousness of motoring offences. Magistrates were asked to place nineteen offences in order of seriousness; these offences included all the motoring offences of the study as well as other indictable and non-indictable offences. Of the 538 who were interviewed, 94 per cent completed this exercise. The second questionnaire was aimed at assessing 'stereotypes' magistrates have of offenders. In the pilot study some magistrates were asked to describe the kinds of people who committed various motoring offences. Their replies were content-analysed and classified into four main groups. Thus, in the main study magistrates were asked, for *each* of the six serious offences and for *persistent* speeding, to say how many out of every ten offenders fell into one of four types:

*Type 1* An average motorist who does something you could imagine yourself doing.

*Type 2* A careless, thoughtless type of person whose offence arises from not paying adequate attention to either his driving or the regulations.

*Type 3* An anti-social person who has no respect for rules and regulations and the safety of others.

*Type 4* The sort of person whose offence arises from a somewhat unstable personality or from emotional problems.

They were invited to add other types if they thought this necessary. Eighty-eight per cent filled in the form.

Finally the subjects were given, after the interview, an Eysenck Personality Inventory, which measures personality in relation to two major variables—'introverted to extraverted ', and 'stable to neurotic'. They were also asked to complete a social attitudes questionnaire adapted from Eysenck's *Psychology of politics*, which measures attitudes along the two dimensions 'conservative to radical' and 'tough-minded to tender-minded'.[1] The meaning of these tests is

---

[1] H. J. Eysenck (1954), *The psychology of politics*, London, Routledge, 122–4. The shortened 24-item scale used by Nagel in his study of American judges was used (except for one change). See Stuart Nagel (1963) 'Off the bench judicial attitudes' in G. Shubert (ed.) *Judicial decision making*, Glencoe, Free Press, 29–53. Nagel did not attempt to relate these social attitudes to sentencing, but did relate liberal attitudes to decisions in civil cases.

described in Chapter 3. Only 12 and 13 per cent, respectively, refused to answer these rather controversial questionnaires.[1]

In addition the chief clerks in 29 of the 32 courts were interviewed and asked identical questions about disparities in sentences passed in their courts. All the questionnaires are reproduced in Appendix I.

## 6. Conferences for Studying Group Decisions and the Use of Information

Conferences were arranged at six courts (there was not time to do more). Two-thirds of the invited magistrates attended. They had been sent two cases—one of drunken driving, the other of dangerous driving. At this meeting they were first divided into 'benches' of three or occasionally two justices (always with one member being more senior through longer experience) and asked to reach a group decision. From this we hoped to see whether group sentences tended to go towards those of the 'senior' magistrates or towards the average.

Secondly, an 'information game' was devised to study how specific items of information about the offence or offender altered the decision. It will be shown that many magistrates when interviewed stated that they considered a very wide range of information to be relevant to the sentence. We were therefore anxious to measure the extent to which a radical change in any one factor in a case might produce a different sentence. After the groups had reached their decision they were told that one aspect of the case was changed and asked if their decision remained the same and, if not, what the new sentence would be. Information about the degree of harm done, the drunkenness of the driver, his attitude in court, and his previous record were all changed one at a time, and the magistrates asked to record their new decision on a specially designed form. For example, they were told 'In this case no-one was harmed, *but* if the facts had read that in ignoring the red traffic lights the defendant had smashed into the side of a car travelling through the green lights and as a consequence the driver of that car was seriously injured so that he was detained in hospital for nine months and suffered permanent disablement . . . what would your decision be?' Similarly, 'In this case the defendant had no previous convictions, *but* if two and a half years ago he had been fined £50 and disqualified for two years for drunken driving . . . what would your decision be?' Using this

---

[1] I am grateful to Professor Eysenck for his advice and for permission to use these tests.

CHOOSING A STRATEGY 79

method it was possible to see the extent to which particular changes in information actually affected the sentence.

## 7. *Court Observations*

In order to check on what happened in court, as much time as possible was spent in court, inconspicuously noting details of procedure on a standardized schedule.[1] Of particular interest was the type of information acquired before sentence was passed, the way it was obtained and the extent of retiring to consider sentence. Details on all types of cases—those in the study, other motoring offences, indictable offences and non-indictable non-motoring offences—were recorded. Altogether over 1,400 cases were observed, including 585 of the eight types of case included in this study.

## 8. *Summary of Methods*

It was decided to use as wide a variety of methods as possible so as to collect information not only on attitudes and opinions (which were obtained by interview, special questionnaires and standard tests) but to simulate decision-making individually and in groups, and to compare the data collected in the research situation with sentences passed in court and, through observation, with actual court practices. The use of such a battery of techniques, approaching the subject from different angles, is helpful in that it provides a check on the validity of information obtained by any one method.

### PLAN OF ANALYSIS

There were two methods of presenting the data. It would have been possible to review all the issues which have been discussed in the last few years in journals, by the Magistrates' Association, in court judgements and the press, and then *separately* to give information from the survey relating to each issue. But this seemed over-cumbersome; to require too much referring-back, and liable to the danger of presenting information from the study out of the context of current debate. Therefore I have attempted to mix material from these sources with research findings so as to show, at each stage, the relevance of the information. This is especially the case in the next

---

[1] As much observation as possible was done before interviewing magistrates so as to try to avoid the presence of the observer influencing court practice. The original collection of 165 cases, from which the 40 used in the study were selected, were not included here.

five chapters, which describe the magistrates, their attitudes, the way they use information, and their sentencing practice.

The plan is to present the descriptive data first and to discuss in the final sections to what extent it can usefully explain different types of sentencing behaviour. The remaining chapters are in the following order:

3. A description of the magistrates, their social and personal backgrounds and motoring experience, in the context of views on the social structure of the magistracy, system of appointments, training and court organization.
4. Attitudes towards sentencing, methods of punishment and treatment. Again, this material will be presented in the context of current debate, especially on such issues as 'basic' or 'suggested' penalties, the use of disqualification, etc.
5. Perceptions of motoring offences and offenders, particularly the issue of their similarity to, or difference from, 'ordinary crime', and the implications for methods of punishment and treatment.
6. The information regarded as relevant to sentencing and the way in which it is used.
7. A description of the range of sentences imposed by the 100 magistrates who dealt with each of the 40 cases. The analysis compares their decisions with those made on matched cases in court, draws attention to the sorts of case which produce the greatest disparities in sentence, and examines the extent to which magistrates vary in their relative severity or leniency over a range of different kinds of offence.
8. An analysis of the factors associated with different sentencing practices, and a discussion of the implications for policy and research.

# CHAPTER 3

# The Magistrates

THERE are two main reasons for beginning the analysis with a description of the social and personal qualities of the magistrates. First, a clear picture is needed of the characteristics of justices, which will later be correlated with sentencing variations. This chapter will examine the 'backgrounds' of the magistrates. Their attitudes and perceptions will be the subjects of Chapters 4 and 5.

Secondly, the information is valuable in its own right. There has been no recent sociological survey of magistrates. In fact, Lady Wootton asked the Lord Chancellor in 1970 whether he would agree 'that there is no source of information at present about the composition of the body of magistrates other than that contained in the Royal Commission Report[1] of more than 20 years ago'.[2] Because of this, the data collected may cast some light on recent debates concerning the social 'balance' of the bench. Indeed, by attempting to see what characteristics are correlated with sentencing (at least for motoring offences, which make up over two-thirds of those coming before the courts) the study might indicate which factors are irrelevant (or perhaps even relevant) considerations in selecting magistrates. To illustrate the point: there is continuing debate about the importance that should be attached to social class, political affiliation and age—as well as motoring qualifications where traffic offences are concerned. But the key question remains unanswered: namely, do magistrates who differ in these characteristics actually sentence offenders differently?

After a general introduction to the debate about magisterial appointments findings relating to social and personal characteristics, status and role as a magistrate, and motoring experience, will be reviewed in turn. Before presenting the data, one point should be

[1] *Royal Commission on Justices of the Peace 1946–48* (1948). Cmd. 7463, H.M.S.O. (Hereafter cited as *Report*, 1946–8.) A postal-survey of all justices was carried out in March–April 1947. Eighty-seven per cent replied. See Minutes of Evidence, Appendix 4, 1948, H.M.S.O.
[2] *H. L. Debates*, Vol. 308 (18 March 1970), col. 1129.

borne in mind. It may be recalled that the sample over-represented magistrates from very small benches (where everyone was included instead of two-thirds). In relation to every item discussed in this chapter, and the next, a comparison was made between magistrates in rural areas from benches which were sampled and those where all magistrates were included, and no statistically significant differences in the distribution of answers to any questions were found. It is therefore legitimate, for descriptive purposes, to ignore this differential sampling fraction.

Of course, it is true that chairmen and deputy chairmen are also slightly over-represented, because at the larger courts they were always included in the sample. A note is made wherever this could affect results—but apart from the fact that these magistrates tend to be above average in age, their inclusion does not seem to have led to any particular biases.

## THE BALANCE OF THE BENCH: GENERAL ISSUES

In recent years there has been a definite attempt by Lord Chancellors to appoint both younger magistrates and persons from a wider range of social backgrounds. At the same time, many commentators have protested that political party affiliation should be an irrelevant consideration in selecting men and women for the bench.

Lord Dilhorne pointed out in 1963 that there was a lack of younger people and that the bench should be more representative of different age-groups.[1] It has been easier to tackle the upper age-range than the lower. The maximum age was reduced from 75 to 70 by the Justices of the Peace Act 1968, but the problem has been to attract those under 40. It is rare for justices to be appointed under 30, and some think this is right. For example, the Law Society's Standing Committee on Criminal Law recently contended that: 'The office of Justice calls both for maturity and experience of life, and accordingly the Committee recommend that the appointment of anyone under thirty years of age should be the exception rather than the rule.'[2]

Of more practical importance is the difficulty of finding 'men and women between the ages of 30 and 45 who can spare enough time',[3] particularly because this coincides with the period of life when effort at work is closely related to prospects of promotion.

Although attempts are made to discuss the issues of social balance

[1] Reported in *Justice of the Peace, 127* (1963), 242.

[2] *Practice and procedure in magistrates' courts,* Memorandum of the Council of the Law Society, May 1967. Appendix 2, 27.

[3] *The training of justices of the peace in England and Wales,* (1965) Cmnd. 2856, H.M.S.O. paragraph 20, 7.

and politics separately, they are inextricably entwined. Ever since the Royal Commission on the Selection of Justices of the Peace of 1909–10, it has been recognized that the bench should be representative of all levels of the community: 'It is in the public interest that persons of every social grade should be appointed Justices of the Peace, and that working men with a first hand knowledge of conditions of life among their own class should be appointed.'[1] For this reason the Commission were:

> Of the opinion that it is not in the public interest that there should be an undue preponderance of Justices drawn from one political party . . . appointments influenced by considerations of political service and interest are highly detrimental to public interests . . . selection should be wide so that the Bench may include men . . . of all shades of creed and political opinion.[2]

The words 'may include' should be noted. The idea of a representative bench has never meant 'proportional representation', simply that members should be appointed from different sectors of the community. The bench should not simply represent those with power in the local community.

But as the 1948 Commission pointed out, this conclusion created a paradox. For how would it be possible to ensure a wide or even 'balanced' range of political views without making sure that the Advisory Committees which recommended appointments to the Lord Chancellor represented different political opinions? And if men were chosen for the Advisory Committees on political grounds was it not inevitable that their choice of candidates for the bench should rest, at least in part, on political criteria? It is not necessary to hold a conspiracy theory to see why this might be the case. In the first place party members are likely to know other party members well, and secondly, political activity is, especially for the manual worker, one of the main ways in which someone can become known in community affairs and show the signs of leadership, independence and intelligent grasp of affairs which are regarded as essential qualities for a magistrate.[3] Even so, the Commission, when collecting information on social background and other factors in their survey: 'considered whether [they] should enquire into the political opinion of justices and came to the conclusion that such information, even if it were desirable to seek it, would not be of real assistance. . . .'[4]

[1] Quoted in Royal Commission *Report*, 1946–8, p. 4.

[2] Quoted in *Report*, 1946–8, p. 4.

[3] Among the qualities mentioned by the Law Society's Committee as essential qualities for a competent justice are: 'reasonable standard of education . . . ability of expression . . . experience of the world'. Op. cit., 27.

[4] Royal Commission *Report*, paragraph 20, p. 5.

The 1948 Commission did, of course, recommend that the 'proportion of members of the [Advisory] Committee who are appointed because of their affiliation with political parties should be restricted, so that their influence shall not be predominant' and that 'no member of the committee should regard himself as "the representative" of any political party'.[1] But Lord Merthyr, Mr Cotton and Mr Watson, in a memorandum of dissent, went further in suggesting that no attention should be paid to the political affiliation of any person appointed to a committee.[2] This was not to say, of course, that political activity should be a bar—only that it was an irrelevant criterion. There is no recent evidence about the importance of politics in local committees, although one recent press report did mention that at least on one committee 'political balance is skilfully preserved. Of the members, four are Conservative, four are Labour and there is one vacancy [the other member being the Lord Lieutenant].'[3] A report in *The Times* suggested (on the evidence of a magistrate) that some committees became 'self-appointed selection committee(s) on which members of one political persuasion may easily become the majority . . . the final bench reflects in its members the political make-up of the advisory committee, and not many are outside the influence of a political party.'[4] That was in 1963, and even two years later a prominent lawyer and former Recorder and Stipendiary Magistrate, Mr J. P. Eddy, Q.C., wrote: 'When there are vacancies on any particular Bench to be filled the first consideration is the preservation of the balance of the parties and not the intrinsic merits of the candidates'.[5]

Whether or not this was, or still is, an accurate reflection of the process (and it is important to note that while Lord Chancellors have denied that it is,[6] bodies such as the Law Society have been unconvinced by such denials),[7] Lord Dilhorne reiterated the import-

[1] Royal Commission *Report*, paragraph 76, p. 19.

[2] Ibid., paragraph 20, p. 5.

[3] Tony Geraghty, 'Quest for cloth-cap magistrates', *Sunday Telegraph*, 2 July 1967.

[4] Report in *The Times*, 24 January 1963.

[5] Article in *The Yorkshire Post*, 27 August 1965.

[6] See Lord Dilhorne's address to the Magistrates' Association: 'I seek to secure that the Advisory Committees are thoroughly representative . . . none of them are representative of political parties . . . the Advisory Committee helps me to find the best people for the bench, irrespective of the candidates' political views . . . I go through [the recommendations] and consider them most carefully . . . the function of the Lord Chancellor is no formality', *The Magistrate*, *19* (1963), 182.

[7] See the Law Society's 1967 memorandum, op. cit., especially the letter to the Lord Chancellor on the appointment of magistrates, which deplores that *greater* weight is given to political considerations than any other factor.

ance of keeping a political balance on the bench. For example, he pointed out the necessity 'to distinguish between the individual magistrate whose politics were irrelevant and the need to keep a political balance on the bench and avoid the predominance of one political colour or another'. Yet at the same time, when asked whether there was justification for the 'widely held view' that appointment as a magistrate was a reward for political or local government services, he said: 'I do not accept, and I do not think my predecessors accepted this view. Appointment depends on evidence of ability to discharge the functions of magistrate—a reward for services of this sort must be sought in other fields.'[1]

Even so, it must be recognized that the title J.P. does provide considerable status based on the authority of the office. While the manifest function of appointments to the bench may not be to give this status, it inevitably is one of the 'latent' functions[2] and must affect decisions about the kinds of person who are considered to have the necessary qualifications for the office. It would seem obvious that those who have already achieved seniority or status in other walks of life will be the main candidates, and perhaps inevitable that appointment as a Justice of the Peace will be seen by many as a confirmation of being a 'worthy citizen'.

In any case, the closeness between political affiliations and social background does of course make it inevitable, as the *Justice of the Peace* pointed out, that 'groupings of those having the same political beliefs are to be expected . . . this is not as a result of any party line but as a manifestation of background and social attitudes.'[3] This point was clear to Lord Gardiner when he started his campaign in 1966 to recruit more wage-earners to the bench, but it brought a good

[1] Reported in *Justice of the Peace, 127* (1963), 242, and *The Magistrate, 19* (1963), 182. Almost precisely the same point was made explicitly by Lord Hailsham in his 1970 Presidential Address to the Magistrates' Association: 'It is not an honour, like a knighthood or an OBE', *The Magistrate, 26* (1970), 184–5. Similarly Lord Merthyr (then President of the Magistrates' Association) said 'the Magistracy should not be regarded as a reward for good service in other spheres. It should be treated as an appointment in its own right, as a specific vocation.' (Reported in an interview with Dr Bolt, *Justice of the Peace, 133* (1969), 102.) As an example of the view which is being attacked here the leading article in a Northern local paper is illuminating: 'it is therefore vitally important that the magistrates *who are made Justices of the Peace as a reward for public service*, but *whose honour*, thus accorded, involves many hours of work, should be as competent as possible.' Leading article on 'Training' in *The Mail*, Hartlepools, 2 June 1964 [my italics].

[2] For a discussion of these concepts see R. K. Merton (1957), *Social theory and social structure*, The Free Press, Glencoe, 19–84.

[3] *Justice of the Peace, 127* (1963), 46.

deal of criticism. In an early interview with 'Brougham' of the *Justice of the Peace* Lord Gardiner said, 'While we do not want politics on the bench it is very desirable that it should be representative of all social classes and there is a strong connection between social class and political affiliation.' He went on to point out that proportionate to the voting figures there was a high percentage of Conservatives among justices, usually, he thought, because of financial reasons.[1]

The issue was brought to public attention by press reports of three incidents in 1966: complaints about the composition of the Bournemouth bench and the Rossendale bench, and a circular about political affiliations which was rejected by the Bromley magistrates. In January of that year the Bournemouth local Labour Party protested that ten of the twelve magistrates appointed had come from the upper or middle classes, and Lord Gardiner then asked the Advisory Committee to 'make a special effort to find suitable candidates from among these [wage-earning] sections of the population'.[2] Similarly at Rossendale in Lancashire, Labour Party officials protested that the bench contained none of their nominees for the third year running, and that the 'great majority of magistrates for the area were drawn from those holding what were, in Rossendale, minority opinions'. Apparently, similar protests came from Sheffield and Tonbridge and from Liberals in Birmingham and Liverpool.[3] But a problem arose from the Bournemouth Labour Party's attitude to the solution. The secretary was reported as saying:

> We have submitted the names of three well known party members and we may be putting up another two. We have also circularised all affiliated organisations and received five further nominations. These will be forwarded in the near future.[4]

In a leading article the *Sunday Times* said that the 'general policy' behind the attempt to draw more magistrates from the wage-earning sector 'is open to grave suspicion. Assuming that wage earners as such are needed on the bench, how are they to be found?' and commenting on the Bournemouth affair stated 'At once the selectivity is shifted from economic class to party politics. This is manifestly wrong in principle.' Furthermore the article pointed out that probably two-fifths of wage earners vote Conservative and so might be eliminated from selection. While admitting that the bench should not be 'manifestly biased by class monopoly' it laid more stress on the 'authority of education or experience'.[5] In the same vein, *The*

---

[1] *Justice of the Peace, 129* (1965), 158.    [2] *The Times*, 7 January 1966.
[3] *The Guardian*, 17 August 1966.    [4] *The Times*, 7 January 1966.
[5] *Sunday Times*, 'Politics and the bench', 9 January 1966.

*Times,* while applauding the attempt to introduce more people with 'different types of knowledge and background', stated categorically that 'training is more important than social balance on the bench'.[1] A Conservative M.P. with particular experience of penal affairs summed up the argument:

> There are, the Lord Chancellor thinks, too many Tories on the bench. That strikes me as the wrong approach to a valid point, which is that magistrates should not be too narrowly drawn. To aim at socially representative benches makes sense. To purge benches of Tories by quizzing magistrates about their political views is objectionable.[2]

And I suppose this was behind the fears expressed by the Bromley bench on receiving a questionnaire about their political affiliations. Questions were raised in Parliament, in which the member for Bromley suggested that a 'political test' was irrelevant to the administration of justice. While generally agreeing that 'merit and qualification for the job are the primary considerations', the Attorney General added that 'we are a political nation and politics cannot be entirely detached from a consideration of this matter'.[3]

One recent measure, aimed to help manual workers, was the introduction, in Section 4 of the Justices of the Peace Act 1968, of a financial loss allowance, which makes possible reimbursement, to a limited extent, for loss of wages. This had been a contentious issue for a long time. Since the 1948 Commission there has been payment

---

[1] *The Times,* leading article, 'Choice of magistrates', 9 May 1967. The same argument was put by the Law Society committee's memorandum, op. cit., p. 27. 'The committee . . . are firmly of the opinion that the need for obtaining a cross-section of the community on the bench must not be allowed to over-ride the paramount need for ensuring that only those best qualified be appointed to this important office.' Other commentators have suggested there would be problems for those with little formal education: 'without being unkind, if Lord Chancellors really do want wage earners of modest education and ability on the bench, these are not always the best equipped persons to articulate a closely reasoned judgement'. Report by a magistrates' clerk on the Justices' Clerks' Society's weekend training course, *Justice of the Peace,* 134 (1970), 756.

[2] William Deedes, M.P. 'When magistrates boob', *Sunday Telegraph,* 16 March 1967.

[3] See *H. C. Debates,* Vol. 737 (7 December 1966), cols 1352–54. The questionnaire had been sent to all magistrates in the area covered by the South-East London Advisory Committee, and only one bench complained.

The Attorney General pointed out that it was necessary to get information on the political affiliations of those already on the bench, so that this could be taken into account when making new appointments. He thought benches had not always been balanced in this respect in the past. See also *H. C. Debates,* Vol. 737 (14 December 1966), 455–7, in which it was pointed out that benches were not always over-weighted with Conservatives: some in the north having mainly Labour party members.

for expenses and a subsistence allowance for magistrates living more than three miles from court, but the Commission rejected reimbursement on the grounds that a magistrate's 'duty can never be satisfactorily fulfilled if justices are not respected by the community . . . impartiality and independence are taken for granted . . . due in part to the fact that it is generally recognized that the work of the justice involves more self-sacrifice and loss'. They were concerned lest the sum paid was equal to what a wage-earner would normally get so that he would become 'a new class of stipendiary magistrate', and also convinced that the main problem, especially for those younger persons in responsible positions, was getting time off from work. In any case the Commission believed the majority of justices would themselves be against payment.[1] It will be interesting to see whether magistrates' attitudes have changed and, more important, whether a loss allowance can be of any help. It is probably true that the main difficulty lies in getting time off from work, not in losing money— although in a few cases this must be important. A Magistrates' Association spokesman is reported as saying:

> The trouble is that the man who is outstanding and has the confidence of his fellows is likely to be invited to serve as a magistrate. He is also the chap likely to be promoted to supervisor or foreman. It is often a case of asking an employer to release one of the key men.[2]

In relation to the findings of this enquiry it seems therefore useful to review the social composition, political affiliations and attitudes of the magistrates in the sample. True, there have been changes since 1965 (and it will be remembered that the last interviews were in early 1967), but these will have been relatively slow to take effect. Lord Gardiner said in 1968 that:

> in the last three years a great deal has been achieved in making benches more representative of the population as a whole . . . now benches are composed of men and women of different shades of opinion and with knowledge and experience of different walks of life to a far greater extent than ever before . . . .[3]

---

[1] *Report* 1946–48, especially paragraphs 206–8, pages 53–4. This is not an entirely outdated view. See for example H. A. Samuels, 'The magistracy: declining?' *Justice of the Peace*, *133* (1969), 71. 'The dangers of such a step [reimbursement] is that the image of the great unpaid may be tarnished. The office of magistrate is one of honour and not of profit. Service may involve sacrifice.'

[2] See report in *Sunday Telegraph*, 12 November 1967. An attempt has certainly been made to overcome the *financial* problems by persuading at least the nationalized industries to allow manual workers appointed as magistrates 18 days' paid leave a year.

[3] 1968 Presidential Address to the Magistrates' Association, *The Magistrate*, *24* (1968), 178.

Without wishing to detract from the progress made, it has been estimated that if every one of the 1,000 magistrates who retire annually 'were replaced by a known wage-earner, it would be almost eight years before the Gardiner policy really began to bite',[1] and this would give wage-earners about a 50 per cent representation. But of course replacement from the 'wage-earning sector' must have been at a slower pace, and so the figures from this survey, which include some magistrates appointed in 1965 and 1966, cannot be too far out.

It seems (as the present Lord Chancellor, Lord Hailsham, said) that *within limits* Lord Gardiner had a quite tangible degree of success' (my italics). But Lord Hailsham appears to regard the major work as complete. Indeed he apparently fears 'the emergence of the "statutory wage earner" just as one had "the statutory woman" [on every Committee]'.[2] Soon after appointment he told the Magistrates' Association that:

> The balance which is required is a natural balance, not one artificially striven after or contrived. The most important thing is not balance at all . . . [but] the judicial temperament . . . [which] does not consist in not having controversial opinions but . . . of having both the determination and the capacity to overcome them when sitting judicially.

After defining the concept further he concluded: 'The candidates [for the bench] were never of a higher quality or better social balance than they are at the moment.' 'The magistracy', said Lord Hailsham, came 'straight from the grass-roots of society', especially from among those devoted to public and social service of all kinds.[3]

## SURVEY FINDINGS

In the analysis of magistrates' social, personal and motoring characteristics we looked not only at each item separately but also at the correlations between them. Obviously it was important to know if

[1] Tony Geraghty, *Sunday Times*, 2 July 1967. Gordon Rose, writing in 1963 of the proposed changes, said, 'since it is difficult to change the balance they [the benches] tend to reflect the balance of the 1920s rather than the 1960s'. ("Can we train the magistracy?" *New Society*, No. 54, 10 October 1963, Page 16.) This is obviously an overstatement, but the point that change is bound to occur slowly is surely valid.

[2] Report of a conversation with 'Brougham' in *Justice of the Peace*, 134 (1970), 849.

[3] Report of Address at the Jubilee Dinner of the Magistrates' Association, *The Magistrate*, 26 (1970), 129–30. See also a recent article on 'The training of magistrates' which, in discussing the demands that may be made, warns that this might deter some from joining the bench and change the character of the magistracy: thus concluding, 'If it changed too much it would no longer be *the representative body* which it now is' [my italics]. *Justice of the Peace*, 134 (1970), 580.

some were highly interrelated: if, for example, age was correlated with political affiliation or sex with driving experience. This was done by looking at the relationship between each attribute and every other one.[1] A 'cluster analysis' made it possible to examine which attributes of magistrates were most strongly associated. The statistical method and a detailed diagram of the associations are shown in Appendix III. It shows, for example, that there is a close association (as one would expect) between occupation, voting behaviour and political attitudes, and that the region of the country a magistrate comes from is more highly associated with attributes such as age and occupation than with sex, personality type and membership of the Magistrates' Association. It is important to note that very few attributes were so closely correlated as to suggest distinctive groups of magistrates sharing a particular set of common characteristics. In fact, none of the attributes is found predominantly in any social, political, age or personality group. While many characteristics are represented in English magistrates, it is as well to remember that magistrates share much in common.

## 1. *Social Class*

This survey indicates that there have been some changes in the composition of the bench—in particular more young magistrates and more women—but there seems no evidence of any significant changes in the social-class backgrounds from which magistrates came in the years between 1946 and the second half of the 1960s.

It was possible to make a rough comparison between my information and that collected by the 1946–8 Commission through a questionnaire sent by post to all magistrates in England and Wales in 1947, 87 per cent of whom replied. But two points should be remembered: first, the categories used in the two surveys are not identical;[2] second, mine is not a guaranteed representative sample from the country as a whole. Table 1 shows the social-class backgrounds of the 538 magistrates compared with the Commission's findings and the general population of England and Wales in 1961 (the nearest census).

In fact, no semi- or unskilled workers on the bench were found in the sample, and many of the skilled manual and clerical workers were

---

[1] Attributes were divided into 2, 3 or 4 categories, and the relationship between attributes was computed using the chi-square test of significance.

[2] Because full details of occupations were collected, they could be re-grouped into the Commission's categories. It was obviously desirable to group P and E and S and W categories together. (See Notes to Table 1.)

TABLE 1

THE OCCUPATION OF MAGISTRATES 1947 AND 1966–7

| Registrar General's Classification | | Royal Commission's Classification [Males] | | | Total Population (1961) |
|---|---|---|---|---|---|
| 1966–7 Sample [N = 538]* | | Sample 1966–7 [N = 377] | | Commission 1947 [N = 11, 279] | England & Wales (Reg. Gen.) |
| Class | % | Class‡ | % | % | % |
| 1. Higher professional | 21·7 | O | 3·5 | 0·8 | ⎫ |
| 2. Managerial and other pro-fessional | 55·2 | | | | ⎬ 3·9 |
| | | P | 21·3 ⎫ 51·3 | 30·8 ⎫ 51·8 | ⎭ |
| 3. Clerical | 9·7 | E | 30·0 ⎭ | 21·8 ⎭ | 14·4 |
| 4. Skilled manual | 12·1 | OA | 16·5 | 14·6 | 49·8 |
| 5. Semi-skilled | 0 | S | 13·7 ⎫ 28·7 | 11·4 ⎫ 27·3 | 19·9 |
| 6. Unskilled | 0 | W | 15·0 ⎭ | 15·9 ⎭ | 8·6 |
| Not classifiable | 1·3 | Other† | | 4·3 | |

* Women are classed by their own occupation if in full-time employment, otherwise by their husband's. The figures for women are difficult to compare with those gathered by the Commission because that survey had an 11 per cent 'unclassified' group. This is why the comparison has only been made for males.
† Farmers, including landlords who farm.
‡ The Commission used a 'simplified form' of the categories employed by the Royal Commission on Population. See *R.C. Report* (paragraph 29, pages 7–8) and Appendix 4 of the *Minutes of Evidence*.
O = Persons without gainful occupations (those who are now retired are entered under another appropriate classification).
P = Professional.
E = Employers (non-professional) of 10 or more people, directors and the higher managerial posts in business and industry.
OA = Persons in business on their own account or employing less than 10 people.
S = Persons paid salaries other than those who fall into any of the above classes.
W = Persons paid wages.

full-time trade-union or local-government officers. Comparing the two sets of figures for men it can be seen that the combined propor-tion of salary and wage earners has not increased.[1] The minority with independent means has decreased at the same time as the

[1] Because of the problems of precise comparison it seemed sensible to bracket the S and W groups.

number of those from professional backgrounds has risen. Bearing in mind the problems of making comparisons for women, precisely the same trends seem to occur: those with independent means fell from 17 per cent to 5 per cent, but women with professional backgrounds (either of their own or their husband) increased from about 30 per cent to over half the number on the bench. At the same time the proportions from the salaried and wage-earning sectors remained static.

Women were much more likely to be in the Registrar General's Class 1 than men, and less likely to be in Class 4.

TABLE 2

A COMPARISON OF THE SOCIAL BACKGROUND OF
MALE AND FEMALE MAGISTRATES

| Registrar General's Classification | % Men [N = 377] | % Women [N = 161] |
|:---:|:---:|:---:|
| 1 | 15 | 39 |
| 2 | 60 | 46 |
| 3 | 10 | 9 |
| 4 | 15 | 6 |
| 5 | 0 | 0 |

Clearly, the increase in the proportion of women magistrates (from roughly 22 per cent in 1946 to 30 per cent at the time of this survey) has not helped to balance the bench in social class terms. On the contrary it has made it even more of a middle class preserve.

The magistrates were predominantly middle-aged, the youngest being 29 and the oldest 74 (75 then being the retiring age). Three-quarters were over 50, only 5 per cent under 40; the average being 56.[1] Nearly a fifth had retired from work. On the other hand magistrates in 1966–7 were younger than in 1947. Then 65 per cent were 60 or older and 28 per cent 70 or more, compared with 38 and 7 per cent. In 1947 the largest group was between 60 and 69; now it is between 50 and 59. But the changing age composition has had little impact on the social balance. This is partly because women magistrates are younger—37 per cent being 50 or less compared with 24 per cent of the men—but also because recently appointed magis-

[1] And the average age is probably slightly higher than would have been found if the sample from each bench had been random, instead of always including chairmen and deputies, who are selected, generally from among older (but not the oldest) magistrates.

trates have been even less likely to come from the clerical or skilled working groups. Of those who had been on the bench five years or less, 12 per cent were from this sector of the community, compared with 28 per cent of those who were appointed 20 or more years ago.

Social class, naturally, is reflected in the educational level the magistrates had reached. A quarter were at elementary school— leaving at the age of 14; nearly a third were at public schools, and most of the rest at grammar or technical schools. Over half had remained at school until at least 17, 35 per cent had continued in full-time higher education, 22 per cent at university, and another 46 per cent had pursued part-time further studies, mostly in profes- sional or vocational subjects. Only a fifth had no higher education. Again, however, it was the younger magistrates who were more likely to be better educated. Of those aged 50 or less only 38 per cent had left school before 17, compared with 58 per cent of those over 60.[1] Again, by this criterion, women were more middle class. A significantly higher proportion had continued in full-time higher education—49 per cent compared with 27 per cent of the men—and more had been to public or grammar schools.

## 2. Politics and Community Affairs

The evidence confirms that magistrates are largely chosen from those who have made a success in political and public life. Despite the assurances that political affiliations are an irrelevant criterion in selection, magistrates were much more likely to be party members than a sample of the general public. A very high proportion, 61 per cent, were actually *members* of a party; 34 per cent Conservative and 24 per cent Labour. This should be compared with a membership of approximately 15 per cent among the electorate in general.[2]

When asked how they would vote if there were a general election, a half said Conservative, just under a third Labour, and 10 per cent Liberal. In terms of the general voting pattern in recent elections, Labour supporters are under-represented.[3] There was no evidence that a higher proportion of more recent appointments were Labour members or voters. Nor has the increased proportion of women made any great difference: for despite being more 'middle-class', the same proportion are Labour voters as among male magistrates.

[1] Similarly, while 22 per cent of those aged 50 or less had been to elementary school only, 35 per cent of those aged over 60 had.

[2] See J. Blondel (1963), *Voters, parties and leaders*, Pelican Books, 88–94.

[3] In 1966, of those who voted, 48 per cent voted Labour, 42 per cent Conser- vative, and 8·5 per cent Liberal. See D. E. Butler and R. King (1966), *The British general election of 1966*, London, Macmillan, 296.

The usual factors were, of course, correlated with political voting intentions—social class, type of school background and full-time higher education. But there was no evidence that the region of the country, size of the bench (whether rural or urban) or length of appointment differentiated between Labour and Conservative supporters.

Besides being likely to be party members, magistrates were also heavily committed in local affairs. Just over half were (39 per cent) or had been (13 per cent) active in public service, for instance as councillors or members of rent tribunals. Over 60 per cent were (50 per cent) or had been (12 per cent) in community services such as social service organizations, and almost 90 per cent had had connections with social activities such as church affairs, charities, men's, women's and young people's organizations. A third were actively involved in all three types of activity. It is perhaps significant that many extended their attitudes towards voluntary work to their conception of the magistracy. When asked whether they were in favour of reimbursement for loss of earnings, just over a half said 'No'—mainly because they believed 'voluntary service is best'.

In order to get a wider perspective of political and social attitudes, magistrates were invited to complete a questionnaire. It was a 24-item version of H. J. Eysenck's test of political attitudes, which had been used in studies of judges in the USA by Stuart Nagel.[1] We originally viewed this with some scepticism because of the possibility of endorsement of items (in this case liberal) which might have been thought appropriate for a university-based sociological study, but the very high correlation between the replies and statements of actual voting intentions indicates that the forms were validly completed.

The main dimensions of the test are 'radicalism to conservatism' and 'tough-mindedness to tender-mindedness'. By 'tough-minded' Eysenck means having opinions based on 'rationalism' and 'empiricism'; the tender-minded are those whose opinions are dominated by 'ethical, moralistic . . . altruistic values', those in fact who 'go by principles'.[2] It is difficult to compare magistrates with the group of

---

[1] Stuart S. Nagel (1963), 'Off the bench judicial attitudes', in G. Schubert (ed.) *Judicial decision making*, The Free Press of Glencoe, 29–53; and (1961), Political party affiliation and judges' decisions, *American Political Science Rev.*, 55, 843–850. The questionnaire is in Appendix I. We changed item 22 in Nagel's questionnaire, [Birth control, except when medically indicated, should be made illegal] to one about abortion, because the statement was obviously not appropriate (the answers were scored, for this question, on the middle of the three weighted scales used by Nagel. See fn. 1, page 55).

[2] See H. J. Eysenck (1954), *The psychology of politics*, London, Routledge, 131–2.

500 middle-class citizens tested by Eysenck, but both samples seem to have similar average scores on both scales. Magistrates seem, then, to represent the range of political and social attitudes held by others of their social class in the community.[1] On the other hand, they do indicate a tendency to think in terms of abstract general principles rather than in pragmatic terms.

If the actual mid-points of both scales were used as a basis for describing the magistrates, 85 per cent have scores in the 'tender-minded' half, and on the other axis 58 per cent in the conservative half: only 11 per cent would be described as both tough-minded and conservative, (veering towards right-wing "fascist" views) and 4 per cent as tough-minded radicals (having communist-orientated views).

FIGURE 2

POLITICAL AND SOCIAL ATTITUDES OF MAGISTRATES

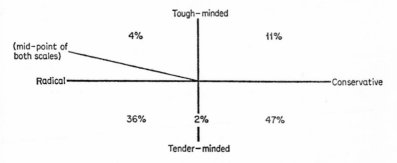

So that the *relative* scores of magistrates could be compared, they were divided, on each scale, into two groups: those scoring in the upper half, and those in the lower half. Further analysis showed that the relatively tough-minded were more likely both to be conservative

[1] Nagel's scoring system was used (see Appendix 2 of his article, pp. 50–1) both for the conservative-radical scale and the tough-tender mindedness scale. This scoring system is based on the correlation co-efficients with these factors given in Table XX, p. 129 of *The psychology of politics*. The mean scores on both scales were compared with the scores given in Table XXI (p. 134) of Eysenck's book, which are based on a sample of 500 middle-class men and women. The comparisons were difficult to make, first because Eysenck's figures are unweighted while those in the study are; second, because Eysenck's scores are based on a 40-item test and Nagel's on a shorter 24-item version. Bearing this in mind, and roughly converting Eysenck's 'averages' to our scale, we found the mean scores to be very similar.

voters and conservative in their attitudes as measured by the Eysenck test.[1]

Conservative attitudes were correlated with being older, middle class, and better educated, but not with sex. The women were as conservative as men, but more likely to be tender-minded.[2]

## 3. *Personality*

Personal qualities of the kind required of magistrates are obviously difficult to measure, especially when they are summarized as:

'Men of the work, men of sense, men of common justice.'[3]
[Chief Baron Pollock]

Among the personality traits mentioned by the Law Society were 'patience and courtesy; firmness without obstinacy; the ability to make up one's mind' as well as integrity, common sense and absence of bias.[4] Lord Hailsham added: 'the capacity to listen, the willingness to be influenced by argument but not stampeded by oratory . . . the ability to be sympathetic without being weak, be generous and kindly without being sentimental and mawkish . . .'[5]

The test most easily completed and useful for this purpose seemed to be the Eysenck Personality Inventory, which has been given to many other subjects in Britain. It measures two main dimensions— what Eysenck calls neuroticism to stability and extraversion to introversion. The relationship of these to more generally described characteristics is shown in the diagram from the Eysencks' manual to the test, together with the proportion of magistrates in each of the four sectors.

The average (mean) 'E' (extraversion) score of Eysenck's 'normal' population is 12·07; for magistrates it was 9·98. Comparing this with a very small sample of 'managers' tested by Eysenck, the magistrates were still more introverted. This may of course be due partly to age— the older ones being significantly more likely to have a lower extraversion score—and partly to the low proportion of women, who in my sample were significantly more extraverted.

[1] Of conservative *voters*, 55 per cent were relatively tough-minded compared with 33 per cent of labour voters: among the relatively tough-minded two-thirds also had relatively conservative attitudes.

[2] Sixty-six per cent of women had relatively tender-minded scores compared to 52 per cent of the men.

[3] Quoted in the Law Society's memorandum on *Practice and procedure in magistrates courts*, op. cit., 26.

[4] Ibid., 27.

[5] *The Magitsrate 26* (1970), 130.

Similarly the 'N' (neuroticism) score is lower than for a 'normal' population—the mean being 7·11 compared with 9·07, much more stable.[1] Again, age is a complicating factor as the younger magistrates were more likely to have a higher neuroticism score and my

FIGURE 3

RELATIONSHIP OF EXTRAVERSION/INTROVERSION AND NEUROTICISM STABILITY TO EARLIER PERSONALITY SCHEMES[2]

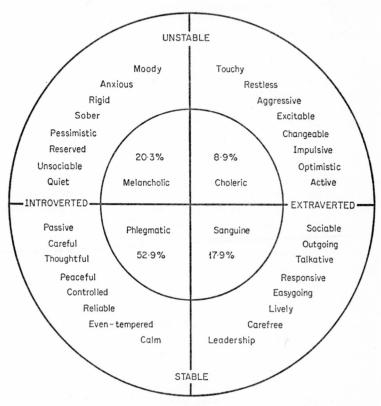

sample was biased towards the relatively old. Yet despite these caveats, Figure 3 shows that magistrates are, on the whole, a stable group: 70 per cent scored below the mid-point of the neuroticism

[1] For the figures on which these comparisons are based, see H. J. and Sybil B. G. Eysenck (1964), *Manual of the Eysenck personality inventory*, University of London Press, Tables 4 and 5.

[2] ibid., 6.

scale. They are also relatively introverted: 73 per cent scoring below the mid-point of the extraversion scale. Less than 10 per cent are in the neurotic—extraverted or 'choleric' sector, and over half are 'stable introverts', whose characteristics—thoughtful, controlled, reliable, etc.—appear to be what most commentators have regarded as the traits desirable in good magistrates.

Of course, it could be that magistrates were consciously giving 'favourable' responses, but the purport of the questionnaire is so disguised that it is unlikely that most people could 'role-play' consistently. And even if this were the case, it would show that a majority do recognize the qualities usually looked for in judges. One incidental problem was interpreting the lie-scale. This was a number of items which it is supposed only liars or 'paragons of virtue' would endorse, such as answering 'yes' to 'Would you always declare *everything* at the customs, even if you knew that you could never be found out?' The average lie-score was higher than that generally acceptable for the test, but I would interpret this so-called 'faking-good' to be a real indication of the magistrates' self-conception as an upright citizen. This was illustrated by frequent comments during interviews about the effect on behaviour of being appointed to the bench. Many magistrates emphasized that they felt it imperative to set a 'good example' even when to do so might be regarded by many as abnormal. As one magistrate said, 'I feel a clot going into town doing 30 down the Great North Road when everybody is passing me doing 50.' Significantly (statistically and otherwise) the older magistrates and those who regularly took the chair in the adult court had higher scores than others.

### 4. *Magisterial Matters*

Some other questions touched on briefly concerned the position of chairmen, the Magistrates' Association, reading and training. Because the study dealt with so few courts the analysis is concentrated on those who were either formally chairmen or the 203 magistrates who regularly took the chair in adult court settings. As expected, they were more likely to be the older, more experienced magistrates: of those over 60, 61 per cent regularly took the chair, whereas only 15 per cent of those under 50 did. A high proportion of chairmen were men—43 per cent compared with 27 per cent women.[1] It is especially interesting that sitting in the chair was *not* correlated with social class, political party, political or social atti-

[1] Women were more strongly represented in the juvenile court, especially those with considerable experience as magistrates.

tudes or personality score. The vast majority of magistrates were happy with the role played by their chairmen and their clerk. Only ten of the 29 clerks said the chairman was 'influential' in affecting general bench policy—other than acting as a chairman at group meetings, although another five said he had a stabilizing role in acting as a link between rotas. Only one clerk said that he thought the chairman's influence at one of his benches (not in the study) should be less. The remainder thought the role of the chairman was what was required.

Three-quarters of the magistrates were members of the Magistrates' Association, 83 per cent of the women and 73 per cent of the men. Membership was lowest in the North-East, only 67 per cent belonging, and there is no doubt that social class is closely related to membership. Percentages of members in the Registrar General's four categories of social class were:

|   | %  |
|---|-----|
| 1 | 91 |
| 2 | 84 |
| 3 | 44 |
| 4 | 42 |

Eighty-seven per cent of Conservative supporters (intending voters) were members compared with only 54 per cent of Labour supporters. Very few who did not join said they thought the Association 'ineffectual'; the usual reason was a combination of expense and 'not getting round to it'. Lord Gardiner was clearly aware of these social implications when he urged the Association in 1967 to abolish the wearing of formal dinner suits at annual dinners.[1]

Nearly all magistrates were in favour of training. As an attempt to get an indicator of 'professional' interest in their task they were also asked about the extent of their reading of professional journals dealing with crime, criminals and sentencing. The findings are interesting in their own right and might have implications for training.

Magistrates were 'quality paper' readers. Nearly three-quarters read *The Times, Guardian* or *Daily Telegraph*, and one of the three 'quality' Sunday papers. Their professional reading was, however, very restricted. They were asked first if they *subscribed* to any of a list of journals dealing with matters relating to sentencing—almost none did.[2] They were then asked, for each journal, whether they read

[1] *The Magistrate*, 23 (1967), 183.
[2] With the exception of *The Magistrate*, which is sent free to members of the Association.

it regularly (i.e., every issue), occasionally, or never, and, if never, if they knew of it and also whether it was accessible. The results were as follows:

TABLE 3

JOURNAL READERSHIP

| | The Magistrate | Justice of the Peace | Criminal Law Review | Probation | British J. of Criminology | Howard Journal |
|---|---|---|---|---|---|---|
| | | | (Percentage) | | | |
| Read regularly | 73·2 | 2·8 | 0·4 | 4·0 | 0·2 | 1·7 |
| Read occasionally | 13·2 | 25·8 | 6·5 | 19·9 | 2·2 | 7·4 |
| Never read, know it, accessible | 3·5 | 7·2 | 3·3 | 4·5 | 0·9 | 0·6 |
| Never read, know it, not accessible | 8·7 | 34·8 | 15·2 | 18·6 | 8·2 | 13·9 |
| Never read, not know it, not accessible | 1·3 | 29·4 | 74·5 | 53·2 | 88·5 | 76·4 |

Not only were a number of journals not read, but a large proportion of magistrates had never heard of them, or knew where they might obtain a copy. On the other hand, a third claimed to have read at least one book on a criminological or penal topic within the last two years.

Of course, these results do not mean that magistrates are necessarily ignorant of articles in professional journals, for their clerks may undertake to circulate information which they consider to be of importance. While this might be done for journals such as *The Justice of the Peace*, which deals with matters of immediate practical concern, it is doubtful whether more academic material is disseminated in this way. Some will, of course, be summarized in training sessions, but unfortunately we were not able to investigate the extent to which this is done. In any case, the fact that such a high proportion of magistrates thought the four 'academic' journals on their list were 'inaccessible' suggests the need for courts to take out subscriptions so that a library is available in the clerk's office—and that once there it is used.

## 5. The Magistrates as Motorists

Nearly 90 per cent of magistrates could drive, and nearly as many owned a car. Over 70 per cent of drivers had been driving for 25 years or more, and 80 per cent drove three or more times a week.[1] There is no shortage of driving experience on the bench.[2]

On the other hand, social class and driving experience are significantly correlated. Nearly all in the top two Registrar General's categories owned cars, but 37 per cent of the 117 in Classes 3 and 4 did not. There were similar differences in the amount of driving done in a year—those in the lower social categories had less experience. When asked to 'rate' themselves as drivers ('better than average', 'average' or 'not as good as most') about half named the top category. But while in Class 1 50 per cent, and in Class 2 64 per cent, rated themselves 'better than average', only 31 per cent and 23 per cent respectively did so in Classes 3 and 4.

While magistrates are experienced drivers, few are enthusiasts. Less than a fifth of the drivers read a motoring journal, and only 16 per cent were members of a motoring club or the Institute of Advanced Motorists or Veteran Motoring Association. Only ten magistrates were members of the Royal Society for the Prevention of Accidents.

All the magistrates were asked about their involvement in accidents, and whether or not they had been prosecuted. Just over 60 per cent had been in an accident as a driver or passenger, the majority of these as a driver. But their experience was largely limited to one accident—only 10 per cent being in two or more. One-quarter blamed themselves (21 per cent) or their driver (4 per cent); most of the remainder blamed the other person rather than road conditions. Twenty-seven per cent of the accidents had resulted in personal injury, but only a handful in death.

A third of all magistrates had, at some time, been prosecuted for some kind of motoring offence, but only 10 per cent twice or more. Of those who had been prosecuted, 17 per cent had been convicted of careless driving, 40 per cent of speeding and 37 per cent of minor offences such as parking and breaches of construction and use of

[1] Either as driver or passenger, 47 per cent drove under 10,000 miles a year, and 48 per cent between 10,000 and 19,000.

[2] It has been noted that in the past motorists have claimed that magistrates do not have sufficient expertise and grasp of motoring problems, and that non-motorists have claimed that magistrates, coming from the 'motoring sector of the community . . . are . . . too lenient with motorists'. D. W. Elliott and Harry Street (1968), *Road accidents*, London, Penguin Books, 86–7. The authors point out that with the general use of motor cars both arguments seem irrelevant.

regulations. For most the incident happened long ago—40 per cent over 20 years ago and 72 per cent ten or more years previously. Nearly a third regarded the decision as either unreasonable, completely unjust, or the result of an unmerited prosecution. By contrast, when questioned about prosecutions of friends or relatives (40 per cent of magistrates had friends or relatives who had been convicted), less than a fifth regarded the decision in such an unfavourable light.

It should be stressed that two-thirds of magistrates had no convictions and that those who had, had not been convicted (with rare exceptions) of offences such as dangerous or drunken driving, or driving while disqualified or without insurance. Even so, there is a substantial minority with experience of the situation facing offenders in the court, and this, presumably, is not the case with 'ordinary' indictable crime such as theft, sexual offences and crimes of violence.

This chapter has provided, for the first time in recent years, a profile of the social, personal, magisterial and motoring backgrounds of a sample of justices of the peace. They are interesting data in their own right, for they may shatter some prejudices about the constitution of the bench, but furthermore, they provide the raw material for the later analyses in which we have attempted to assess the effect of individual attributes on the sentencing behaviour of magistrates in motoring cases.

CHAPTER 4

# Purposes and Practices

BEFORE trying to distinguish between magistrates who impose different sentences I shall describe the range of views held by the sample as a whole on a number of important and often controversial topics. First, the aims of sentencing, including the idea of equality and individualization in fining; second, the complex issues surrounding the use of disqualification either for deterrent or preventive purposes; third, views on possible new approaches to the problem—in themselves reflecting attitudes to the basic aims of the penalty.

## IMPRISONMENT: ITS LIMITED USE

For the three offences for which imprisonment could be imposed in the mid-sixties, dangerous driving, drunken driving and driving while disqualified, sentencing practice was affected by the Criminal Justice Act 1967, which made it mandatory that prison sentences of six months or less be suspended unless the offender had previously served a term in prison. In fact, the only offence substantially affected was driving while disqualified, imprisonment being rare before 1967 for the other two offences.[1] The proportion actually imprisoned for all three offences fell. But if, for 1968, prison and

---

[1] The Court of Appeal has upheld prison sentences for dangerous driving even for a young offender. See *R.* v. *Hazell* [1965], *Crim. L.R.*, 120. In this case, though, the length of disqualification was reduced from twenty to five years. For the converse situation (in a case of causing death), where disqualification was increased after a reduction in prison sentence, see *R.* v. *Worrell* [1965] *Crim. L.R.*, 561. Sentences of imprisonment for drunken driving have been upheld on appeal only for persistent offenders, see *R.* v. *Wilson* [1969], *Crim. L.R.*, 158. In *R.* v. *Lavin* [1967], *Crim. L.R.*, 481–2, the court reversed a sentence of six months' imprisonment passed as a deterrent sentence on the grounds that 'a major departure in sentencing policy should have been made only after consultation with . . . brother judges . . . It might be that the time would come when for every offence of this character the courts will feel bound to impose imprisonment. But before it took place there should be consultation to ensure some degree of uniformity throughout the country.' A fine of £50 was substituted. See also *R.* v. *Whelan, The Times*, 15 July 1969.

suspended sentences were added together the proportions for which a custodial sentence was thought appropriate increased from 2·1 per cent to 2·8 per cent for dangerous driving and 31·6 per cent to 36·2 per cent for driving while disqualified—falling very slightly for drunken driving. The provisions of the 1967 Act have both enabled and perhaps encouraged magistrates to make more use of their power to send offenders convicted of driving while disqualified to Quarter Sessions. Under Section 56 of the 1967 Act offenders tried summarily, for summary or hybrid[1] offences, may be committed for sentence if on another indictable charge they are also committed under section 29 of the Magistrates' Courts Act 1952. They may then receive a prison sentence, but not exceeding the maximum penalty that could have been imposed by the magistrates: in this case six months.[2] In 1966 20 per cent were listed as 'otherwise disposed of', probably the majority being young offenders (aged up to 21) sent for sentence with a recommendation for borstal training.[3] In 1969 the proportion was 29 per cent, and this probably included offenders over 21. Combining immediate imprisonment and committals for borstal or prison sentence, the proportions sentenced to custodial sentences only fell from 55 per cent to 43 per cent. If one adds to this latter figure the 18 per cent given suspended sentences, presumably mainly because of the mandatory restriction on imprisonment, it is clear that magistrates have become more severe since 1967 in their policy towards these offenders. It should be remembered that before the Road Traffic Act 1962 imprisonment for driving while disqualified was mandatory (with exceptions), and that in 1966 the Magistrates' Association Road Traffic Committee and Council

[1] A hybrid offence is an offence for which separate penalties on indictment or on summary trial are provided in the Statute creating the offence.

[2] The law here is very complicated. Firstly, if a case of driving while disqualified began on 'indictment' by the magistrates taking depositions and then switching to summary trial under S.18(3) of the Magistrates' Courts Act 1952, Quarter Sessions would have power to give the maximum penalty for this offence when charged on indictment, which is 12 months. Secondly, Quarter Sessions are also bound by the suspended sentence provisions of the 1967 Act, and any sentence of six months or less would have to be suspended unless the offender had a previous prison record, or he was given a sentence of longer than six months for an indictable charge dealt with at the same time. See *R. v. Fullerton*, [1969], *Crim. L.R.*, 383, and *Justice of the Peace, 133*, (1969), 395.

[3] A few may have been adult offenders, but before 1967 they could only be committed for sentence if the charge of driving while disqualified had begun on indictment in the magistrates' courts: a practice which appears to have been relatively rare. This provision did not apply to committals under section 28 of the Magistrates' Courts Act 1952 for consideration of borstal training. See G. S. Wilkinson (1963), *Road traffic offences* (4th edition). London, Oyez Publs., 307–9.

urged that this should again be the law.[1] Furthermore, in 1969 the *Justice of the Peace* called for a reform of the 1967 Act 'to exclude from the mandatory [suspended sentence] provisions at least the offence of driving while unfit ... [and] driving while disqualified' and in 1970, commenting on the Act abolishing compulsory disqualification (see page 84), the journal emphasized that this did not represent a shift to a lenient policy: 'It is to be firmly hoped that the criminal courts will continue to regard the offence as one which warrants a custodial sentence, even on first conviction.'[2]

Of the five driving while disqualified cases sent to magistrates in this research, three involved offenders with previous convictions for non-motoring indictable offences, including prison sentences. Most magistrates sent them to prison again. There was a widely held view that such offenders, who deliberately flout the court's authority, need a severe penalty both as an individual and general deterrent. But, of course, for the other kinds of offence the penalty used in nearly every case is a fine, and it is here that problems of disparity in sentencing are felt to be particularly important.

EQUALITY AND THE TARIFF IN FINING

Where fines are concerned one issue, common to all sentencing, stands out above the rest: the conflict between the notion of what is variously called 'equality', 'the tariff' or 'just proportion', and the idea of 'individualizing' the sentence in relation to its effect on the offender. It has already been pointed out that this is an especially complex problem where motoring offences are concerned because many people regard them as a kind of technical infringement, often accidental, lacking the characteristics common to 'real crime' such as *mens rea* and therefore only calling for a penalty relating to the offence. The characteristics of the offender are considered unimportant because in this light the idea of general deterrence seems

[1] See A. J. Brayshaw, 'Hard case', *The Magistrate*, 23 (1967), 54–5; a comment on the 'Mrs Baker affair'. She was a pregnant woman whose sentence of three months' imprisonment for this offence led to a public outcry (see *Daily Express*, 15 February 1967, and its page one headline 'CAR MOTHER JAIL SHOCK'), but whose sentence was only reduced to one month on appeal (with no adverse press comment).

[2] *Justice of the Peace*, 133, (1969), 736 and 134 (1970), 544, Also report by *The Times* motoring correspondent, 16 February 1967, quoting Mr Gott, the Chief Constable of Northamptonshire, and Mr J. Eddy, Q.C., on the seriousness of the offence. Mr Eddy said 'Magistrates have a duty to send these men to prison.' Compare Elliott and Street's comment that since the 1962 Act 'it is curious that the proportion of defendants sent to prison still remains high', op. cit., 123.

redundant—for how can one deter the truly accidental occurence?—
and the concept of specific deterrence irrelevant, for the offences are
not committed 'on purpose'. Obviously this view carries more
conviction for some offences than others, and the next chapter will
discuss the problems magistrates face in distinguishing between those
offences which are more like 'real crime', and simple breaches of
regulations. At this stage it is only necessary to point out that
the lack of unanimity on this issue is what makes the debate so
important.

The arguments for and against 'basic' or 'suggested' penalties
were examined as well as the problem of relating fines to the offender's
income and the difficulties associated with taking account of extraneous variables such as costs and lists of multiple charges.

## 1. Basic Penalties: the Arguments

In July of 1964 the Council of the Magistrates' Association issued
a statement that it had 'for some time been concerned over wide
variations in sentences', and that road-traffic offences offered the
best opportunity for action.[1] After consultation with the Lord
Chancellor and the Lord Chief Justice a confidential circular was
sent to magistrates in February 1965 which set out for certain
offences a list of 'basic penalties', which was intended as a sentencing
guide. The idea of a basic penalty has been widely misinterpreted as
an attempt to apply a tariff, but the Association made it clear that its
aim was simply to provide a basis for discussion: its notional
penalties would be 'starting points'—'appropriate for an ordinary
offence committed by an ordinary average person'—which could be
varied accordingly to circumstances. It was made clear that the
Association 'has no power to desire to tell courts what they ought to
do and would resist any pressure from any quarter that would inter-
fere with the vital principle of the independence of the judiciary'.[2]
Yet a press leak of the Association's suggested penalties brought an
outcry that the discretionary power of magistrates was being eroded.
Lord Gardiner later pointed to the paradox:

> The public and the press cannot have it both ways. In one breath they
> object to variations in sentence and in the other they attack a genuine
> and quite proper attempt to lessen the variation. There can be nothing
> wrong in justices themselves getting together and discussing the problems

[1] See the Association's *Annual Report* for 1963–4, Appendix VIII, Statement by
the Council on consistency of penalties, 75, and the circular to members of the
Magistrates' Association, February 1965.
[2] Report in *The Times*, 25 September 1964.

of sentencing and indicating the level of penalty which they think right for certain of the more straightforward minor offences, where the facts reveal neither extenuating nor aggravating circumstances.[1]

But the 1965 list of penalties which was in operation throughout this research only partly dealt with the problem. Firstly, the national circular was not used everywhere. Local lists existed at only 16 of the 32 courts in this study. Secondly, there was no consistent policy about which offences were suitable for the basic penalty approach. The Magistrates' Association excluded dangerous, drunken and careless driving, but included driving while disqualified.[2] Only four of the 16 courts with local guides excluded dangerous and drunken driving, only two excluded careless driving, and 14 included driving while disqualified. Thirdly, local lists varied in their suggested starting points. For example:

| | Dangerous driving | Drunken driving | Driving while disqualified | Careless driving |
|---|---|---|---|---|
| Court A | £25 + 6 months' disqualification | £35 + 12 months' disqualification | Imprisonment or £25 + 12 months' disqualification | £10 |
| Court B | £35 + 6 months' disqualification | £50 + 2 years' disqualification | £25 + 5 years disqualification | £15 |
| Court C | £30 | £50 | No suggested penalty | £20 |

The 14 courts which included driving while disqualified varied in their suggestions from a fine of £25 with no stated period of disqualification to 'imprisonment or a heavy fine plus at least twelve months' disqualification'.[3] Of 10 courts with local suggestions for careless driving, three recommended specific periods of disqualification and another three said, 'consider disqualification'; the remainder simply suggested a licence endorsement. Similarly the recommendations for offences of failing to insure ranged from a fine of £10 to £25 plus disqualification. Six courts recommended specific disqualification periods ranging from three to twelve months.

[1] Lord Gardiner, Presidential Address to the Magistrates' Association, *The Magistrate*, 23 (1967), 183. See also *The Magistrate*, 20 (1964), 172.

[2] It was originally intended to include dangerous and careless driving, and as the distinction between them 'was largely artificial' a 'combined scale of penalties was drawn up covering four types of cases which were "very bad", "bad", "not so bad" and "negligent not involving danger"'. See *Annual Report* for 1963–4, 18.

[3] At four of these 16 courts the list was regarded as so confidential that we failed to obtain a copy from the clerk. This is why it was only possible to examine the recommendations for careless driving at 10 courts.

The extent to which a scale was used varied enormously. Beside the 16 benches with their own lists, another two appeared to have some 'unwritten' agreements on penalties for a few of the less serious offences. The remaining courts used no list at all. As might have been expected, all but one of the eight courts with fewer than ten magistrates serving on the bench had no schedule—presumably because they sat together so often. At some of the courts where a basic-penalty schedule existed the majority used it—so often at one place that it was known as 'the menu'. But the practice was certainly not universal, for at quite a few courts there was a deep division of opinion on the value of this device.[1]

Apparently the decision on which offences to include, and what amounts to suggest, was arrived at by a variety of procedures. Sometimes all magistrates would meet; at other courts the chairman and deputy chairman would decide with or without the clerk; in one area the chairman of Quarter Sessions drew up a list in consultation with the chairmen of each petty sessional division and it was sent to all courts in the county (although it was rejected by the bench we studied); in others a penalties sub-committee was appointed to review the situation; and in a few it was left for the clerk to prepare the scheme and submit it for ratification to the chairman. The fines and disqualifications recommended might be the average over the last one or three years, or a reflection of what was being done at adjacent courts, or the result of a special discussion on the 'average case' and its appropriate penalty.

Naturally, the Magistrates' Association were aware of this situation and made strenuous efforts to get the views of local benches. The penalties suggested in the 1965 circular were sent to all branches for comment and during 1965 opinions were collated by the Association's Road Traffic Committee. Amendments were subsequently incorporated in two revisions of the schedule, circulated in 1967 and 1970.

The 1967 circular stressed the need for *voluntarily* adopting a common policy and rejected 'any idea of a tariff with set penalties which enable a potential offender to calculate the exact penalty that will follow a particular offence', omitted the word 'basic'[2] in favour of the concept of 'starting points', which would be 'a normal penalty which is regarded as appropriate for an ordinary offence committed by an ordinary or average person', and drew attention to the particular

---

[1] The full analysis of the importance of court schedules is discussed in Chapter 8.

[2] Which members of the Association have said 'suggested a minimum on the analogy with basic wages', *Annual Report*, 1964–5, 13.

importance of considering the gravity of the offence and the circumstances and record of the offender. The circular sent in 1970 stressed these points even more by underlining them, increased the suggested penalties in line with rising incomes and, more important, included the offence of careless or inconsiderate driving.[1]

It is impossible to estimate the extent to which the efforts of the Magistrates' Association have reduced disparity. But it must be recognized that during the whole period in which the fieldwork for this study was being conducted, the 1965 circular was available to all members of the Association. Furthermore, the question of local scales and the way in which the schedule is interpreted are still live issues. A recent article in the *Justice of the Peace* stated that:

> Nationally agreed figures are not enough. Each area has its own traffic problems and local magistrates their own views on the gravity of different offences. It is right that these should be reflected in their penalties . . . And yet, how many petty sessional areas, we wonder, still have no standard penalties generally agreed among their justices?[2]

Also it seems that there is no necessary correspondence between the starting points and average fines imposed. The *Justice of the Peace* compared these figures for one bench and found:

|  | Fines suggested | Average actually imposed |
|---|---|---|
| No insurance | £15 | £11·1 |
| Careless driving | £20 | £11·1 |

It concluded that:

> In practice it was found that the suggested penalties were used as 'starting points' by the bench in the sense of figures to be reduced by the

---

[1] 'The Lord Chancellor and Lord Chief Justice waived their earlier objection subsequent to attention being drawn to the special importance of taking the means of the defendant into account in these cases,' *Minutes of the 31st meeting of the Magistrates' Association Road Traffic Committee*, 11 September 1969, minute 322b. (hereafter referred to as *R.T.C.*) But apparently the Lord Chief Justice reconsidered his view and 'expressed the gravest doubts' about including careless driving. 'He had said he would prefer if it was excluded but if it was to be included he felt the starting penalty should be £35 not £25.' But as the leaflet had already been printed the Road Traffic Committee resolved 'respectfully to note the views expressed by the Lord Chief Justice', 34 *R.T.C.*, 3 September 1970, minute 363a(2).

[2] *Justice of the Peace*, Consistency of penalties in traffic cases, *134* (1970), 243. There was some local reaction along these lines. The chairman of the Billericay (Essex) bench was reported to have said, 'We will impose such penalties as we think fit . . . we are not being told what to do and will not stick to a system laid down by an Association which has no local knowledge,' *Daily Telegraph*, 17 May 1967.

triviality of any offence and the limited means of the offender and never increased in the more serious cases.[1]

Yet despite the help of these attempts to persuade benches to adopt a 'common policy which they accept as fair, just and reasonable', there is probably still a long way to go. As we shall see, it may be easier to agree on common starting points than about what constitutes a 'normal' or 'serious' offence, or what is an 'average' person, or what weight should be given to income or previous record in calculating the sentence.[2]

## 2. *The Question of Means*

This variation in procedure and in practice from court to court was reflected in the answers to questions about the process of fining. Only half the magistrates stated categorically that they used a 'basic penalty' as a guide in serious cases: 40 per cent claimed not to use them at all. How then did they operate? Sixty per cent said they began with the *maximum* in mind and adjusted it to suit the particular case: 'We have the legal maximum in mind. I take into account the degree of seriousness of the offence, previous record, means of the defendant, mitigating circumstances, and arrive at a figure and then we discuss it.'
Or some start at a proportion of the maximum: 'We start with half the legal maximum and then adjust to the circumstances, usually downwards.'

These answers indicate that there may be what some call 'rough and ready guides', but that a genuine effort was being made by a substantial minority to overcome the most obvious objection to the basic penalty scheme—the danger of regressing to what some described as a 'rubber-stamp justice'.

Even so, the desire for flexibility might be seen as a need mainly to reflect in the sentence the varying gravity of the offence rather than the circumstances of the offender. In an effort to discover to what extent the income of the defendant was considered relevant the following problem was posed:

Imagine two motorists have had exactly the same accident and have been found guilty of the same offence arising out of it. Both have the

---

[1] Loc. cit.
[2] An example of an attempt to arrive at a scale based on the perceived seriousness of a case is Dr E. J. Anthony's suggestion of '25 per cent of the maximum for a first or trivial offence; 50 per cent of the maximum for a second or more serious offence, and 75 per cent or over for an outrageous offence with no redeeming features'. Letter to *The Magistrate*, 26 (1970), 81.

same record of previous offences and have appeared apologetic in court. *Motorist No. 1* earns £3,000 a year, say £60 per week, is a married man with his wife at home and two school age children. *Motorist No. 2* earns £15 per week with the same family considerations, paying £2·50 per week rent and £1 per week hire purchase. The only difference between them is income. Would you fine both these offenders the same, *first*, if it were one of the serious offences,[1] *secondly*, if it were not so serious an offence, say speeding or a pedestrian crossing offence?

Thirty-two per cent said they would give the same fine, mainly because the offence should be punished equally:

'The fine is for the offence whether it is for a rich man, poor man, beggar man or thief' . . . 'In the serious offences the penalty attaches to the offence and reflects the gravity of it' . . . 'It would be unfair to give one more than the other merely on grounds of income' . . . 'Why should one man's earnings come into a question of an offence?'

These views were expressed even though statute directs magistrates to 'take into consideration . . . the means of the person, so far as they appear or are known to the court' when imposing a fine.[2] Their interpretation of this is to consider the question when deciding the amount of time the offender will have to pay. The poorer man is simply given a lesser weekly burden.

The majority of magistrates, though, saw this type of equality as unequal. To them the penalty should be in proportion to income. It would only be *fair* if the poorer man paid less. And at the same time the deterrent *effectiveness* of the fine could only be equivalent if the richer man paid proportionately more: 'I would be harder on the rich man because it would hurt him more and it should' . . . 'one is concerned with the impact on the individual' . . . 'what would punish the poor man would not punish the other' . . . 'the hardship must be the same'.

But magistrates did not hold this view for all circumstances. It depended on the 'relative poverty' of different offenders and the seriousness of the offence. An attempt was made to discover to what extent magistrates would impose a heavier fine *because of wealth* and not simply fine less in mitigation for a poor man. In principle it seems they should not. D. A. Thomas, examining the Court of Appeal's (Criminal Division) policy, states:

. . . the ability of the offenders to pay is relevant only as a mitigating factor, reducing the amount which might be fixed by reference to the gravity of the offence alone; it would be inconsistent with basic tariff

---

[1] See Appendix I (p. 165) for the list. It included six offences and excluded speeding and pedestrian crossing offences.
[2] Magistrates' Courts Act, 1952, S.31; previously in the Criminal Justice Administration Act, 1914.

principles to impose a heavier fine than can be justified on the basis of the offence, on the grounds of the offender's wealth. Thus, while there may be discrimination between offenders of different financial standing in respect of similar offences, this discrimination is the result of mitigating the fine imposed on the less affluent offender, rather than by increasing the fine imposed on the wealthier man beyond the amount which can be justified by reference to the gravity of the offence.[1]

This has not, however, stopped magistrates from disagreeing. For example, in a letter to *The Magistrate*, a lady magistrate observes:

> It seems that too often [taking means into account] . . . operates only in one direction . . . whereas in the case of the better-to-do defendant the punitive effect of many fines must be relatively insignificant. Indeed the maximum for many offences is not high enough to allow a flexibility upwards to give something like equal punishment to defendants of widely differing incomes.

She acknowledges that this would increase the level of disparity perceived by the press and other observers, but remarks that 'this should certainly not deter us from doing what is right'.[2] Most of the magistrates in the sample, however, appeared to agree with the Court of Appeal. When given another example in which one man earned £5,000 and the other £1,800, 79 per cent said they would fine the same amount, because:

> 'Both would be able to pay without hardship' . . . 'I can't see a good reason why one shouldn't. There is a limit of income below which a man can't be allowed to go. Here they are both above it and can pay' . . . 'You can't argue about £50 fines at that level of income.'

This seems to reflect a tariff view of sentencing with mitigation allowed—and not an individualized approach aimed at deterring the offender. For if this had been the case surely they would have wished to fine the richer man more.

[1] D. A. Thomas (1967) 'Sentencing—the basic principles', *Crim. L.R.*, 523, and (1970), *Principles of sentencing*, London, Heinemann, 221–3. This view has recently been criticized in the Report of the Advisory Council on the Penal System on *Non-custodial and Semi-custodial Penalties* (under the chairmanship of Lady Wootton) which would like to see upward adjustment of fines in the case of the better-off offender. H.M.S.O. 1970, paragraph 18, 6–7. According to the *Justice of the Peace*, the Lord Chancellor 'has now taken the view that the Wootton approach is consistent with the existing law and has advised magistrates accordingly. If so this is an important departure from previous thinking and an example of Judge-made law,' *134* (19 December 1970), 937. In the light of this, the opinions of the magistrates interviewed in the survey are especially interesting. See also, in general, K. W. Devlin (1970), *Sentencing offenders in magistrates' courts*, London, Sweet & Maxwell, 67–74.

[2] Letter from Mrs M. R. Barton, *The Magistrate*, 26 (1970), 101. On the other hand, Elliott and Street suggest that there is probably a limit on the use that can be made of fines in terms of their effectiveness; *Road accidents* (1968), 118.

Policy for the serious offences is probably rather unclear and reflects the tension between regarding them as 'crimes' or as 'breaches of regulations'. But the matter seems less complicated when speeding and pedestrian offences are considered. Given the same examples, the vast majority said they would give the same fine: 'Because the fines for minor offences are such that it would not make any difference to the rich man and it would be wrong to increase it just because he has more money' . . . 'the fines are nominal rather than punitive.'

An indication that these views are still widely held is the following letter published in *The Magistrate* in 1969:

> Discussing this question of fines for speeding with two senior magistrates a few days ago, I put it to them that making the punishment fit the criminal was just as important as making it fit the crime and that, where the means of the offender are known to the court, these should be taken into consideration when deciding the fine to be imposed. This opinion was strenuously opposed by my two fellow magistrates and also by one other participant to the discussion who is not a magistrate. At a sentencing exercise, held by the East Yorkshire Branch of The Magistrates' Association about 18 months ago, thirteen syndicates were asked to say what fines they would impose on two persons found guilty of exceeding the speed limit in a built-up area. The circumstances of these two offences were identical except that the means of the offenders differed. One was a rich man and the other a man of modest means. The fines imposed by 12 out of the 13 syndicates were the same for each.[1]

This issue was followed up in the interview with questions about the use of the Magistrates' Courts Act procedure (1957) under which a substantial proportion of guilty pleas are received by post. Magistrates were asked whether offenders should be made to state their financial circumstances (which at present they may do if they wish in mitigation). About half wanted this information because they felt that without it some advantage might be gained by those who did not appear. The other half regarded income as entirely irrelevant to such minor cases.[2] Another indication that this latter view is becoming more widespread is that a third of the magistrates were in favour of 'on the spot' fines for speeding offences.[3]

[1] Letter from Brigadier H. A. Macpherson, *The Magistrate*, 26 (1969), 22.

[2] Other points were also raised. For example, some magistrates doubted whether the information would be at all reliable.

[3] In 1967 the Road Traffic Committee of the Magistrates' Association resolved that 'it should be made clear to the Home Office that the Association adheres to its previously expressed opinion that all endorsable offences should continue to be brought before the court', 26th meeting R.T.C., 7 September 1967, minute 263b). But in 1969 the Committee agreed to the extension of the fixed penalty system for speeding offences where the speed is not more than 10 m.p.h. above

Obviously, variability in defendants' incomes is a major problem in gaining uniformity. One of the bravest schemes so far put forward to overcome it was Roy Weeks' 'Formula' by which, first, the gravity of the offence was estimated and then a percentage figure calculated in relation to the defendant's means.[1] This was published in 1963 and is set out in the chart below:

| | | | | | | | | | | Weekly means and circumstances of defendant |
|----|----|----|----|----|----|----|----|----|-----|----------|
| 10 | 20 | 30 | 40 | 50 | 60 | 70 | 80 | 90 | 100 | Indefinite means |
| 9 | 18 | 27 | 36 | 45 | 54 | 63 | 72 | 81 | 90 | £25 |
| 8 | 16 | 24 | 32 | 40 | 48 | 56 | 64 | 72 | 80 | £22·50 |
| 7 | 14 | 21 | 28 | 35 | 42 | 49 | 56 | 63 | 70 | £20 |
| 6 | 12 | 18 | 24 | 30 | 36 | 42 | 48 | 54 | 60 | £17·50 |
| 5 | 10 | 15 | 20 | 25 | 30 | 35 | 40 | 45 | 50 | £15 |
| 4 | 8 | 12 | 16 | 20 | 24 | 28 | 32 | 36 | 40 | £12·50 |
| 3 | 6 | 9 | 12 | 15 | 18 | 21 | 24 | 27 | 30 | £10 |
| 2 | 4 | 6 | 8 | 10 | 12 | 14 | 16 | 18 | 20 | £7·50 |
| 1 | 2 | 3 | 4 | 5 | 6 | 7 | 8 | 9 | 10 | £5 |
| 10% | 20% | 30% | 40% | 50% | 60% | 70% | 80% | 90% | 100% | |

Gravity and circumstances of offence

For example, 60% gravity + £17·50 means = 36% maximum penalty. In dangerous or careless driving under the new Act this could be £36. In juxtaposition with monetary penalty must also be the question of disqualification.

But there are two problems. It is probably not as easy as Weeks suggests to get unanimity on the percentage of gravity. His long list of factors to be considered—ranging through twenty-two items about

the prescribed limit, provided that, (a), endorsement should not apply to fixed penalties for speeds up to 10 m.p.h. above the limit, and (b), the driver should always have the option of accepting the fixed penalty or contesting the charge in court, (31st meeting *R.T.C.*, 11 September 1969, minute 322a). Of course, this will not have a great effect as few police forces appear to prosecute unless the offender has *exceeded* 10 m.p.h. above the limit.

[1] Roy Weeks (1963) 'A formula for uniformity in penalties', *Justice of the Peace*, *127*, 75–6.

the nature of driving, eight about the defendant, and many others about the vehicle's condition, weather and road conditions—testify to this. More important though, it is certainly contentious whether the person of indefinite means who commits an offence of 20 per cent gravity should be fined the same as a man earning £15 per week who commits one of 40 per cent gravity.

## 3. *The Problem of Costs*

Problems of equality, unrelated to the question of individualization arise where costs are concerned. There is a great deal of controversy over awarding prosecution costs against a convicted defendant. They may include solicitor's fees, costs of photographs, doctor's fees and witnesses' expenses, and total more than £30.[1] Some courts assume that costs should automatically be awarded against the defendant; others argue that they should be borne, as in most criminal cases, by the State.[2] Apart from doctor's fees, which might be legitimately regarded as a cost brought about by a drunken driver, other costs are largely fortuitous. Some courts employ prosecuting solicitors, others do not; in some cases witnesses come miles, in others they live close by. There is certainly a danger, when costs loom large, that defendants might plead guilty to avoid them— knowing that the fine itself might be moderate.[3] The matter is further complicated because some advocate imposing an appro- priate fine and then adding the costs, whereas others wish to regard fines *plus* costs as the penalty and divide them accordingly.[4] For example, in 1963 the Annual General Meeting of the Magistrates' Association defeated a resolution that 'courts should award what is considered to be an appropriate fine without regard to costs and thereafter consider costs as a separate matter'. It was referred to the

[1] For example, it was reported in *The Wakefield Express*, 23 June 1966, that costs in a careless driving case had amounted to £55 18s. 9d. It will be seen that in two cases sent to magistrates in our research costs were approximately £30 and £35.

[2] Costs are rarely awarded against the defendant in motoring cases dealt with by the Higher Courts. See *Justice of the Peace*, 130 (1966), 125. Provisions relating to costs are set out in Section 55, Magistrates' Courts Act 1952.

[3] See *Justice of the Peace*, 127 (1963), 768, on this point.

[4] See the comments of a prosecutor in *Justice of the Peace*, 129 (1965), 677, 'Some courts take the view that a case brought by the public for the benefit of the public should be paid for by the public and refuse to order payment of any expenses or advocate's fee in addition to the penalty. I take the view that in cases such as these the bench on finding a case proved should fix a penalty and then that sum of money should be apportioned three ways as the court thinks fit as to fine, costs and advocate's fee.'

Council of the Association for consideration who, seeing the implications of such a policy, in 1966 sent a memorandum to the Home Office stating:

> that the Association [urges] that public funds should bear advocates' fees and witnesses' expenses in all criminal prosecutions (other than private prosecutions) in magistrates' courts, less such contributions by convicted defendants as the courts may order them to pay in appropriate cases.

The object was to 'remove the fortuitous burden of costs',[1] while at the same time agreeing with the *Justice of the Peace* that in some cases the defendant should 'pay the costs of his own misdeeds'.[2]

But until such a policy is accepted, defendants who have committed similar offences may receive different penalties because of costs. The magistrates interviewed were deeply divided on what to do in these circumstances. They were given an example of two offenders committing similar offences and with similar personal circumstances, but one incurring £10 costs or even £20.[3] At least half the magistrates wanted to impose the *same* fine as they would on the offender with no costs. In their view it was 'the offence that mattered' and costs were an extraneous issue. It appears that many magistrates would oppose the burden of costs being placed on the Exchequer but are frightened that if they reduce the fine it will *seem* (as this is the official *recorded* penalty) that there is inequality in sentencing. The

---

[1] A. J. Brayshaw (1967), 'Motoring fines and costs: the jigsaw puzzle', *The Magistrate*, 23, 121.

[2] *Justice of the Peace*, 131 (1967), 127, and 131, 66. In 1968 the Legal Committee of the Magistrates' Association (hereafter cited as *L.C.*) resolved 'that the Home Office should be urged to consult the police with a view to their not applying for prosecution costs after convictions in summary cases, nor stating their amount, save in exceptional cases (such as those where the defendant's conduct has unreasonably increased the prosecution costs) (*Minutes of the 94th meeting of the Legal Committee*, 18 January 1968, minute 1164). The Home Office replied agreeing with the Association's views in principle but pointing out that they could not be implemented in the circumstances of extreme economy. It was therefore resolved that in the 'meantime magistrates' courts should be encouraged . . . to order convicted defendants to pay a reasonable contribution towards the costs of prosecution witnesses and not necessarily the whole of the costs' (95th meeting *L.C.*, 16 May 1968, minute 1175). Lord Merthyr has put his finger on the main issue: fines go to the Treasury, costs come from local funds. Attempts will be made to reclaim them from defendants until they are borne by the Treasury.

[3] Costs were fixed at a substantial sum, but smaller amounts may also be taken into account. For example, at one court it was observed an offender was fined £5, after which the prosecutor said he had a claim for £5 5s. 7d. witnesses' expenses. The clerk remonstrated about the delay and the bench decided to reconsider the matter. Each witness was asked to justify his claim for costs. Then the chairman announced the decision as a fine of £3 with the costs added, saying, 'we realize this is an unusual thing to do but we feel it was necessary in this case'.

remaining magistrates took a less 'legalistic' view and wished to mitigate the fine in order to ensure more equality in practice. In fact, they are more likely in these circumstances to reduce the amount of costs than alter the fine.[1]

In the cases sent to magistrates, costs were asked for by the prosecution in all five cases of both dangerous and drunken driving, in one case of careless driving and in one of failing to stop and report an

TABLE 4

THE EXTENT OF AWARDING COSTS AGAINST OFFENDERS

| Offence | Group | Amount of costs £ | All costs | Per cent awarding less than half costs | no cost |
|---|---|---|---|---|---|
| Dangerous driving | A | 11  1s.  1d. | 86·5 | 1·9 | 6·7 |
| | B | 8  8s.  0d. | 74·4 | 4·9 | 9·7 |
| | C | 10  6s.  6d. | 80·2 | 2·8 | 8·5 |
| | D | 5  5s.  0d. | 72·6 | 0·8 | 19·6 |
| | E | 11  7s.  3d. | 70·9 | 5·8 | 16·5 |
| Drunken driving | A | 4  4s.  0d. | 88·5 | 1·0 | 10·5 |
| | B | 11  4s.  6d. | 85·6 | 2·9 | 8·7 |
| | C | 7  0s.  6d. | 88·7 | 0·9 | 8·5 |
| | D | 29  8s.  6d. | 56·0 | 10·0 | 5·0 |
| | E | 14  14s.  6d. | 77·3 | 11·7 | 4·9 |
| Careless driving | D | 34  14s.  0d. | 35·3 | 34·3 | 10·8 |
| Failure to stop and report | B | 2  11s.  0d. | 91·5 | — | 8·5 |

accident. Table 4 shows the amount of these costs, and the proportions of the 100 magistrates dealing with each case that awarded all the costs against the defendant, less than half, or none at all.

It can be seen that, except in the two cases where costs were £29 and £34, at least 70 per cent[2] (and often over 80 per cent) of magistrates awarded the entire costs. In these cases with very high costs a

[1] In a local penalties schedule circulated in a southern county it was specifically stated that where 'a fine plus costs is thought to impose too heavy a financial burden, any reduction should be made in the assessment of costs and not in reducing the fine'.

[2] In two cases (D and E) of dangerous driving a sizeable minority ordered that the defendant pay no costs. The reasons seem to have been that in D the only

smaller proportion of magistrates had awarded the total. But there is an interesting difference between the case of drunken driving and the case of careless driving, especially as both were dealt with by the same 100 magistrates (i.e., group D). For the careless driving case only

FIGURE 4

THE EFFECTS OF HIGH COSTS ON TOTAL FINANCIAL PENALTY

The spread of fines and costs awarded by 102 magistrates on exactly the same case of Careless Driving. Costs amounted to £34·14s. The highest *fine* imposed was £30.
24 *fined* under £10
44 *fined* £10
22 *fined* £15

Total financial penalty imposed (£)

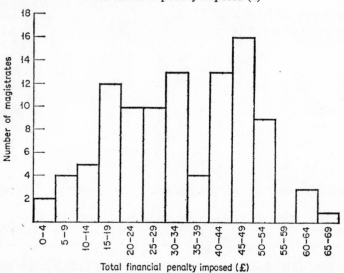

Total financial penalty imposed (£)

35 per cent gave all the costs and more than a third gave less than half of them: for the drunken driving case the figures were 56 per cent and 10 per cent respectively. The difference may well reflect the fact that this careless driving offence was rated by many magistrates as not serious, and witnesses' expenses were purely fortuitous. On the other hand, the drunken driving case had been 'fought' even though there was a proved blood alcohol reading of 216 milligrammes.

costs were for the prosecution's advocate (see the discussion on page 76) and in E the defendant had been granted legal aid and he was an unemployed married man.

Differences in the policy over costs had an enormous effect on the total amount of money the defendant in the careless driving case was expected to pay. Leaving costs aside, the hundred magistrates had varied little in the fine they thought appropriate (see Table 3, Appendix IV), but the addition of costs in various proportions caused an enormous variation in the actual financial burden imposed on the offender (see Figure 4 on page 78). It seems that varying policy in deciding whether or not to mitigate the costs rather than the fine might be a major cause of disparity.[1]

## 4. *Multiple Charges and the Total Penalty*

Multiple charges pose similar problems for equality. If the total fine is decided and then 'parcelled out' between offences, the fine for any one of them may appear small in comparison with a similar offence dealt with on its own. This is an explanation often given for the relatively low average fines listed in the official statistics for offences which quite frequently appear as part of a multiple charge—for example, failing to stop or report accidents, driving while disqualified, driving without insurance, and driving without 'L' plates or a licence. Magistrates disagreed about the way to approach this dilemma. Some (21 per cent) favoured reaching a 'total penalty' which would be distributed accordingly; others (38 per cent) decided that each offence should be dealt with separately and then totalled; the remainder used some combination of these systems.

Thirteen cases involving multiple charges were sent to magistrates. These were analysed and the amounts of total fines actually given by those magistrates claiming to use each method were compared.[2] With only one exception[3] the 'adding up' method was *not* associated with larger amounts of fine being imposed, neither was one method or the other associated with higher fines for the main charge. There could be at least two explanations for this result. Either other factors are much more powerful determinants of the size of fine given, or the method is irrelevant, the total fine having ultimately to be tailored to

[1] This is reinforced by the finding that those who said they would fine less if high costs were asked for did not give lower *fines* in practice. (With the exception of one case of dangerous driving, the Mann Whitney 'U' test was used: $z = -2.55$, $0.01 < p < 0.02$.). For those cases with costs a chi-square ($\chi^2$) test was used to see if those who said they would reduce fines gave lower than average fines. In all cases $p > 0.5$.

[2] Using the Mann-Whitney 'U' test, see S. Siegel (1958), *Non-parametric statistics for the behavioral sciences*, New York, McGraw Hill, 116–27.

[3] A case of dangerous driving in which the co-charges had been driving without a licence and having no insurance.

the magistrates' perception of the seriousness of the case as a whole and to the financial circumstances of the offender.

Nevertheless, it should be recognized that the problem of reaching a total 'payable fine' does make it difficult to apply a basic penalty system,[1] so as to give the *appearance* of uniformity and at the same time an impression of sufficiently severe fines for offences considered out of their 'multiple charge' context. The Magistrates' Association has pressed for the reform of the law to allow *concurrent* fines, so that the penalty given for each offence can reflect its gravity without making the total excessive,[2] but their proposals have been rejected by the Home Office mainly because of substantial criticisms from the Justices' Clerks' Society.[3]

## DISQUALIFICATION: FOR WHAT PURPOSE?

Willett has asked of disqualification: 'does it fall within the category of a retributive, a preventive, a deterrent or a reformative measure?'[4] It is not, technically, a sentence but an addition to the penalty.[5] In principle it probably had its roots in a preventive philosophy—to remove dangerous persons from the road. But there can be no doubt

[1] Consistency of penalties in traffic cases, *Justice of the Peace, 134* (1970), 243.

[2] A. J. Brayshaw, 'Motoring fines and costs', op. cit. In the case of imprisonment, concurrent sentences must be passed for offences arising from the same incident except where they are 'essentially different offences, such as driving while disqualified and drunken driving', *R.* v. *Smith* [1961] *Justice of the Peace, 125*, 506.

[3] In 1966 the Legal Committee of the Association adopted a resolution of the 1965 A.G.M. on concurrent fines with the amendment that the word 'cumulative' would be more appropriate (86th meeting *L.C.*, 27 January 1966, minute 1109). A meeting was arranged with the Home Office and a subsequent letter stated that the Association's views had been studied in the light of the Justices' Clerks' Society: 'In addition to pointing out technical difficulties, the Society had stressed the added complication which a system of concurrent fines would bring to enforcement, accounting and audit procedure.' The Home Office considered 'the concept of "concurrency" in relation to a motoring penalty could not be made analogous with that of the concurrent prison sentence. While the adoption of a "concurrent" fining system might mean that the amount of a fine better indicated the court's view of the offence and the offender, it was felt that some courts might tend to assess a non-payable fine less carefully than one which would actually fail to be paid.' So, in view of the Clerks' Society's views on practicability and Home Office doubts '. . . the advantages of the proposed changes were not likely to be commensurate with the difficulties involved.' Following this letter the Association agreed that no further action could be taken (98th meeting, *L.C.*, 8 May 1969, minute 1212).

[4] Op. cit., 266.

[5] The Divisional Court in *R.* v. *Appeals Committee of Surrey Quarter Sessions ex parte Commissioner of the Police for the Metropolis* [1963], 1 Q.B.990.

that a strong specific and *general* deterrent element now also plays a part. This can be seen clearly in the statutory provisions making disqualification mandatory for the offence of drunken driving. In discussions about the need for discretion in 'marginal' cases of drunken driving it has frequently been argued that despite the merits of any particular case, the law gets its deterrent effect through the mandatory element.[1]

The penalty may be supposed to have a preventive effect on an offender's future behaviour through the specific deterrence of the shock and inconvenience of the ban on driving. Its only reformative provisions lie in the possibility of disqualifying the offender until he takes another driving test.

## 1. *Balancing the Penalty and Disqualification*

The relationship between a fine and the period of disqualification seems to be very unclear. If disqualification is not part of the penalty but a separate matter, should they be considered in isolation or should the effects of a period of disqualification be taken into account in deciding on the fine? The Magistrates' Association's 1970 circular on penalties suggests that it should:

> The same period of disqualification may have a very different impact as between one offender and another, and this should be taken into account in deciding *both the fine* and the period of disqualification, particularly when 'totting-up' applies [my italics].

According to Elliott and Street the legal position is that 'if the court thinks that the normal fine plus disqualification is too heavy a penalty it is allowed to remit or lower the fine, but it is not allowed to avoid disqualification by the device of raising the fine'.[2] Yet at one court the local list of 'average fines' for no-insurance cases stated '£15–£20 disqual. unless mitigating circumstances. If disqual. is a hardship increase fine.' From the sentences given by magistrates it was possible to test whether *in fact* fines and disqualification lengths went up together as equal indicators of the severity of the case; or if it had been decided to give a long period of disqualification the fine was lowered in compensation. Correlations between amounts of fines and lengths of periods of disqualification showed a *positive* relationship for cases of dangerous driving and driving while

---

[1] See report on the views of the Magistrates' Association in relation to a criticism of mandatory disqualification by the chairman of the Yeovil bench, *Justice of the Peace*, *133* (1969), 552–87.

[2] (1968), *Road accidents*, 126.

disqualified[1] but not for drunken driving,[2] no insurance[3] or careless driving. On the other hand, in the 'information game', which is described in more detail on page 121, magistrates were presented with various new pieces of information about a case of drunken driving and asked to record whether they would change their initial fine or disqualification. The results showed conclusively that when the penalty was increased both fine and disqualification usually went up together.

Thus, for some offences there were positive correlations—when the fine was relatively high so was the disqualification; but for others there was no association. Certainly there was no evidence to support the 'compensation' theory.

Similarly, no clear relationship was found between length of imprisonment and length of disqualification. Looking at the penalties for the offences of driving while disqualified alone,[4] in one case there was a significant *negative* correlation, in another no significant relationship, and in the third a significant positive correlation. In examining the cases no ready explanation for these differences came to mind.

A few exceptional cases apart, it seems that the question of penalty and the question of disqualification are regarded as separate matters. In the most serious cases a high penalty and a long disqualification may go together.

[1] Kendall's rank correlation coefficient $\tau$ (tau) was used. Out of the four cases of dangerous driving examined, $p < 0.001$ in one ($\tau = 0.23$) and $p < 0.01$ in three. Out of two cases of driving while disqualified $p < 0.01$, $p < 0.05$.

[2] This may have been because the majority of magistrates imposed the mandatory 12 months' disqualification. In the information game it had been possible to observe the changes in fines and disqualifications as items of information were altered. Then it was found that when the fine was increased so also was the amount of disqualification. The results for the few offences involving multiple charges were conflicting, but again showed no evidence of *negative* correlations. But these results are not particularly meaningful because for dangerous and drunken driving any additional disqualification for other offences would have been *concurrent* with that imposed for the main offence (i.e., disqualification could not be increased) whereas fines are consecutive and the total does increase.

[3] In only one of four cases of no insurance was there a positive relationship at $p < 0.05$.

[4] One could not correlate imprisonment and disqualification for 'overall' penalties, because some of the charges in the list would have incurred fines, making the total penalty an imprisonment and fine combination. Of the five cases of driving while disqualified, only the three in which imprisonment had been frequently imposed were examined.

## 2. *How Long?*

Attitudes towards disqualification were sounded by asking magistrates what they considered the purpose of disqualification to be—how long they considered appropriate, to what extent they were in favour of disqualifying persistent offenders, and how frequently they would use their powers to order tests.

They were first asked what should be 'in general' the optimum (i.e., the most appropriate) period of disqualification for a typical case of each of the following offences: driving while disqualified (first and second offenders); drunken driving (first and second offenders); and dangerous driving (second offender). Table 5 shows the range of periods suggested.

TABLE 5

OPTIMUM PERIODS FOR DISQUALIFICATION

|  | Driving while disqualified | | Drunken driving (*Percentage*) | | Dangerous driving |
|---|---|---|---|---|---|
|  | *1st* | *2nd* | *1st* | *2nd* | *2nd* |
| 6 months or less | 16 | 1 | 24 | 2 | 9 |
| 1 year | 47 | 11 | 53 | 11 | 27 |
| 18 months or 2 years | 23 | 24 | 16 | 21 | 29 |
| 3 years | 6 | 23 | 2 | 29 | 19 |
| 5 years or more | 5 | 37 | 1 | 35 | 15 |
| Others | 3 | 4 | 3 | 2 | 1 |

The answers relating to drunken driving and driving while disqualified are especially interesting, and they seem authentic as they roughly reflect official statistics.[1]

In a first offence of drunken driving a quarter thought disqualification should be shorter than the statutory minimum of one year,

[1] In 1967, 80 per cent of those convicted of drunken driving (not within 10 years of a previous offence) were disqualified for one year or less. The proportion for driving while disqualified was 50 per cent (although it had been 55 per cent in 1964). The lengths suggested for dangerous driving cannot be compared with official statistics as it is not possible to tell how many offenders of those disqualified had been convicted for a second time of this offence. For dangerous drivers as a whole disqualification periods tend to be shorter. In 1967, 50 per cent received six months or less and 82 per cent one year or less. Only 1·8 per cent were banned for five years or longer.

and for a second offence over a third thought it should be less than the statutory three years. But of course not to invoke the minimum entails giving special reasons relating to the offence. (The kind of reasons magistrates consider relevant are discussed on pages 86–88.) For first offenders few were in favour of periods over two years.[1] But over a third considered five years or more the right penalty for a second offender.

Similarly, for a second offence of driving while disqualified 37 per cent chose five years or more and only 12 per cent one year or less. It is in cases such as these that the debate about disqualification has been hottest. There is increasing uncertainty both about the *effectiveness* of long terms[2] and about the appropriateness of barring certain types of 'compulsive' drivers from one area of activity in which they show interest and where often they have not proved a danger to other road-users. There are offenders who collect increasingly long periods of disqualification for driving while disqualified and taking and driving away vehicles. Until 1970 there was a minimum period of 12 months' disqualification *consecutive* to any other periods already in force or imposed at the same time.[3] The object of the new legislation is to make long periods not *inevitable*. Pressure had come from both the Magistrates' Association (especially the late George Wilkinson) and from the Court of Appeal. They had been disturbed by the futility of periods of disqualification which were virtually bans for life. How long such periods could be is illustrated by the 1967 headline:[4]

'Driver banned until 2047'

[1] This is in line with D. A. Thomas's analysis of the Court of Appeal's views, *Principles of sentencing*, 295–9. Although in *R.* v. *Lavelle* [1965] *Crim. L.R.*, 176, three years' disqualification was upheld for a first offender who had consumed four pints of beer and in whose case two doctors had disagreed on whether he was unfit to drive.

[2] See T. C. Willett (1966), *Some aspects of a current research on serious motoring offences and offenders*, paper to National Conference on Research and Teaching in Criminology, Cambridge, *mimeo*. Elliott and Street go as far as to say, 'whatever the outcome of Willett's research it seems that very long periods of disqualification are futile', op. cit., 120. Another expert, Dr J. J. Leeming, a traffic engineer, is reported as saying, 'As a matter of observation [deterring the driver from another offence by disqualification] is not a very high probability. If we observe people who have been thus penalized we see that it has not a great deal of effect on their conduct. Even if it did, the probability of its preventing an accident is still remote.' See report '2,000 banned drivers on Britain's roads', *The Times*, 16 February 1967.

[3] This was abolished by the Road Traffic Disqualification Act 1970, Section 1.

[4] Headline about a 34-year-old driver in *The Guardian*, 1 April 1967.

The problem has been outlined most cogently in the Court of Appeal by Lord Justice Davies in the case of *Bond* [1968].[1]

It has been said more than once that excessive periods of disqualification do more harm than good, particularly in the case of a man whose occupation is that of a motor driver and whose offences, many and multifarious though they may have been, do not include any offences for careless driving or dangerous driving or anything of that kind, indicating, as in the present case, that he is probably a skilful and good driver but that, possibly by force of circumstances, he will not refrain from taking and driving many motor cars and driving them while not insured, as a result of which he now finds himself in the position that as things stand he may never be able lawfully to drive a motor car again. Presumably he will go on driving motor cars, presumably he will go back to prison and remain disqualified all the time. It seems to the court that, although inevitably in the circumstances of this case he is bound to be subject to considerable periods of disqualification, subject to any right that he may have to apply for the restoration of his licence, it is not right to slam the door permanently and for life in his case, and that it would be proper in so far as the court has the power to do so to reduce the overall periods of disqualification to such a time as gives him at least some hope that in the future he may be able to drive a motor car.

Similarly, in the case of *Johnson*[2] the court spoke of a 'position so hopeless as to sow the seeds of an incentive to disregard the law: however wrong such an attitude may be, it springs from a human factor it is wise to take into account'.[3]

To what extent the change in the law will actually affect lengths of disqualification for most cases of driving while disqualified it is difficult to say, since, as the analysis below shows, many magistrates regarded prevention as their aim.

The reasons given for disqualifying varied, as one would expect, according to the kind of offence. For first offenders prevention or removal from risk was mentioned by a minority, coming far below punitive and individual deterrent views. Prevention was a major reason, however, for second offenders.

[1] *Cr. App. R.*, [1968] *52*, 505. See also A. Samuels (1969). 'The motoring offender: what can we do about him?' *Crim. L.R.*, 133–5.

[2] *R.* v. *Johnson* (1969), *Crim. L.R.*, 443–4. Also, *R.* v. *Evans* [1965], *Crim. L.R.*, 737–8, 15 years reduced to five; *R.* v. *Measham* [1967], *Crim. L.R.*, 661, 10 years reduced to five; *R.* v. *Shirley* [1969], *Crim. L.R.*, 497–8, 11 years reduced to one: 'long periods of disqualification might prove a severe handicap to a man coming out of prison wanting to lead a new life . . . and might become an incentive to break the law.'

[3] This point has been made in relation to disqualification in general. Now that many people live in suburban areas they have become dependent on private motor transport. As Laurence Ross (1960) points out, any suspension of a licence now 'runs the risk of forcing the driver into the more serious violation of licensing laws because of his dependence on his automobile for his livelihood'. See, 'Traffic law violation: a folk crime', *Social Problems*, 8, especially 239.

D

TABLE 6

REASONS GIVEN FOR CHOOSING AN OPTIMUM PERIOD OF
DISQUALIFICATION

| | Driving while disqualified | | Drunken driving (Percentage) | | Dangerous driving |
|---|---|---|---|---|---|
| | 1st | 2nd | 1st | 2nd | 2nd |
| Simple punitive views | 56·8 | 70·1 | 36·5 | 39·8 | 37·9 |
| Individual deterrence | 58·4 | 41·0 | 70·8 | 44·2 | 56·8 |
| General deterrence | 6·7 | 7·9 | 9·9 | 10·1 | 9·7 |
| Prevention (removal) | 17·2 | 40·1 | 23·9 | 59·1 | 49·5 |
| Reform of attitudes | 2·3 | 1·9 | 8·6 | 3·6 | 5·7 |

(Multiple answers: all reasons mentioned are included.)[1]

Two things are perhaps surprising. First, that 40 per cent said that
their aim in dealing with those who continue to drive while disqualified would be to *remove* them from the roads. Surely the offence
itself indicates what a pious hope this is. Yet it was not intended as an
empty threat, for those who named removal as a reason were much
more likely to say that the optimum disqualification should be five
years or more.[2] Secondly, the low proportions mentioning general
deterrence as even one of their reasons, although it might of course
have lain behind some of the more straightforward punitive statements such as: 'To show the offender he must not do this'. . . 'punishment—flouts the law' . . . 'ten years—should NOT be on the road'
. . . 'attitude to law all wrong—antisocial behaviour' . . . 'more
severe penalty' . . . 'teach him a lesson'. It may also be that general
deterrence is of prime importance in considering whether or not to
disqualify, but a less potent influence when it comes to fixing the
actual length.

## 3. *Special Reasons for not Disqualifying*

In cases of drunken driving (and a second conviction for dangerous
driving within three years), disqualification is mandatory unless
there are 'special reasons'. These reasons are supposed to be restricted

[1] Percentages exclude those for whom we had no information on this question:
N = at least 519 in any column.

[2] $\chi^2$ 2df = 29·31, p < 0·001; highly significant. It should be noted that
when the sample was divided into those specifying under three years, and three
years or more, the difference between those giving removal as their reason was not
statistically significant.

to those concerned with the *offence* and cannot relate to the circumstances of the offender. The interpretation of this rule has led to some curious decisions,[1] but the intention is to make disqualification virtually automatic so as to act as a deterrent.[2] Therefore appeals on the grounds of a 'small excess' over the prescribed limit, or because of hardship due to loss of employment, have been dismissed, and attempts to amend the law and to take such factors into account have been resisted by the Magistrates' Association.[3]

The research design ensured that five different types of drunken-driving cases were each 'sentenced' by about 100 magistrates. In two of these cases substantial minorities of 17 and 24 did not disqualify because of special reasons. Both offences were committed in rather

[1] See, in general, D. A. Thomas (1970), *Principles of sentencing*, 288–290. For example, *Brewer* v. *Metropolitan Police Commission* [1969], *Crim. L.R.*, 149, in which the defendant 'had drunk three small whiskies only, but before doing that he had been leaning for hours over a tank containing trichlorethylene, fumes from which. unknown to him, contained alcohol which cumulated with any alcohol drunk, rendered him unfit without his realising it.' Held to be a special reason for not disqualifying. Compare, though, cases in which the defendant has a physical (usually liver) defect of which he is unaware. For example, *R.* v. *Jackson and Hart* [1969], *Crim. L.R.*, 321, in which it was held that although the defendant (Jackson, who had been convicted of driving with an excess of alcohol in the blood) was *not unfit* to drive, because of a liver defect alcohol had been retained in the blood longer than normal and for that reason was over the prescribed limit. The appeal was not allowed. Thus, Brewer's inhalation of fumes was taken to relate to the offence and Jackson's liver defect to the offender. The reason for this is that Brewer's case was dealt with under Sec. 6 of the Road Traffic Act 1960 (driving while unfit), while Jackson was convicted under the Road Safety Act 1967. The Court of Appeal suggested that 'special reasons' for driving while unfit might not apply to cases of driving with alcohol over the prescribed limit. See *R.* v. *Jackson and Hart* [1969] *Cr. App. R.*, 53, 341.

[2] In general, for this offence the full obligatory disqualification is imposed. The returns for 1967 were analysed by Brigadier Appleton who found that overall only 4 per cent of those convicted of driving while unfit (not within 10 years of a previous conviction) were either not disqualified or given less than 12 months. However, for the small number convicted of a second offence within 10 years, 14 per cent were not disqualified for the statutory three years. See *The Magistrate*, 25 (1969), 52, and leading article in *The Guardian*, 26 April 1969.

[3] See report in *Justice of the Peace*, 133 (1969), 552, and 133, 587. Since the introduction of the breathalyser test in the Road Safety Act of 1967 appeals have been made both by defendants (*Gillingham* v. *Wright* [1968], *Crim. L.R.*, 276) and by prosecutors relating to the allowance of a 'small excess' as a special reason for not disqualifying. Lord Parker decided in *Delaroy-Hall* v. *Tadman, Earl.* v. *Lloyd, Watson* v. *Last* [1969], *1*, All E.R., 25, that it could not be allowed, although in Watson's case the excess was only 2 milligrammes: 'To introduce the principle would open the door to variability which the positive provisions of the Act are designed to keep shut.' See also 30th meeting of the *Road Traffic Committee*, 16 January 1969 minute 310e; also the same issue relating to employment in the 26th *Road Traffic Committee* 7 September 1967, minute 265.

peculiar circumstances. In one, a lorry driver in a private car hit another car which was sticking out into the road. He complained of the way that vehicle was parked and went to fetch the police (in the meantime driving friends home and returned to the scene). In the other, an airport catering manager had crashed on an airport driveway. The main reason given for not disqualifying was, in both cases, the belief that this would deprive the offender of his 'means' of livelihood; they were found drunk on occasions unconnected with their work. In the airport case, where 24 magistrates did not disqualify, other reasons were often also given. The defendant had driven a mini van on a service road connecting airport buildings to a main road on Christmas Eve in order to collect someone from a 'bus stop. On the way he drove at a parked van in an erratic way, the driver of that van switched on his headlamps, at which the defendant swerved but failed to clear the other vehicle, collided and damaged it slightly. His windscreen was iced-up and he was found to have 210 milligrammes of alcohol per 100 millilitres of blood—equivalent to about 7 to 8 pints of ordinary beer or 5 to 6 pints of best beer. He received a supporting letter from his employers who stated he needed a licence for his work. Of the 24 who gave special reasons, 14 mentioned the threat to his job and 14 his clear record—another seven stressed that the offence had not occurred on the main highway. Usually there were two or more reasons, such as:

'(1) he had not driven in the main stream of traffic; (2) 99 per cent of first offenders would believe that 7 pints on a service road at Christmas was reasonable; (3) [the fine] will be as good a deterrent as is required; (4) good record.'

It is interesting that none of these would probably, in law, have amounted to acceptable reasons connected with *the offence*. But they do indicate what some magistrates regard as the kind of circumstances which *should* be taken into account.

How did magistrates react to the idea of disqualifying less serious but persistent offenders under the 'totting-up' provisions of Section 5 of the Road Traffic Act 1962?[1] In general the vast majority were in favour of the law, their reasons being:

|  | % |
|---|---|
| He deserves punishment | 22·9 |
| He deserves punishment *and* it will deter others | 46·3 |
| It will deter him | 1·7 |
| It will deter others | 3·4 |
| All three reasons | 18·7 |

[1] Under this Act, anyone convicted for the third time within three years of an offence for which his licence was endorsed must be disqualified for at least six

Thus there was a punitive and general deterrent approach predominating, although in emphasizing deterrence and punishment to the individual a number of magistrates mentioned that such a penalty would 'give persistent offenders a sharp pull-up' and so affect their behaviour in future. Not surprisingly, no-one thought that periods as short as six months could protect the public from the dangerous driver.

However, when given a specific set of circumstances to consider, opinions were very divided. To what extent do magistrates find mitigating circumstances for not invoking the mandatory period of disqualification, and what reasons are given?[1] In 1965 in England and Wales, of those convicted under Section 5(3), 22 per cent were not disqualified and a further 8 per cent were disqualified for under six months.

The following example was given to each magistrate: 'Within the last three years a driver has been convicted of careless driving and speeding and his licence has been endorsed on both occasions. He now appears before you on a charge of exceeding the speed limit.' They were asked what circumstances they would consider amounted to reasons justifying a decision not to disqualify him. Forty-five per cent considered he should be disqualified automatically. The majority of the others said they would consider the effect on the offender, primarily on his employment, but they would also take the nature of the previous offences into account as an indication of the general seriousness of the man's record. These concerns were again seen when they were given another example, this time of a lorry driver with two previous speeding offences which had been just above the speed limit and who was now charged with travelling at 38 m.p.h. in a restricted zone. Sixty-eight per cent said they would not disqualify him, and the main reasons were: (a) that the offences were too trivial (89 per cent); (b) that it would affect his livelihood (66 per cent). It was this point which was at issue in the *Baker* v. *Cole* appeal when the Lord Chief Justice commented, 'One of the mischiefs aimed at by Section 5 was the persistent relatively trivial offender.'[2] Elliott and

---

months unless there are mitigating circumstances. See, G. S. Wilkinson (1963), *Road traffic offences*, London, Oyez Publications, 292 ff.

[1] Under the 1962 Act 'mitigating circumstances' have been interpreted wider than 'special reasons' and can relate to the offender as well as the offence. See the discussion on *Baker* v. *Cole* in J. C. Brooke-Taylor (1966) 'Mitigating circumstances and the Road Traffic Act 1962', *Justice of the Peace, 130*, 336; also comments on *R.* v. *Sixsmith ex parte Morris* by B. Harris (1967), 'The totting tangle', *Justice of the Peace, 131*, 5, and B. Strachan (1966), 'Recent road traffic cases on totting up', *Justice of the Peace, 130*, 766.

[2] J. C. Brooke-Taylor, op. cit. Of course, another point of view which is frequently mentioned is that the 'professional driver' does not necessarily deserve

Street on the other hand support more flexibility, and suggest that 'different weights [be] given to different offences'.[1] Obviously this remains an open issue, but such schemes seem to be preferable to alternatives such as the Law Society's suggestion for suspended disqualification, which we are told, would 'create a state of "fluid anxiety" on the part of drivers'.[2] Such a scheme would probably not be flexible enough to take into account the wide variety of circumstances which might surround the reappearance in court of a driver already 'on' a suspended disqualification.

Short terms of disqualification, then, are imposed mainly on a tariff basis, mitigated by special defence pleas, but rarely tailored to the likely impact on the future conduct of the offender. With so little information on the effects of disqualification such a policy is, at present, probably the only viable one.[3]

## 4. Driving Tests

The last question about disqualification relates to the use made of the power to order new driving tests. This can be in addition to a specific period, or the offender can simply be disqualified until a further test is passed.[4] Few tests were ordered in any of the cases sent to the magistrates. This result is not untypical—Patchett and McClean have already pointed out how rarely this power is used in the country as a whole.[5] The reasons emerge from the respondents. Sixty-three per cent said that a driving test would be appropriate for dangerous

---

special treatment: in fact, as he is more 'at risk' he could be considered more dangerous. See *Justice of the Peace*, 133 (1969), 552. It has also been suggested that if the statutory minimum were reduced to three months there would be less recourse to 'special reasons', i.e., mitigating considerations. 'Disqualification is meant to inconvenience and even to hurt, but it should not be unnecessarily harsh. The halving of obligatory periods would go far to remove at least some of the unnecessary hardship which may be caused to professional drivers and the like.' G. L. Appleton (1969), 'Special reasons', *The Magistrate*, 25, 54.

[1] Op. cit., 128. For a general discussion on 'totting-up' see 124–7.

[2] The Law Society, *Motoring offences*, June 1965, paragraph 13.

[3] More studies of the kind being carried out (in connection with this research) by Willett on drivers' reaction to disqualification are urgently needed. As Elliott and Street (1968) suggest, it is possible 'that there is an optimum period of disqualification, probably between six and twelve months.' *Road accidents*, 118.

[4] Powers to order tests were first introduced in 1934 and extended in 1956 to driving under the influence of drink and another 23 kinds of offence.

[5] K. W. Patchett and J. D. McClean (1965), 'The power to order new driving tests', *Crim. L.R.*, 265–72; also, J. F. Beashel (1970), 'Disqualification pending test', *The Magistrate*, 26, 35. Elliott and Street (1968), *Road accidents*, 134. Patchett and McClean say that up to 1963 the order was made only in 0·5 per cent of dangerous driving cases and 0·33 per cent of careless driving.

driving and 60 per cent said it would be so for careless driving. But only a tiny proportion thought them suitable for drunken driving or speeding. Even so, among those who favoured tests almost all (80 per cent for dangerous driving, 95 per cent for careless driving) said they should be ordered only for a second or subsequent offence. When it is realized how infrequent second or subsequent offences of dangerous driving are in any one year,[1] it is not surprising that the tests are so rarely ordered.

Of those favouring tests in these circumstances, between 85 and 90 per cent thought them necessary to test skill, but a third *also* thought the order had a deterrent value—'they should be subject to a test, it would act as a deterrent'—a view that has been dismissed by at least one judge[2] but is supported by Patchett and McClean as a means of 'reminding the offender of the more unpleasant consequence of outright disqualification'. But of course they stress that it should not be used for this purpose alone.

Many magistrates thought the provision was of little value because a new test would be irrelevant to ordinary driving conditions. For example: 'Motoring offenders in general might be incompetent only at one particular time—the rest of the time they are O.K.' And, of course, the dangerous or reckless driver is unlikely to misbehave in the test. Patchett and McClean recognize this argument and therefore suggest 'a more exacting and extended test of an advanced nature . . . [with possibly] a course of tuition before being tested . . . at some place along the lines of an adult attendance centre'.[3] This and other ideas were examined in questions about new approaches, especially of a constructive kind.

NEW APPROACHES

Two-thirds were in favour of new methods of dealing with motorists. Only a handful were against, but the remainder were unsure—having

---

[1] In 1967 the number convicted of a second offence within three years amounted to 273. This figure is not particularly accurate. The fact was recognized when the practice of providing separate figures for these offenders was dropped in the statistics for 1969.

[2] In the case of *Ashworth and Johnson*, Mr. G. J. Waller (now Waller, J.) said, 'These powers were to be contrasted with the powers of disqualification for a specified period which was part of the penalty imposed by the court. [This section] on the other hand was not a punitive section but was intended as a section for the protection of the public against incompetent drivers.' Quoted in Patchett and McClean, op. cit., 735. Beashel, op. cit., suggests this judgement has (unjustifiably) caused some courts to be reluctant to use their powers.

[3] Op. cit., 271.

no specific ideas themselves. Those with views mentioned the following:

|  | % |
|---|---|
| A more punitive approach | 13 |
| New ideas relating to court procedures and practices | 37 |
| 'Constructive penalties' | 11 |
| Suspended sentences | 2 |
| New legal regulations—fixed-penalty systems, etc. | 11 |
| Preventive measures relating to traffic and driver safety | 28 |
| No particular ideas, but generally in favour | 18 |

(These are multiple answers.)

Most related to procedures in court or to accident prevention rather than new penalties—although 11 per cent thought 'constructive penalties' aimed at changing the offender's attitudes or skills would be valuable. Their specific reaction to the idea of a traffic school were sought. Such schools have been in operation in the United States for some time, and have proved relatively effective.[1] An example of one

[1] Some evidence that these schools may be effective comes from an experiment carried out in California by Judge Claude M. Owens. To test the efficacy of the court's drivers' school, four groups of 100 offenders with three 'moving' offences in the previous 12 months were given four different types of sentence: group 1 a fine only; group 2 fine plus suspended sentence of five days imprisonment; group 3 fine plus drivers' school; group 4 fine plus drivers' school and suspended sentence.

The only criterion for determining which sentence an offender received was chronological. The first 100 were fined, the second 100 given suspended sentence, and so on. In this way obvious disparities in sentences from day to day were avoided.

All offenders were followed for up to two years. At the end of the first year those sent to drivers' school and those given a suspended sentence both had considerably fewer convictions than those who were just fined. However, a combination of the school and a suspended sentence did not produce a very marked improvement.

After the second year (i.e., after the suspended sentence period had ended) those who had been to drivers' school had much better records than those given suspended sentence or fined. Sixty-two per cent were not guilty of a traffic violation compared with 48 per cent of the suspended sentence cases and 42 per cent of those simply fined.

When the total number of convictions recorded against offenders in each group was computed the former drivers' school group had 92·4 per cent fewer than those in the fine only group. In other words, suspended sentence works well for a year, but the drivers' school has the most lasting effect. A combination of drivers' school and suspended sentence was less effective than drivers' school on its own. Judge Owens suggests that this may be because the threat of gaol carried such an impact that it diluted the positive effects of the drivers' school.

Clearly the study indicates that for persistent offenders, experiments with new methods may produce significantly better results than a policy of continued fining. See C. M. Owens, *Interim report (March 1966) on the three years study of*

operated by the Metropolitan Police Department in the District of Columbia in the early sixties is described by Judge Neilson:

When a defendant convicted of a traffic violation appears to be a co-operative person, whose clash with the law resulted perhaps from ignorance or momentary carelessness, he is referred by the Court to the traffic school. Final disposition of his case is postponed for approximately one month. Attendance is purely voluntary, and in most instances the driver is eager to avail himself of the opportunity to attend the school when its purposes and functions are explained to him.

His case is then referred to the probation department of the court, where the facts in his case and other pertinent information are recorded. He is given a registration card, authorising him to attend school on the day or night of his choice, on successive Tuesday or Wednesday nights or Saturday mornings, for two 3-hour sessions. He is instructed to report to the probation department at the end of his period of instruction. The statement of facts in his case, together with the instructor's report from traffic school, indicating the defendant's success or failure, is then submitted to the trial judge for his further consideration, before a final sentence is imposed.

As an incentive to serious and diligent study at the school, the judge, at the outset, indicates to the defendant that if he attends the school and successfully passes the final test—a carefully planned and comprehensive examination of the subject matter covered during the course—he will be given credit and this will be reflected in a reduction of any penalty which might otherwise have been imposed.

[the programme is as follows]:

Through lectures covering a wide range of traffic subjects essential to an adequate comprehension of sane and safe motor vehicle operation, and supplementary motion pictures and photographs, the student is instilled with good driving practices on the one hand and the tragic results of irresponsible driving habits on the other. He sees portrayed before him a terrible accident that might have been caused by the same infraction as his own. Perhaps for the first time he is fully conscious of the fact that his own violation could have easily snuffed out his own life or the life of some other person. The deep impression thus made is one he is not likely to forget.

---

the effectiveness of the Anaheim-Fullerton Municipal Court Drivers Improvement School (mimeo).

For an interesting study of an experiment on young traffic offenders in Utah with contrasting results, see G. D. Mecham (1968), 'Proceed with caution: which penalties slow down the juvenile traffic violator?' Crime and Delinquency, 14, 142–54. Boys were randomly allocated to fines, traffic school, 'restraint from driving', and an order to write a paper on traffic safety. After a follow-up of one year, the last-named order was found to be by far the most effective: 16 per cent committing additional violations as against 52 per cent who were fined and 48 per cent of those sent to traffic school. The author is careful to point out that these results should not be taken as criticism of all traffic schools. On other new approaches, such as the sending of 'advisory letters', see Elliott and Street, op. cit. 132–4.

It is interesting to note that a session of the school is devoted to a lecture on the subjects of utmost importance to good driving practices, but too often found wanting. These include courtesy, attitude, and self-discipline. Obviously, if a person is to become a good and safe driver he must bear these things in mind constantly, and reflect them in his actions while driving. It is impossible to estimate the number of accidents caused simply by lack of courtesy, or by an indifferent attitude on the part of the operator. Every motorist should keep in mind that courtesy in operating a motor vehicle will prevent automobile accidents. The driver who is thoughtful enough to show proper regard and consideration for a fellow motorist is likely to be a careful driver. Of course, this presupposes that he has a thorough knowledge of traffic rules and regulations and understands the mechanics of motor vehicle operation.[1]

A summary of the first two paragraphs of this quotation was read to magistrates and they were asked whether they favoured such a scheme. Forty-seven per cent said they were in favour although many added caveats like: 'for serious offences only' . . . 'for careless driving' . . . 'for young offenders', or stressed the practical difficulties. It was the practical problems which influenced many who were opposed: 'I am appalled at the thought of the complications . . . cumbersome . . . too long-winded, expensive . . . laborious . . . unwieldy . . . and delaying.' Besides this, many doubted its likely effectiveness and some suggested it would certainly cause resentment. One said simply, 'It's a load of rubbish!' But even so, measures aimed at affecting the offender's attitudes towards, and competence in, driving were favoured much more than a standard probation order, which 86 per cent were opposed to for motoring offences.[2] The idea of traffic attendance centres has now been supported as worthy of an experiment by Lady Wootton's Committee on non-custodial and semi-custodial penalties.

More punitive ideas got little support. Less than a quarter were in

---

[1] G. D. Neilson (1964), 'Traffic courts should educate while they adjudicate', *Federal Probation*, *28*, No. 1, 18–23.

[2] It was not of course legal to impose both a period of probation and disqualification for the same offence until the 1967 Criminal Justice Act (see Sec. 51). *The Magistrate* commented that it would 'no doubt be . . . useful . . . for the more criminal motoring offences, such as taking and driving away, having a ride in a stolen vehicle, driving while disqualified, and also possibly in the case of young offenders, driving or being in charge whilst unfit through drink', *23* (1967), 146. Of course, in cases of driving while disqualified it had often been possible in practice to impose a period of probation for one of the offences in the list of charges (such as taking and driving away, having no insurance) before the 1967 Act, but it seems that it was rarely done. Lord Goddard had stated that probation was inappropriate for serious motoring offences except where special reasons existed, *Surtees* v. *Benewith* [1954]. 3 All E.R., 261. See also A. Samuels, (1969), 'The motoring offender: what can we do about him?' *Crim. L.R.*, 136–7.

favour of such drastic innovations as 'P' penalty plates fixed to the cars of persons convicted of some serious offences.[1] Slightly more than a third favoured higher maximum fines, although it will be seen that they rarely used the upper half of the present scale. Less than 10 per cent wanted an extension of the power to disqualify, but 70 per cent said they would like to see more use being made of their present powers—the remedy there, of course, lay in their own hands. And yet it is curious that in the years since the fieldwork began there has been, on the contrary, a restriction in the use of disqualification. Lengths imposed have got steadily shorter, and for dangerous driving[2] and driving without insurance the proportion of offenders actually disqualified at all has fallen by over 12 per cent between 1965 and 1969.[3] For other offences it remains about the same; although for careless driving a decrease from 5·6 per cent to 4 per cent in the proportion disqualified is certainly significant.

While magistrates consider disqualifications to be an important deterrent they are also aware of the tremendous problems of effectively enforcing the order—and this would apply perhaps even more to ideas like intermittent weekend disqualification, which was suggested by the Wootton Committee.[4] From the magistrates' point of view the task has been made even more complex by the Criminal Justice Act of 1967, which has restricted the use of immediate imprisonment for some of these offenders.[5]

Bearing in mind the danger of doing injustice to the detailed and complex arguments reviewed in this chapter, there are three points which need briefly to be stressed because they recur in the discussion which follows. First, there is the development of a basic penalty system aimed at achieving more uniformity. We have seen that there are different opinions about its value, which may reflect more fundamental disagreements about the use of a 'tariff' approach, which favours the same penalty for those who commit the same offence irrespective of their financial means, the costs against them or any

[1] It was reported that in surveys of people all over Britain 'many people felt that . . . every convicted drunken driver should have to display a "D-for-Drunken" plate for 6 months', *Sunderland Echo*, 17 September 1965; also Leading Article, 'Why not a "P" penalty plate', *Yorkshire Post*, 5 August 1964.

[2] Not including those convicted of a second offence of dangerous driving within three years, for which the statistics were so unreliable that they were dropped from the official returns in 1969.

[3] For dangerous driving the proportions were: 1965—44·2 per cent; 1969—30·6 per cent. For no insurance: 1965—28·5 per cent; 1969—16·3 per cent.

[4] Report of the Advisory Council on the Penal System on *Non-custodial and semi-custodial penalties*, H.M.S.O. 1970, paragraphs 105–11, pages 35–9.

[5] Ibid., paragraph 132, page 45.

personal factors. A crucial question is whether these different views are held by magistrates scattered over a variety of courts or whether they are shared opinions of magistrates at particular courts—thus indicating major differences in court policies.

Secondly, it is clear that the purposes of disqualifying as well as the period of disqualification which should be imposed are an area of great dispute in all but drunken driving. Opinion is especially divided on what to do with those who drive while disqualified.

Thirdly, there is a substantial minority of magistrates willing to try new methods of changing some offenders' attitudes towards driving. But is the system geared to providing the information so that those for whom such measures might be appropriate can be selected?

CHAPTER 5

# Motoring Offences as Crime: the Problem as Magistrates see it

MAGISTRATES are faced with a dilemma.[1] On the one side they are pressed by both motorists and pedestrians to regard traffic offences as a serious threat to the safety of thousands of people and their motor cars. It is widely believed that firm law-enforcement and effective action by the courts can make drivers more responsible and careful[2] and remove the dangerous ones from the road. Yet, on the other hand, those who are prosecuted as well as the large 'dark number' who are often 'at risk' are reluctant to be dealt with in a way which would imply that they are criminals, with all the stigma attached to that term. Willett suggests that the police and the public have:

> little or no inclination . . . to apply the term criminal or any social stigma to these motoring offenders. The police had a clear-cut but indefinable concept of a distinction between what they called crime—meaning usually offences handled by the CID—and motoring offences, a concept which was, generally speaking, shared by members of the public. It is also interesting that the offenders interviewed who had criminal records were careful to distinguish between motoring offences and what they called 'real crime', which they defined as 'breaking, burglary and assault'.[3]

---

[1] This incongruity is called by social psychologists 'cognitive dissonance'. A clear review of Festinger's theory is given in R. Brown (1965), *Social psychology*, New York, Macmillan, 584–604.

[2] Speaking at the 1964 Law Society's Conference, Mr R. Wyeth said: 'the vast mass of traffic offences were temporary lapses of ordinary men and women and the aim therefore was not so much retribution as making them more careful drivers'. Reported in *The Times*, 22 October 1964.

[3] *Criminal on the road*, 302. For a very ironic comment on the disrespect with which traffic laws may be held if the principles of *mens rea* are abandoned and strict liability substituted, see G. O. Mueller (1960), 'How to increase traffic fatalities: a useful guide for modern legislators and traffic courts', *Columbia Law Review*, 60, 944–65. Professor Mueller's thesis is that only if these offences are dealt with as other criminal charges, so as to allow pleas of mistakes of fact, genuine error, etc., will offenders respect the courts and law-enforcement agents. See also, P. J. Fitzgerald (1969), 'Road traffic law as the lawyer sees it', in J. J. Leeming, *Road accidents, prevent or punish?* London, Cassell, 161–75.

Their idea of a fair solution is to purge an offence by a penalty which is equivalent to the harm (or potential harm) caused. It may be that penalties lose some of their effectiveness when there is little stigma attached to the conviction, but this situation certainly cannot be changed through magisterial policy. When offences become wide-spread, when many are conceived as omissions, accidents or bad luck, and are committed by persons from all social classes, the action is unlikely to be congruent with the normal stereotype of a criminal—for he is generally a person from 'another' inferior social group who acts with malice and intent against the social order. As Terence Morris points out, 'crime is in the last analysis what the other person does', and the reaction 'whether tolerant or a punitive rejection will depend on how far the crime threatens the observer'.[1] In the case of most motoring offenders (and exceptions will be noted) these conditions do not apply and there is therefore a resistance to what the Americans call 'criminalization'. These attitudes will no doubt be reflected in the views of laymen who are also magistrates, but they, through their experience of the consequences of these offences, naturally have to come to terms with the conflict—and find some way of accommodating both viewpoints. In such a situation one can certainly expect quite a wide divergence in opinions.

The questions are, therefore, how do magistrates regard various kinds of motoring offence when they are compared with other 'crimes', and what sort of person do they think commits these offences? The answers have important implications both generally, in relation to the system of penalties which may be regarded as appropriate, and specifically because they will help us understand what information will be collected about the offence and offender and the way in which it will be interpreted and used in deciding on the penalty. This is discussed fully in the next chapter.

Just as there are stereotypes of motoring offenders, there are stereotypes of magistrates and their opinions. Barbara Wootton, for example, has said:

> Apparently on the Marxian principles that law is made and operated in the interests of the well-to-do, motoring offences in general, and infringements of the speed limits in particular, are not ordinarily thought to 'count' as crimes at all.[2]

---

[1] Terence Morris (1966), 'The social toleration of crime', in H. J. Klare (ed.), *Changing concepts of crime and its treatment*, London, Pergamon, esp. 28–34. See also, generally, D. Chapman (1968), *Sociology and the stereotype of the criminal*, London, Tavistock.

[2] B. Wootton (1959), *Social science and social pathology* London, Allen & Unwin, 25–6. For a good discussion of different viewpoints see Willett (1964), *Criminal on the road*, 3–5.

They are what one American sociologist calls 'folk crimes': relatively numerous, unstigmatized and 'differently treated in the legal process'.[1] This question of differential treatment is one which was specifically inquired into, and it is discussed on pages 105–8. But first, what are magistrates' views on the key issue: the relationship between motoring offences and ordinary crime? Because of the importance of distinguishing between perceptions of the offence and views on the offenders, they are dealt with separately.

THE RELATIVE SERIOUSNESS OF MOTORING OFFENCES

Each magistrate in the sample was asked to rank all eight of the motoring offences in the study in relation to eleven other crimes, including both indictable and non-indictable offences. They were instructed to imagine a typical case of each offence when making comparisons. The overall result of the ranking was:

TABLE 7

THE ORDER OF SERIOUSNESS OF VARIOUS OFFENCES

| Offence | Rank Order | Mean Rank | Standard Deviation |
|---|---|---|---|
| Robbery with violence | 1 | 1·74 | 1·42 |
| Grievous bodily harm | 2 | 3·95 | 2·52 |
| Indecent assault on female under 16 | 3 | 4·04 | 2·94 |
| Drunken driving | 4 | 4·62 | 2·43 |
| Dangerous driving | 5 | 6·00 | 2·78 |
| Housebreaking and larceny | 6 | 7·23 | 3·44 |
| Driving while disqualified | 7 | 7·46 | 3·15 |
| Driving without 3rd party insurance | 8 | 9·69 | 3·52 |
| Possession of offensive weapon | 9 | 9·74 | 4·21 |
| Larceny by a servant | 10 | 10·88 | 3·63 |
| Obtained goods by false pretences | 11 | 11·12 | 3·48 |
| Careless driving | 12 | 12·15 | 3·22 |
| Taking and driving away | 13 | 12·29 | 3·27 |
| Failing to stop after an accident | 14 = | 13·07 | 3·42 |
| Common assault | 14 = | 13·07 | 4·34 |
| Shoplifting | 16 | 14·06 | 3·26 |
| Pedestrian crossing offence | 17 | 14·87 | 3·22 |
| Speeding | 18 | 16·16 | 2·82 |
| Drunk and disorderly | 19 | 17·72 | 2·14 |

[1] L. A. Ross (1960), 'Traffic law violation: a folk crime', *Social Problems*, **8**, 231–41.

It is extremely interesting that two motoring offences are ranked above housebreaking and larceny, four above larceny by a servant and six above shoplifting. This seems to discredit the belief that most magistrates do not regard average offences of this sort as serious matters.

It is also clear that drunken and dangerous driving, driving while disqualified, and driving with no insurance are regarded as a category of offences more serious than others. And contrary to Willett's view, careless driving was placed in this general way above failing to stop after or report accidents on the list of 'serious offences'—although, of course, particular cases of failing to stop may be among the most serious of crimes. The low rating given to taking and driving away is rather curious in view of the fact that since the Theft Act 1968 it has become an indictable offence.[1]

By examining the size of the standard deviations, in Table 7, it is apparent that among the non-motoring offences the most variation in ranking occurred for the offences of common assault and possessing an offensive weapon, the least for robbery with violence, which nearly everyone ranked 1st, 2nd or 3rd. The motoring offences which produced the greatest divergences on ranking were: no insurance, failing to stop or report, pedestrian crossing offences, and careless driving. The least variation was for drunken driving, which 83 per cent of magistrates ranked within the range 2 to 7.

Yet although there was variation, it should be emphasized that it was a lot less than would be expected to occur by chance. Put another way round, the level of agreement in ranking all nineteen offences, or just the eight motoring ones, was better than if magistrates had placed them in random order. The coefficients of concordance between the ranks given were quite high—being 0·66 and 0·72 respectively; a coefficient of 1·0 would be reached if all magistrates had ranked the offences in exactly the same way.[2]

In addition to this comparison between offences of different kinds, every magistrate was asked to rate each of the eight offences

---

[1] Even so, it is often considered as a 'motoring offence'. For example, it was included in the schedule of basic penalties by the Magistrates' Association, and is similarly labelled by the press. A report in *The Times*, Feb. 22, 1967, under the headline 'Three young drivers gaoled' revealed that two of them had been convicted of taking and driving a car without consent and stealing the petrol.

[2] Kendall's Coefficient of Concordance measures the extent of association between the ranking of several items by different subjects. See S. Siegel (1956), *Non-parametric statistics*, New York; McGraw-Hill, 229–39: 'A high or significant value of W [the coefficient] may be interpreted as measuring that the observers or judges are applying essentially the same standard in ranking the N objects under study.'

he received by post, as 'of its kind', very serious, serious or not serious. Thus about a hundred magistrates rated exactly the same set of circumstances for all forty cases. The detailed findings are discussed in Chapter 7, in relation to the penalties imposed. There were some marked variations, especially for the more serious cases involving injury or previous convictions (see pages 129–30). But when the ratings of 100 magistrates were compared over all eight offences (in each of the five groups) there was considerably more agreement (about which were the very serious or serious ones) than would be expected to occur by chance. In all five groups coefficients of concordance between 0·5 and 0·6 were found.[1] Thus although there *was* considerable variation in rating particular cases it would be wrong to underestimate the amount of general agreement that does exist.

The question that remains unanswered, of course, is whether similar levels of concordance would have been found had *non-magistrates* been asked to rank the nineteen offences and rate each case.

### THE MOTORING OFFENDER—A CRIMINAL IN A CRIMINAL COURT?

The conclusion that many magistrates regard motoring *offences* as relatively serious must be compared with answers to the special questionnaire designed to test what types of *person* magistrates thought, in general, committed serious motoring offences. The results, shown in Table 8, indicate that very few offenders were characterized as 'being like the magistrates.' In fact a relatively high proportion were classed as 'anti-social'. This was especially true of those who drive while disqualified (63 per cent), and even accounted for 43 per cent and 45 per cent of drunken and dangerous drivers and 47 per cent of those who fail to insure or persistently speed. Conversely, though, it should be noted that over half of these serious offences were not considered to have been committed by the anti-social type, and only a relatively small proportion of careless drivers were regarded in this light.[2]

There is also a good deal of reluctance to call these offenders 'criminal'. When asked whether they regarded persons who had committed *any* of the six serious offences as 'criminals in the same

[1] $\chi^2$ is significant, p. $< 0·001$.

[2] In relation to the discussion in the next chapter on the provision of information it is important to note that 30 per cent of drunken drivers and 20 per cent of dangerous drivers and those who drove while disqualified or failed to stop after an accident were regarded as suffering from an unstable personality or from emotional problems.

## TABLE 8

### STEREOTYPES OF MOTORING OFFENDERS

The question was: under each of the offences listed along the top of the page write in how many out of every ten people convicted of that offence you think fall into each of the types.

| Types of Motoring offenders | Mean percentage falling into each category | | | | | | |
| --- | --- | --- | --- | --- | --- | --- | --- |
| Description of type | Driving while disqualified | Drunken driving | Dangerous driving | Careless driving | No Third Party Insurance | Failure to stop after accident | Persistent speeding (3rd or subsequent conviction) |
| 1. An average motorist who does something you could imagine yourself doing | 0·5 | 3·0 | 3·1 | 18·4 | 3·1 | 3·8 | 3·0 |
| 2. A careless, thoughtless type of person whose offence arises from not paying adequate attention to either his driving or the regulations | 12·7 | 18·7 | 25·6 | 33·5 | 30·8 | 20·4 | 28·2 |
| 3. An anti-social person who has no respect for rules and regulations and the safety of others | 63·4 | 43·3 | 45·4 | 26·3 | 47·2 | 47·6 | 47·1 |
| 4. The sort of person whose offence arises from a somewhat unstable personality or from emotional problems | 19·7 | 30·7 | 20·5 | 17·2 | 14·4 | 23·9 | 15·7 |
| PLEASE WRITE IN, IF YOU THINK NECESSARY, ANY OTHER TYPES NOT DESCRIBED ABOVE | | | | | | | |
| 5. All other types of person mentioned, e.g. 'young hot-heads' | 3·2 | 4·1 | 5·0 | 4·4 | 4·3 | 4·0 | 5·0 |

sense as those who steal, rob, commit violent or sexual offences', as many as 40 per cent said no. The majority, who thought motoring offenders equally deserving of the label 'criminal', stressed the potential danger of these offences:

'they have a high degree of risk to life for other members of the community' . . . 'obviously they put other people in danger—they disregard the rights of other people, as do criminals.'

These magistrates mentioned, in particular, drunken and dangerous driving. Those who stressed the element of deliberateness, flouting of the law, or intent, illustrated their argument by referring to driving while disqualified and no insurance offences in particular—while some others mentioned failing to stop or report an accident:

The thing which defines a motorist as a criminal is the DELIBERACY of the offence—except in the case of SPEEDING which is not *yet* recognised by society as a serious offence.

It was precisely this assumption of intent which was denied by those who thought the 'criminal' label inappropriate:

'I don't think they are criminals, although they commit a crime of equal seriousness, but motorists don't commit offences with intent' . . . 'Serious motoring offences don't emanate from such premeditated circumstances. They are crimes, but of a lesser standing than crimes against the person' . . . 'they may be stupid or foolish but not deliberate.'[1]

The dilemma was most clearly expressed by a magistrate who said:

I don't accept the original premise that there is a distinction between crimes and motoring offences, but if you want a general answer my head says 'yes' but my heart says 'no'. I'm loath to put them into this category, but I'm sure they are.

This issue was clarified further by asking about each offence individually. The following answers were given to the question: 'For [these] offences do you consider the majority of those convicted to be criminals?'

|  | % answering 'yes' | |
|---|---|---|
|  | *1st offence* | *2nd offence* |
| Drunken driving | 19 | 56 |
| Dangerous driving | 12 | 52 |
| Driving while disqualified | 50 | 75 |
| Careless driving | 0·2 | 4·5 |
| Failing to stop, or to report an accident | 10 | 43 |
| Failing to insure | 17 | 60 |
| Speeding | 0·6 | 4·5 |

[1] See Professor P. J. Fitzgerald's remark that 'society's refusal to regard traffic offences as real crimes may well stem from a refusal to see anything

It was only for driving while disqualified that as many as half the magistrates called the majority of first offenders 'criminal'. Where second offences were concerned higher proportions were willing to do so, but there were obviously considerable differences of opinion, especially about drunken and dangerous driving, failing to stop and report an accident and failing to insure, where at least 40 per cent of magistrates rejected the term as inappropriate. As one magistrate said, 'any calculated dangerous act, as opposed to doing something silly [is criminal]. If he does it twice it must be calculated—calculated in the sense of knowing he is breaking the law whether or not it is intentional.' On the other hand, for careless driving and speeding (which often involves deliberate intent) there was virtual unanimity that the 'criminal' label was undeserved: thus supporting Lady Wootton's opinion of how magistrates view such motoring offences.

It seems significant that 75 per cent of magistrates thought those who persisted in driving while disqualified were criminals, for, as Willett's sample showed, the majority convicted of this offence are working class and also have convictions for non-motoring crime. Furthermore, their offence is often thought to be 'dishonest'.[1] The criminal label is therefore only thought to be appropriate by a large majority of magistrates where *other* criteria of the criminal stereotype are evident. In general, magistrates seemed unaware of the proportion of offenders with convictions for other indictable offences. Willett estimated that overall (including driving while disqualified and no insurance cases) it was as high as 20 per cent, and, similarly, in a pilot study for this project in the North East of England 28 per cent of 195 offenders convicted of the six serious offences were found to have a previous indictable conviction. Despite the widespread (and at that time, recent) publicity given to Willett's book, 38 per cent of magistrates thought that less than one in ten offenders convicted in the serious cases had criminal records, and only 13 per cent put their estimate as high as three in ten.

Thus many offenders are not considered to be real criminals. Yet the paradox is that when fines for indictable offences, such as theft, are compared with those for careless driving or failing to insure, it is often the motorist who receives the heavier penalty. He may both resent and fail to comprehend this.[2] The point is illustrated by a

---

immoral in offences of negligence or in violations of regulations which seem arbitrary'. In a review of *Criminal on the road*, *Law Q. Rev.*, *82*, (1966), 121–4.

[1] D. J. Steer and R. A. Carr-Hill (1967), 'The motoring offender—who is he?' *Crim. L. R.*, 214–24.

[2] There may of course be good reasons, for example the motoring offenders could be much wealthier. Even so, motorists may not agree that this should

few cases observed in various courts during the course of fieldwork:

| Court A | Larceny | Fined £10 |
| | Careless driving | Fined £15 plus £10 3s. 9d. costs |
| Court B | Office-breaking and larceny | Fined £5 |
| | Careless driving | Fined £20 |
| Court C | Simple larceny | Fined £10 |
| | Failing to insure | Fined £30 |
| Court D | Assault occasioning actual bodily harm | Fined £15 and bound over for 12 months |
| | Failing to insure | Fined £15 |
| Court E | Possessing an offensive weapon (a knife confiscated) | Fined £5 |
| | Careless driving | Fined £15 plus £4 4s. 0d. costs |

It is these disparities which have persuaded some observers that all but the most serious offences should be dealt with in separate traffic courts: particularly, it seems, because they feel that punishing 'non-criminals' in criminal courts might consequently adversely affect public attitudes towards law-enforcement.[1] In June 1965 the Law Society issued a memorandum on motoring offences which was widely debated. Its key recommendations, which were endorsed by the Magistrates' Association, were that a distinction should be made between 'offences' and 'breaches' of the Road Traffic Acts. The former would include 'deliberate, conscious or vicious breaches of the law and reckless acts or omissions'. The offences mentioned were 'reckless' driving, drunken driving, knowingly driving while uninsured 'and similar offences'. The remainder would be dealt with at Traffic Courts. It is worth noting however that when magistrates were asked to rank offences in order of seriousness both careless

---

automatically increase their penalty to a level above that imposed on 'real criminals'. See J. Cohen and B. Preston (1968), *Causes and prevention of road accidents*, London, Faber and Faber, 213–14.

[1] Elliott and Street (1968), *Road accidents*, 70–77, 99. It is precisely this point which has led some magistrates to regard the fine as inappropriate for many cases. See the letter from His Honour Judge David, Q.C., Chairman of Chester Quarter Sessions, in *Justice of the Peace, 134* (1970), 885. Commenting on the deliberations at magistrates' meetings he said: 'Members doubted the value of fining except in a minority of cases. Obviously the fine must be retained for use in serious cases and also for "administrative" offences. But in the great mass of offences the fine, it was felt, had little or no deterrent effect and *tended to cause ill-feeling among convicted motorists*, many of whom might find that they were being fined, for example, £25 for careless driving, whereas a person convicted in the same court for dishonesty or violence might be fined a much smaller amount or might not be fined at all.' [My italics.] He suggested more use of disqualification, including short terms and suspended periods.

driving and failing to stop after an accident were ranked higher than common assault and shoplifting. Yet under these proposals they would be dealt with as a different class of offence from property crime and assaults.

These new courts were to be manned not by traffic 'specialists' but by a panel (like juvenile panels) elected for a three-year period from among existing magistrates: 'the standard . . . set . . . should be that of the ordinary reasonable road user'. The main object of this proposal was to remove the bulk of motorists from 'criminal courts'.

In the opinion of the Council, the stigmatising as criminals of more than 62 per cent of those who came before the courts has the inevitable consequences of diminishing, in a substantial manner, the obloquy which ought properly to attach to those who commit what the public normally regard as *truly criminal offences* . . . it brings within the ambit of criminal procedure a large and growing body of *respectable citizens*, who find themselves for the first time in conflict with the police; this occasions, due primarily to the confusion of thought and uncertainty of recollection so commonly associated with motoring offences, distrust of the veracity of police evidence and disrespect both of the police force and the judicial system. [My italics.]

It is enlightening that concern should be felt for 'confusion of thought' leading to 'distrust of police evidence' where respectable people are involved. The same consideration is rarely given to those accused of offences in which the majority who are prosecuted are working class—such as drunkenness, disorderly conduct and many varieties of assault.

The Magistrates' Association supported the proposals for two separate categories of offence, but did not consider that specially constituted courts were necessary. Instead they suggested that magistrates could allocate traffic cases to certain sittings.[1]

It is perhaps not surprising that the Law Society also suggested the creation of a special traffic police, Some lawyers agreed with, at least, the tenor of the proposals. Foremost among them were Elliott and Street, who particularly emphasized the need to distinguish

---

[1] *Annual Report*, 1965–66, page 13. Lord Devlin made a similar point in discussing the prosecution of dangerous and drunken driving in the Higher Courts. He suggested that juries were acquitting many defendants because a conviction would entail the possibility of imprisonment and public opinion would not accept this as the right punishment for the 'bad' rather than the 'wicked' driver. Imprisonment, he said 'should be reserved for people who do what public opinion accepts as disgraceful or for those who defy the law' . . . The criminal law . . . had lost much of the respect which it ought to have, because we failed to distinguish between what was sinful and disgraceful and what was a failure to measure up to a required standard of conduct.' He therefore wished to see a clear distinction made between the 'wicked' and the 'errant' motorist. *The Times*, 21 October 1960.

between trivial and inadvertent acts—the result of 'bad' motoring or a breach of administrative regulations—and truly dangerous and deliberate acts. By doing this, they argued, it would 'widen the gulf between Everyman and the abandoned creatures who indulge in those [serious] offences by declaring that the lapses and imperfections to which Everyman on the highway is prone are *not* criminal.'[1] But the criteria to be used in making such a distinction are not generally agreed. Elliott and Street suggest 'triviality is perhaps a requirement to be stressed even more than the absence of deliberation'. On the other hand, some bodies, such as the Pedestrians' Association, stressed the likely consequences of many inadvertent acts (which Elliott and Street would 'try to reduce . . . by education and propaganda')[2] and objected most strongly to taking offences likely to cause injury out of 'the category of culpable and reprehensible criminal acts' and to 'pandering to law-breaking drivers'.[3] From a more legal viewpoint the editors of the *Criminal Law Review* declared that 'whether criminality is present in a case may not be clear until the facts have been investigated'.[4]

When the magistrates were asked whether they thought there was a case for a separate traffic court, nearly 60 per cent said yes: but only 16 per cent of these wanted completely separate institutions along the lines of a different court room, the others preferring 'traffic days' or 'traffic magistrates' (drawn from among those with driving licences). The major reason for wanting such a change were both to make administration easier and to ensure that 'experienced' magistrates dealt with the cases. Only 37 per cent—or 18 per cent of *all* magistrates—said they wanted to separate motorists from criminals because of the stigma of appearing in a criminal court.

> Generally motorists are the backbone of the country and they will never accept these are criminal offences. It causes resentment and harms the

---

[1] *Road accidents*, 76–77, 144–7, 155–7, 159, and P. J. Morrish (1970) 'Should traffic offences be classed as crime?' *Justice of the Peace, 134*, 361.

[2] Op. cit., 146.

[3] Reported in *The Daily Telegraph*, 15 Nov 1965. Barbara Wootton has also remarked that even holding separate court days for motoring offenders has the 'regrettable effect of putting motoring offences in a class apart from other crime' (1953), *Social science and social pathology*, 26. Laurence Ross, commenting on the American practice of dealing with more and more traffic violations by 'administrative methods', remarked that 'it is extremely unlikely that a committee of the American Bar Association would recommend the use of such procedures in cases of petty theft or disorderly conduct as they do in the case of minor traffic infringements' (1960), 'Traffic law violation: a folk crime', *Social problems, 8*, 231–41.

[4] *Crim. L.R.* (1965), 457.

image of the court—we should have specialists, technical specialists, sitting with lay people.

The majority of the 40 per cent who were opposed to the suggestion of separate days or 'motoring benches' regarded the mixture of cases which normally occurred to be beneficial in reaching decisions. They felt particularly that:

'specialists would get biased' . . . 'danger of getting cranks and cranky' . . . 'get stale and a one track mind, mixing up gives a better standard of justice' . . . 'it gets the mind in a "traffic groove" but its disadvantage is that the J.P.s cease to compare motoring and non-motoring offences.'

Although it appears that there is some support for dealing separately with motorists,[1] magistrates as a whole are obviously deeply divided on the question of whether these offenders should be considered as 'criminals'. In later chapters it will be possible to see whether holding one view or the other discriminates between those whose sentences are relatively severe or lenient. But, at the very least, it is hoped that the findings outlined in this chapter will have put into clearer perspective magisterial views on matters which are fundamental to an appraisal of sentencing policy for traffic offenders.

[1] For a detailed discussion on Traffic Courts see Elliott and Street (1968), *Road accidents*, 33–34, 160–77.

# CHAPTER 6

# Information: its Relevance and Uses

OBVIOUSLY, decisions are influenced by information received and sought, and the way in which it is interpreted. In recent years, and especially since the Streatfeild Report of 1961,[1] it has become almost a platitude to say that sentences should only be pronounced after comprehensive relevant and reliable information has been collected. As the report pointed out: 'In view of the controversy which the sentencing of offenders can excite, it is important that the sentences imposed by the courts should have a sound factual basis and should not appear to be in any way speculative or based on vague impressions.'[2] A catalogue of information that would normally be relevant to the Higher Courts was outlined, but it can safely be assumed that the Committee had in mind 'ordinary' indictable crime rather than motoring offences. And so, while the general recommendations may apply to theft, violence and sexual offences in magistrates' courts there is no guideline so far as the motoring offender is concerned. Not only is there no knowledge of what information magistrates think is relevant, there is also no evidence of what is, *in fact*, likely to influence the decision.

For these reasons, three main questions were asked. They were: What information do magistrates consider might be relevant, and where should it be collected from? What information is made known in court, and from what sources does it come? What information is actually used in the sense that it affects decisions? The data were gathered in four ways:

1. From direct questions at interview.
2. By observation of court practices.
3. From the cases sent 'for sentence' to each magistrate, and
4. Through an 'information game' in which items about a case were changed in order to see the effect on the penalty.[3]

[1] *Report of the Interdepartmental Committee on the Business of the Criminal Courts* (1961), H.M.S.O., Cmnd. 1289, Part II, esp. Chapters 10 and 11.
[2] Ibid. para 292, p. 84.
[3] See Chapter 2, page 38 for a description of these exercises.

There is a good deal of evidence that personal characteristics, attitudes and experience, affect both the items of information which are chosen as relevant, and the way that information is interpreted and used. Examples in the criminological literature are Wilkins and Chandler's,[1] and Carter's[2] studies of probation officers. In both, a group of officers were asked to select which pieces of information they wished to know before making a decision. Not only were relatively few items chosen before decisions became firm, but the order in which information was used and its effect on decisions varied. Wilkins and Chandler noted that there were some items which were important and weighty, in the sense that they were more likely to change initial decisions, and they concluded: 'It may be that such items of information are related by the decision maker to his background and the item makes an impact,' causing the decision to be changed. This phenomenon, they say 'may be related to stereotypes and prejudices'. In this small study, however, Wilkins and Chandler were not able systematically to relate individual characteristics to information use and decision-making.

The present enquiry was not designed to assess the interaction between personal characteristics and the stimulus of information about offenders; but by providing data on the kinds of information required, and the way in which it might be used, it attempts to shed light on a most important element in understanding exactly how decisions are reached.

## THE GENERAL ISSUES

What is considered relevant information will depend on the aims of the sentence, assumptions about the reasons why the offender has committed the act, and what needs to be known in order to predict his conduct in future. It has already been shown that in the case of motoring offenders the aim is mainly punitive, but, of course, this may vary from the simple application of a penalty which wipes the slate clean, to an attempt to deter the offender in the future or deter others likely to commit the offence. Naturally, the information considered relevant varies depending on which position is taken. Good examples of this point are the discussions in Chapter Four on the extent to which an offender's financial means would be taken into account and the use of mandatory disqualification for offences

[1] Wilkins, L. T. (1964) 'Confidence and competence in decision making', *Social deviance*, Appendix IV, London: Tavistock; and with Ann Chandler (1965), *Brit. J. Criminol.*, 5, 22–35.

[2] Carter, R. M. (1967), 'The pre-sentence report and the decision-making process', *J. Research in Cr. and Delinq. 4*, 203–11.

such as drunken driving (pages 71 and 88). One might also expect that the differences in opinion on the relative seriousness of motoring offences, and particularly on the appropriateness of the 'criminal label' would be reflected in the use made of information about previous criminal convictions.[1] The question of previous convictions for non-motoring indictable offences has been widely debated. The Magistrates' Association, until very recently, consistently argued that *all* previous convictions should be made known in open court. But magistrates everywhere recognized two related problems with this policy. First, in many courts, the police used their discretion in deciding which convictions should be cited, especially for offences such as careless driving (although it was usually clear that this was being done, since phrases were used such as 'nothing of a similar nature known, your worships' or 'his convictions for motoring offences are . . .').[2] Secondly, magistrates do not wish offences which occurred long in the past, or were of an entirely different nature, to be known to the public. There are plenty of examples: the man whose previous conviction for murder 16 years earlier was cited in a traffic case—a conviction which his wife knew about, but his children did not; a sexual offence, unknown to the offender's wife, being made public after conviction for a comparatively minor offence and thus bringing the stability of the marriage into danger.[3] Thus, at the 1968 Annual Conference of the Magistrates' Association, the following resolution was passed by a narrow majority.

> After a conviction on a serious motoring offence any criminal record of the defendant should be given; and that if the defendant so requests this record should be handed in writing to the Bench instead of being announced in open court, and the Bench should have the right either to divulge the record publicly or to state reasons where the sentence substantially varies from the norm.[4]

---

[1] It will be seen that it was not possible to correlate views on criminality with desire for information on previous convictions, as almost all said they regarded this as relevant. However, analysis in the 'sentencing game' casts doubt on the extent to which such information actually affects decisions already reached on other grounds.

[2] Willett interviewed some seventy police officers during the course of his research in 'one of the Home counties'. He reports that their attitude towards motoring offenders is implicit 'with regard to the production of evidence as to previous convictions: non-motoring offences are not revealed since they are regarded as irrelevant. The practice was accepted without question by the officers interviewed. . . Some officers thought that they would be rebuked from the Bench if they produced evidence of non-motoring convictions ("crime" as they called it), and the practice of not doing so appears to be universal.' *Criminal on the road*, 109.

[3] Reported in *Justice of the Peace, 133* (1969), 662.

[4] *The Magistrate, 24* (1968), 176.

At first the Council of the Association did not endorse the proposal, but in May 1970 the Legal Committee agreed to a similar resolution, which had the effect of placing the matter entirely at *the court's* discretion.[1] The only problem remaining is that of agreement on a national system for recording previous convictions, especially those for minor offences. At present, what is in police records varies from county to county, and it seems that a national register with an agreed list of offences will not be feasible for some years.

Some of those who favour traffic courts would make 'only previous convictions involving traffic offences . . . admissible in evidence and in the antecedents'. The offences covered by such a rule would include dangerous and drunken driving and failing to insure as well as the less serious offences, for which there may, perhaps, be a case.[2] While many magistrates might not agree with this, it will be interesting to see if, in practice, they use their discretion any differently from the way the police have generally used theirs.

Leaving convictions aside, there is even less general consensus about what other information besides income and expenditure (and we have already seen the extent of disagreement about this) should be taken into account. Many may consider other details of the offender to be unnecessary because, as one useful guide says: '[For] the great bulk of regulatory offences, mainly in the field of road traffic . . . any meticulous examination of the offender would be impracticable and out of place, the principal function of the penalty is simple deterrence.'[3] This is backed by a leading probation officer's view that pre-sentence reports 'for many motorists' are unnecessary as 'an appropriate sentence is already clear in the court's mind'.[4] Such an opinion may well be based on the assumption that for these offences, any 'pathological' features in the offender's life and environment are likely to

[1] In 1963 the Council announced that it could not agree to this practice. Reported in *Justice of the Peace*, *127* (1963), 671. It was clear that the Legal Committee agreed, but the Council rejected the proposals. See *Annual Report* 1968–69, p. 40. However, the 1970 resolution of the Legal Committee read:

After conviction the court and the defendant should be given written records of previous convictions, and the court should direct which convictions it intended to take into account for the purpose of deciding sentence: these convictions alone should be cited; in other words the decision as to which convictions should be read out in open court should rest with the court itself, as in the case of the higher courts. 101 *L.C.*, 7 May 1970 (Minute 1247).

[2] P. J. Morrish (1970), 'Should traffic offences be classed as crime?' *Justice of the Peace*, *134*, 361–2.

[3] B. Harris (1969), *The Criminal Jurisdiction of Magistrates*, London, Butterworth, 117.

[4] F. V. Jarvis (1965), 'Inquiry before sentence', in T. Grygier *et al.* (eds.), *Criminology in transition*, London, Tavistock, 51–2.

be irrelevant to the act and to his future behaviour—an assumption not usually made for people who commit 'conventional' crime. Willett, in particular, has vividly illustrated how in some cases, indications of gross disturbance may be overlooked:

> There was the not out of the ordinary case of an unemployed public relations man convicted of drunken driving about whom the police surgeon said that he was a killer if he had ever met one; this man had displayed marked aggression on arrest yet no medical report was called for before sentence which amounted to a fine of £50 and one year's disqualification. Another drunken driver was a known alcoholic yet this was not brought out in evidence and he was treated as a straight-forward case.[1]

Whether or not one would agree with the diagnoses, the simple fact is that such evidence probably would have been considered relevant in an indictable case.

An enlightening example of public outrage at the 'personal' questioning of a 'motoring offender' occurred in 1967. A nineteen-year-old had been convicted of fraudulently using a road fund licence, and six other offences. He had several previous convictions for motoring offences and had just come out of borstal. The probation officer said the boy came from a broken home and added, 'I think that the girl has a steadying influence on him and that he is now turning over a new leaf.' Questioning the defendant, the Chairman of the Magistrates, Mr Otto Shaw, asked him if he loved the girl and if he planned to marry her. The defendant answered 'Yes'. He was then asked, 'Have you slept with her?' Defendant, 'No'. Mr Shaw, 'How do you know you love her?' Defendant, 'I just know I love her because I feel differently about her.'[2] It is perhaps worth speculating whether there would have been such a strong reaction had the ex-borstal boy, who was now being considered for probation because of evidence about his new attachment, been found guilty of, say, a crime of violence, although of course I am not by any means implying that the magistrate was right to ask such questions in open court, in *any* kind of case.

Nevertheless, while the range of methods for dealing with motoring offenders remains limited—simply a question of fixing the level of

---

[1] T. C. Willett (1966), 'The motoring offender as a social problem', *Medico-Legal Journal*, *34*, 150. Willett comments that one of his research assistants with psychiatric nursing experience 'very guardedly classified thirty of 300 offenders [interviews after conviction] as being at least disturbed personalities'. See also M. H. Parry (1968), *Aggression on the road*, London, Tavistock, for a pilot study of the personality of drivers.

[2] *The Sun*, 6 April 1967; also *Daily Mail*, 7 April 1967 (report and leading article), reflect strong criticism of the magistrate's behaviour.

fine and deciding whether to disqualify and for how long—it is unlikely that a large amount of information about offenders will prove useful. Yet it should be realized that this is part of a vicious circle. One of the major reasons why the range of methods is so narrow is because knowledge about the motoring offender is so limited. The penalties thought to be appropriate are based on *assumptions* about the factors associated with these offences and offenders. While it is true that these assumptions, resting on common sense, may be correct even for a majority of offenders, they are just as probably *not* correct for a significant minority who might respond to other methods of punishment or treatment. It will only be possible to know the size of this minority if more information is gathered—at least on some offenders, say those who appear before the courts more than once or for one of the very serious offences such as drunken driving. Not until that stage has been reached will it begin to be possible even to try to assess the relative effectiveness of alternative penalties for motoring offenders with different characteristics. The importance of this issue can be assessed by contrasting the small use made of enquiries (described on pages 115–17) with the answers to the questionnaire asking for estimates of the proportion of offenders who were 'the sort of person whose offence arises from a somewhat unstable personality or from emotional problems' (See Table 8, page 102). Magistrates said 30 per cent of drunken drivers were in this category, and even 17 per cent of careless drivers and 16 per cent of persistent speeders. But information about the *offender* is not the only issue. Even if magistrates take an entirely punitive approach, there still remains the problem of deciding what information about the *offence* is relevant to an assessment of its gravity. In motoring cases there are usually detailed descriptions of what actually happened, including plans and photographs, but what weight is given to such factors as potential danger, the actual degree of harm done, the amount of irresponsibility, or recklessness, and the degree of remorse? In the 'information game' it was possible to examine the extent to which these factors influenced a number of different benches.

Thus, in the following sections the questions that will be explored are: What did the magistrates consider to be relevant information? When did they feel they needed more? What did they actually get? What did they do with it?

## WHAT IS RELEVANT?

Magistrates were asked what information they thought was useful in sentencing the motoring offender. Not many items were mentioned

spontaneously by a large proportion of the sample. The most
frequent were:

|  | % |
|---|---|
| Previous convictions (not defined specifically) | 99 |
| Occupation | 51 |
| Income | 75 |
| Financial commitments | 73 |
| Marital status and number of children | 73 |

When asked specifically about individual items the total agreeing
they were important to know was:

| Previous convictions (unspecified) | 100 |
|---|---|
| „     serious motoring convictions | 99 |
| „     indictable convictions | 98 |
| „     non-indictable convictions | 61 |
| All previous convictions | 61 |
| Occupation | 81 |
| Income | 85 |
| Financial commitments | 85 |
| Marital status and children | 85 |
| Employment record | 55 |
| Attitude of offender to offence | 77 |
| Family relationships | 45 |
| Physical health | 55 |
| Mental health | 62 |
| Age-group | 66 |

When asked how this information could be obtained, nearly all
said they would ask the defendant directly. Just under two-thirds
said that if this were inappropriate they would either 'stand the case
down' for a while for an inquiry to be made or make a remand for
a report. However, over 90 per cent admitted that, in practice,
remands for inquiries were made in fewer than one in a hundred
cases. When asked about specific kinds of offence 22 per cent said
they 'frequently'[1] found remands useful for drunken driving, 16 per
cent said this for driving while disqualified, but only 11 per cent for
dangerous driving. The proportions were much smaller for other
offences; for example 5 per cent for failing to insure and 2 per cent
for careless driving.

Asked why the power to remand was used so infrequently, most
said it was because the necessary information was almost always
available. A minority mentioned that it was 'a tradition' not to

[1] Actually, either frequently, usually or always.

remand such cases and that, in any event, the practice only caused administrative problems. Some comments were:

'Motoring offences are very prevalent and I cannot see anything to be gained by putting cases off for these enquiries. It's better for all, including the offender, that the punishment should be quick' . . . 'It has become accepted practice not to ask for it. I think we have tended to separate motoring offences from criminal offences—we may have to rethink this segregation' . . . 'It's never been thought of.' . . . 'I don't think it serves any purpose, only in very isolated cases' . . . 'You don't need to see what is wrong with them, it would be a waste of time' . . . 'Because I don't think probation reports will help even these offences. One is expected to be in control of one's feelings when driving' . . . 'A man's background has no relation to a motoring offence' . . . 'One seldom thinks that a motoring offence is connected with a defect of character' . . . 'Because in the main the facts before us provide us with a full picture including the character of the man'.

When dealing with each of the eight cases of different kinds sent to them, magistrates were specifically asked whether there was any further information *about the offender* which they would have requested before deciding on the penalty. In two of the five cases of *dangerous driving* there was no indication, in the case material, of the offender's income, yet 35 and 54 per cent respectively did not want further information. In the other three cases 72 per cent or more were satisfied with what they had, even though in one case the defendant, aged 23 and an unemployed man, had driven a Jaguar car in a very dangerous manner and already had three court appearances within three and a half years and had been to a detention centre. This case is reproduced in Appendix II (Case 2).

In one case of *drunken driving* there was no information about income and 47 per cent did not ask for it. In all other cases over two-thirds wanted no other information. Yet, in one the driver of the car had been found drunk over the wheel of his vehicle, revving the engine, after drinking the equivalent of nine pints of ordinary beer. His statement of mitigation was as follows:

The defendant said that he did not dispute the facts as outlined by the prosecutor. He had no witnesses he wished to call. He said that at the time of the offence he had been severely distressed. The business of which he was a director was being wound up. It was a family business and the man on whom he had been relying to take over part of the business had backed out on the day of the offence. There was a severe family quarrel over this, which had depressed the defendant considerably and he had gone out on his own in the evening. He had been driving for 28 years and had never been convicted nor had an accident. The defendant asked the magistrates not to disqualify him. He was now virtually unemployed and it would severely limit his chances of obtaining suitable employment if he could not drive a car.

He told the magistrates that his wife had a small private income, there were three children in his family, one 1, one 7½ and the other 14. He was now virtually without a job.

If this story had been told in the context of an 'ordinary' criminal offence, it is highly likely that a social enquiry report would have been called for.

Probation reports were available in only two of the five cases of *driving while disqualified*. In the other three, between a half and two-thirds said they did not require to know anything more.

Similarly, for *careless driving*, although four of the cases contained no details of income, fewer than half the magistrates asked for any more information. In one case where two-thirds of the magistrates wanted to know nothing more, the offender had not appeared in person, had many previous convictions and was described by his solicitor as follows:

> This was a case . . . which could be briefly summed up as the case of a red-haired man and his past. Had the defendant appeared the magistrates would have seen that he had a shock of bright red hair, and he, the solicitor, was bound to say immediately that the defendant's record was a clear indication that he possessed the temperament usually associated with red-haired men . . . (Case 8, Chapter 1)

The solicitor went on to point out that the man had kept out of trouble for four years. But again there are clear signs that the case might have benefited from further investigation.

In all other offences, with a few exceptions, such as where the offence was serious or the offender had previous convictions, only a small minority of magistrates wanted to know more about the offender. In most of the cases of failing to stop or report, speeding, and neglect of pedestrian-crossing regulations, the offender pleaded guilty by letter or by the Magistrates' Courts Act procedure. In no instance did more than a quarter of the magistrates indicate their need to know more than the defendant's simple statement of mitigation.[1]

This analysis indicates clearly that many magistrates are prepared to reach decisions without full details of an offender's means. Nor do they seek information even when there are clear indications of unusual personal circumstances.

---

[1] Previous convictions cannot be made known in the defendant's absence unless he has been served with a statement of the convictions by the police. There seems to be considerable difference of opinion on whether such offences as careless driving and failing to stop after an accident should be disposed of in the absence of the defendant.

E

WHAT IS ACTUALLY KNOWN?

The research worker attended court as frequently as possible and recorded every item of information heard in court about the offender. Overall, the information (other than previous record, age and address) known before sentence was pretty scant, as the following table shows:

TABLE 9

INFORMATION KNOWN TO THE COURT BEFORE SENTENCE (AS OBSERVED IN COURT)

|  | All cases | Four serious offences[1] | Careless driving | No insurance | Indictable non-motoring cases |
|---|---|---|---|---|---|
|  | (N = 585) | (N = 48) | (N = 151) (percentage)* | (N = 91) | (N = 183) |
| Driving experience (Any information) | 22·7 | 31·3 | 44·4 | 3·3 | Not Appl. |
| Present occupation | 41·5 | 70·8 | 58·3 | 59·3 | 76·5 |
| Work record | 5·1 | 18·8 | 0·7 | 20·9 | 61·8 |
| Marital status | 19·3 | 52·0 | 28·8 | 39·6 | 74·9 |
| Education | 4·4 | 16·7 | 0·0 | 18·7 | 54·1 |
| Income | 23·4 | 60·4 | 33·1 | 48·4 | 67·8 |
| Expenditure | 14·7 | 29·2 | 20·5 | 33·0 | 37·7 |
| Physical health | 1·0 | 4·2 | 0·7 | 2·2 | 12·6 |
| Mental health | 1·2 | 6·3 | 0·7 | 2·2 | 9·8 |

* As more than one item could be 'known' for each offence, the percentages are not cumulative.

Even though more information was known for the more serious cases, a considerable proportion were decided with scanty data on a number of items magistrates claimed, in the interview, were important. The data relating to income confirm, from another angle, the differences in opinion about relevance which were noted above and discussed in Chapter 4.[2] Even for the four serious offences, no detailed information on income was given in 40 per cent of cases; although, of course, some indication of the man's financial standing might have been surmised from his employment (but even here it was not known for 30 per cent) and appearance. It is interesting and

[1] Driving while disqualified, drunken driving, dangerous driving and failing to stop after an accident were grouped together, as the numbers of each were small.

[2] See pages 70–73. Another example was recorded in observing court practice. A man had been fined £10 for careless driving and costs of £27 7s. 0d. agreed to *before* the court were told of any personal circumstances of the defendant. This was at the point when they were considering the question of time to pay.

perhaps surprising that such a large proportion of cases were decided without information on driving experience—such as number of miles travelled and type of driving done.

Probation reports were requested in 2·7 per cent of all cases and 17 per cent of the 'four serious offences'. The figures for psychological or psychiatric reports were 1 per cent and 8·4 per cent respectively— all for driving while disqualified. It was possible to compare what was known for motoring offenders with the procedure for the indictable non-motoring offences which were observed. It was noticeable that a higher proportion of decisions in these latter cases were reached with the aid of details on work record, marital status and occupation. What is more revealing is that in 41 per cent of cases there were probation reports—although a lower proportion, 2·7 per cent, had psychiatric reports.

In interpreting all these figures the reader should remember that at many urban courts there is every day a long list of cases to be dealt with. Magistrates, naturally, wish to proceed with business as efficiently as possible and this constraint of time may have an important bearing on the decision whether or not to seek further details of cases. For example, at one court near London the nine magistrates on a rota, sitting in three separate courts, had to deal with more than thirty cases in a day. These cases ranged through shoplifting, possessing dangerous drugs, taking and driving away, breaking and entering, a complex case of driving while disqualified and dangerous driving involving many charges and various orders for non-payment of fines. The situation in a Midlands urban court was the same. Under such pressure it is perhaps not surprising that those offences which are regarded as relatively less serious by the magistrates are sentenced on the basis of the available information. This does not mean, however, that this situation should be allowed to continue *faute de meux*.

Records were kept of the proportion of cases in which previous convictions for indictable offences were made known to the court. The figures are compared below with Willett's findings. Care should be taken in interpreting the table, not only because Willett's enquiry was in only one county, but also because the numbers in the present study are small.

Leaving aside the offence with small numbers, the only major difference between what was made known and what Willett found in Criminal Records occurs for the offence of having no insurance.[1]

---

[1] The figures in the Durham pilot study (mentioned later in this paragraph) for no-insurance cases were very different from Willett's. Out of 55 cases *44 per cent* had a conviction for an indictable offence. This should be compared with the *14 per cent* of 91 cases observed in courts.

TABLE 10

THE COURTS' KNOWLEDGE OF INDICTABLE PREVIOUS
CONVICTIONS

|  | N | % with indictable convictions read out in court | % with indictable convictions recorded in Willett's study |
|---|---|---|---|
| Driving while disqualified | 11 | 54·5 ⎫ | 77·0 ⎫ |
| Drunken driving | 4 | 0 ⎪ | 18·3 ⎪ |
| Dangerous driving | 17 | 17·7 ⎬15·9 | 13·4 ⎬20·7 |
| Failure to stop or report | 16 | 6·3 ⎪ | 5·1 ⎪ |
| No insurance | 91 | 13·9 ⎭ | 24·5 ⎭ |
| Careless driving | 151 | 2·7 | — |

Bearing in mind the rough nature of this comparison, there is some evidence that in the more serious offences the police do make indictable convictions known. But careless driving is a different matter. Only a tiny proportion had crimes disclosed. Willett does not include comparable figures, but a pilot study in County Durham of convictions in 1963–4 revealed that out of 82 cases, indictable crimes could be traced in 16 per cent of the records.

THE WAY INFORMATION IS USED

After the main fieldwork was completed six courts were revisited and magistrates were invited to a conference. Beforehand they were sent two cases—one of drunken driving and one of dangerous driving. These are both cases (on which the analysis below is based) reproduced in Appendix II. After making an individual decision, they were divided into groups of three or two, making altogether twenty-five 'benches', and asked to reach a joint decision.[1] At each court the groups were spread around the court room and the 'information game' began. One item of information was changed at a time and after each change the benches were asked to record their decision—either 'no change', or whatever new penalty the two or three magistrates agreed upon. The changes were *not* cumulative; after every one they were told: 'Go back to the original facts'—thus *each* change was intended to measure the impact of *one* item of information

[1] The analysis of this part of the exercise is described in Chapter 7, page 126.

on the sentence. The items changed, in a case of drunken driving, were:

(a) potential harm—(i) in the town, (ii) on a deserted country road;
(b) actual harm—(i) slight injury, (ii) serious injury;
(c) extent of drunkenness—(i) lower level of alcohol, (ii) 'marginal' level of alcohol;
(d) defendant's attitude to his offence—aggressive and uncontrite;
(e) previous record—items were varied systematically in the following way: (i) same type of offence—10 years ago, 5 years ago or 2½ years ago—previous high penalty, previous low penalty; (ii) other motoring offences (careless driving), 5 years ago, 6 months ago—previous high and low penalties; (iii) previous indictable offences—violence, larceny (once and twice); (iv) previous non-indictable—drunk and disorderly (once and twice). These previous offences were dealt with both separately and in various combinations with each other.

The analysis of the data gathered from possible changes in sentence for a total of twenty-nine items was complex. Each of the twenty-five 'benches' noted their decisions on the original case, and this 'basic' decision varied; in other words each bench did not begin from the same base. For example, some had fined £25 and disqualified for a year while others had imposed a £50 fine and disqualified for two years. It was apparent that the possibilities for increasing the sentence in the light of new information would vary according to the basic starting point. All changes that occurred were therefore plotted and the distributions of 'steps' in the pattern of increases in penalties was recorded for each starting point. This complicated system (which is described in more detail in Appendix III) enabled the increases to be put on roughly the same scale, whatever base they started from. A similar scale was devised for increases in length of disqualification. Each item was examined to see if the change had led to an increase in penalty. It was also possible to compare the amount of change engendered by different items of information. Some information did not affect the sentence at all, other items universally led to a large change, and for others the amount of change varied substantially between different benches.

In the case given to the magistrates, the offender had driven along a busy road in an erratic manner and gone through red traffic lights before being stopped by the police. There had been no accident. The offender had a blood alcohol content of 267 milligrammes of alcohol per 100 millilitres of blood. He had no previous convictions and was penitent in court.

The magistrates were told in the 'game' that an accident had happened, and were given two instances: in one the driver of the other car had sustained bruised ribs, and in the other he had been seriously injured so that he was detained in hospital for nine months and suffered permanent disablement. For slight injury nineteen of the benches did not increase their penalty, and the others very slightly; but for the severe injury case there were wide variations in practice: six benches raised neither fine nor disqualification, five did not raise the fine but increased the disqualification and five raised the fine but did not increase the disqualification. The remaining nine raised both. The difference between the pattern of changes for slight and serious injury was found to be statistically highly significant.[1]

When the level of blood alcohol was dropped, first to 150 milligrammes, and then to 100, twenty-three of the benches changed neither fine nor disqualification; nor did they change them when told the offender was not contrite. These are both factors which might be considered relevant to the offender's culpability or sense of responsibility.

The changing pattern of sentencing in relation to previous convictions was most interesting. Certain convictions made little impact on the sentence, in particular previous convictions for larceny (two convictions), being drunk and disorderly (two convictions), and causing grievous bodily harm. Even when two convictions of larceny were added to convictions for drunken and careless driving, the penalty was not increased more than it had been for the motoring offences alone: only when grievous bodily harm and two convictions for drunkenness were also added was the penalty increased. This is interesting in view of the fact that nearly all magistrates claimed that previous indictable convictions were relevant.

In relation to drunken driving the two factors which appeared to make the most difference to sentencing were the penalty for the last offence, and the period since the last conviction. When the previous conviction was also for drunken driving the penalties were higher when the last conviction had incurred a large fine than when it had incurred a small one—even when the conviction was relatively recent. It was the same when the previous conviction was for careless driving. When the previous conviction for drunken driving had been 5 years ago rather than $2\frac{1}{2}$ years there was no difference in penalty, but there was a marked difference when both $2\frac{1}{2}$ and 5 years

[1] The test used was the Sign Test. See S. Siegel (1956), *Non-parametric statistics*, pp. 68–75.

were compared with 10 years. There was also a change in penalty when a conviction for careless driving had been 5 years ago instead of 6 months (although the difference was significant only at the 5 per cent level). A previous conviction for careless driving alone led about half the benches to change their decision, even when it had occurred about 5 years previously. But such a conviction when added to a recent offence of drunken driving did not increase penalties already passed for that offence (except when a very recent and serious offence of careless driving was added to a recent conviction for drunken driving—and even then the difference was only significant at the 5 per cent level).

A similar exercise was carried out in respect of one case of dangerous driving, but here only items describing the driving and harm done were changed.[1] In this case (see Appendix II) the driver had overtaken another vehicle on a sharp bend, causing a police car coming in the opposite direction to brake sharply. Two other descriptions were given, indicating that no other car was coming the other way and that it was early morning on a deserted road (the police car having witnessed the incident as a following vehicle). In neither case did more than two benches change their decision—and even then only slightly. When they were told that a collision had actually occurred, a description of minor injury made 15 of the 25 benches change either fine (9), disqualification (4), or both (2). The size of change varied from an initial £5 to £10 on one bench to from £15 to £50 on another. Serious injury made 23 benches change: 16 of them put their fines *and* disqualification up. Thus chance injury (for the police car *could* have been nearer) is seen as a factor to be considered in sentencing. When a clear indication of recklessness was given: 'A following motorist had given evidence that the defendant overtook three other vehicles, cut in on them and caused oncoming motorists to take evasive action so that they had to brake sharply and swerve off the road,' all but one bench increased the penalty—19 increased the fines and disqualifications. Often the increases were substantial; of the 12 benches who had not disqualified on the original facts, 10 did on the new ones. It seems that the courts may not imply recklessness from one dangerous manœuvre—seeing it perhaps as more akin to careless driving— but with concrete evidence of gross recklessness they view the offence much more seriously. Even so, the penalties actually imposed varied substantially. This aspect of the material will be briefly referred to in the next chapter.

Finally, two warnings should be given. First, it would be dangerous to draw too many firm conclusions from this enlightening game, for it

[1] Our 'subjects' having reached the limit of endurance!

was played with only two cases at six courts. Second, the way information was considered may have been unusual; one has the impression that many magistrates would not 'weigh-up' the importance of an item on its own but see it, more vaguely perhaps, as 'part of the picture'. The technique does, on the other hand, enable both the researcher and magistrate to consider carefully what impact particular pieces of the picture have, and it could probably be developed as an effective part of training programmes.[1]

Nor is it possible in many cases to know what reasons the court had for its decision. With the exception of driving while disqualified a reason was not given to the defendant in open court in more than 40 per cent of motoring cases. For non-motoring crimes reasons were also not given in half the cases.

The only indicator that could be collected about the way decisions were reached in court was the extent to which benches retired to consider the sentence rather than conferring in open court. Taking all the observed 48 serious offences grouped together (see page 118), 63 per cent were decided without retirement. The figures for insurance offences and careless driving were 78 and 93 per cent respectively.[2] Even in non-motoring indictable cases (of which we observed 183), 65 per cent of sentences were decided in this way.

The findings of this part of the study are especially important in the light of the evidence in the remaining chapters. They show conclusively that where complicating factors are introduced into cases, such as accidents and previous convictions, there are large differences in the way these circumstances are acted on. We would expect therefore that cases including these factors would be more likely to be dealt with in differing ways than those which appear more 'normal' or ordinary.

[1] A recently completed pilot study of changes in decisions made when alternative and additional items of information are added to a case of theft was carried out through a mailed questionnaire by Keith Devlin. Although there was a low response rate (100 out of 334 magistrates returned the questionnaire), Devlin's work supported the potential value of this research and training technique. See Keith Devlin (1971), *Sentencing offenders in magistrates' courts* (a study of legal factors affecting the sentencing process), *mimeo*, School of Social Sciences, Brunel University.

[2] The proportions who said they would have liked to retire with their colleagues to consider the cases sent to them individually is not really relevant for this purpose, but is discussed in Chapter 7 as an indicator of the extent to which the case was regarded as a problem.

CHAPTER 7

# Disparity in Sentencing

SO FAR the analysis has described, at a general level, the magistrates and their views on the sentencing problems posed by the motoring offender. Certain aspects of policy have been discussed, which may explain why these offenders are dealt with rather differently from other types of criminal, but the research design does not make it possible to pursue this question further. Instead, the remaining chapters concentrate on the issue which prompted the research— disparity in sentencing similar kinds of motoring offences. This chapter shows the extent to which divergent practices existed even when magistrates were given *exactly* the same case to sentence.

Three main questions were investigated:

1. To what extent were the variations in penalty produced by a research design based on a 'game situation' (decisions being reached by individuals, rather than groups, in their own home on the basis of written transcripts) similar to the kinds of variation found in the courts? In other words, are the research findings a valid reflection of 'real life'?
2. Which 'types' of each 'kind'[1] of case produced the most variation in penalties, and which the least?
3. To what extent were magistrates consistent in the relative severity of their imprisoning, fining and disqualification as they went from one kind of case to another? In other words, are there some magistrates who consistently fine or disqualify more than others— or do they only do so for certain groups of offences?

COMPARING SENTENCES IN THE RESEARCH WITH REAL LIFE

It will be remembered that about 100 magistrates dealt with each of five *types* of eight different *kinds* of offence.[2] Thus decisions were made in forty cases by about one hundred magistrates, making over

---

[1] For a reminder of the distinction made between types and kinds see page 34.

[2] Although 538 magistrates were interviewed, not all of them completed their set of eight cases. The numbers varied from case to case but were usually very close to a hundred. See Note 1 to Table 3, Appendix IV.

4,000 decisions altogether. The research design made it possible to compare the distribution of penalties given for each of these forty cases with a distribution of penalties for similar (matched) cases which had been dealt with in court. (The method of this analysis is described in Appendix IV.) This showed conclusively that the variations in decisions imposed by magistrates in cases sent to them *reflected* variations in penalties imposed in court. They were in other words, not a *product* of the research. In general, fines were higher and periods of disqualification lower in the research situation. The variation in (or range of) fines was only substantially greater for careless driving and speeding, which rarely receive high fines in court. In all cases the variation in disqualifications was *less* than that normally found in court. The comparisons for all cases are set out in Appendix IV.

Of course, it could be argued that decisions reached alone could vary more than those reached after group discussion. It was possible to examine the range of penalties given for the *same* case by twenty-five groups of three or two magistrates at the six courts where the 'sentencing game'[1] was held. They each dealt with one case of drunken driving and one of dangerous driving, and the fines they gave varied substantially. When the cases were made more complicated the variations were even greater. For example, when evidence was given that the drunken driving case had involved an accident causing serious injury to another driver the penalties imposed varied enormously—ranging from £25 plus twelve months' disqualification to six months' imprisonment with two years' disqualification. Similarly, when evidence in the dangerous driving case indicated recklessness and deliberate dangerousness the penalty given ranged from a £20 fine with twelve months' disqualification to £50 and two years' disqualification, and even to three months' imprisonment. Thus, especially in serious cases, the disparity in sentences imposed by 'benches' of magistrates was very substantial. It will be shown that it was precisely for such serious cases that magistrates, when questioned individually, differed most in their sentence.

## WHICH CASES PRODUCED THE GREATEST VARIABILITY IN SENTENCING?

### 1. *Comparing Cases*

Obviously some kinds of case are regarded as more serious than others. For example, driving while disqualified is the only offence for

[1] See page 120.

which imprisonment is commonly imposed,[1] and the majority of persons convicted of careless driving, failing to stop, speeding, and breaches of pedestrian-crossing regulations are not disqualified. Yet within any one kind of offence the circumstances of cases can be very different. Each of the five cases of one kind (e.g., dangerous driving) sent to magistrates differed in some way or another, either in the way it was presented in court (whether there was a guilty plea, legal representation, a personal appearance by the accused, etc.); in the circumstances of the offence, such as the existence of an accident or the degree of drunkenness; and in the facts about the defendant, for example whether he had previous convictions or his means or family circumstances were known.[2] Some cases were clearly more serious or complicated than others. Earlier it was explained that with each decision magistrates were asked to record how serious they regarded the offence 'of its kind'. In addition, there were questions on whether they would require more information before sentence,[3] whether they would retire to consider sentence, and to what extent they thought their colleagues would agree with them. These data were primarily collected to see whether it would help to explain different sentences. But they are useful also as a series of broad indices of the seriousness or problematic nature of the case, and the results are therefore set out in Table 6 of Appendix IV. Details of cases, along with those indicators, will be used to describe the different sentencing problems posed for the magistrates.

## 2. What is Disparity?

Each magistrate's decision in a case could be compared with the decisions reached by at least one hundred other magistrates *who were given exactly the same facts to judge*. The distribution of penalties imposed—both in range (lowest to highest) and shape—indicates the degree of unanimity among magistrates.[4]

---

[1] It is interesting to note that at the time of the field work the maximum penalty for driving while disqualified was imprisonment or fine (in that order), whereas for other serious motoring offences the penalty was fine or imprisonment.

[2] For details of the design see pages 33–6.

[3] Although this is not a particularly good measure, as it is affected greatly by whether the offender's income was included in the case summary rather than by the complexity of the case alone.

[4] Where distributions are relatively 'normal' or 'bell-shaped', the most useful measure of spread is the *standard deviation*. In these instances about two-thirds of the cases fall within one standard deviation either side of the mean (average); about 95 per cent of cases fall within two standard deviations. Thus if the mean fine is £20 and the standard deviation £5, about 66 per cent of magistrates will fine between £15 and £25, and 95 per cent between £10 and £30. But many

The main difficulty in presenting these data is to decide what constitutes substantial variation. The problem partly involves value judgements. For example, people may quite justifiably disagree on whether the difference between a £10 and a £15 fine is substantial. But it is also a problem inherent in the methods which have been used. One has to decide whether different amounts of fines required by different magistrates are due to real differences in their practice or to the 'random' choice of one figure rather than the amount next to it. For example, if the average fine is £30, it may be partly arbitrary, or due to 'random factors', whether a magistrate picks this amount or a fine at a point just below or above it. When fines are in this range the next alternative amount of fine that would be chosen would normally be either £25 or £35, a variation of £5 either side of the average. This is because there are 'natural numbers' for amounts of fines. Almost no one chooses 'odd amounts' like £27 or £32.[1] Should one regard, then, £25, £30 and £35 to be roughly equivalent amounts of fine; the choice of one amount rather than another not constituting *real* or *substantial* variation? The problem is, of course, that £35 is 40 per cent more than £25. And where the range is £10–15–20, the higher fine is 100 per cent greater than the lower! Even so, many may wish to say that this is not substantial variation, and I have therefore (in Table 3, Appendix IV) shown the proportion of magistrates who have chosen either the fine which the largest number chose[2]—i.e. the mode of the distribution—or the next 'natural number' either side of it.[3]

With the serious offences this is easy because the natural numbers

distributions are too 'skewed' for this measure to be reliably used, and some are bi-modal (double-peaked), in which case the standard deviation is a useless measure. Even in relatively normal-looking curves a few extreme values (say a few £80 fines when the mean is £25) greatly affect the standard deviation. It will only be mentioned therefore where it is statistically justified.

[1] Although when costs are added, or the total penalty calculated where there are multiple charges, odd numbers are frequently found.

[2] Of course even if the same fine were given magistrates could vary in the time they gave the offender to pay it. For example, of 23 magistrates who ordered an offender to pay a £50 fine plus £4 costs in a drunken-driving case, 7 said he should pay at £1–£2 per week, 5 at £3 or £4, 6 at £5 or £6, 3 at £7 or £8 and 2 at £13–£14: a substantial difference in the weekly impact on the offender. Under the Magistrates' Courts' Act 1952 the means of the offender should be taken into account in assessing not only the fine but also the length of time given to pay. Clearly different assessments of the offender's ability to pay were being made.

[3] In those instances where the distribution was 'skewed' so that few magistrates gave the next fine above the mode, the fines are grouped around the three 'values' chosen by most magistrates. For an example see Figure 5, p. 131, where the 'mode' is £30–34, but the fines are grouped £20–24, £25–29 £30–34.

are clear. But with minor offences, where only a short range of fines
is given (usually only up to a maximum of £15 or £20), the range of
penalties has been restricted to £2 either side of the mode, namely
£8–10–12 or £3–5–7. Even with this restriction one fine within the
range of 'similar penalties' may be twice as high as another. Many
may still consider it unreasonable to say that such a range indicates
little disparity and therefore ultimately it must be for the reader to
decide what he considers to be disparity in practice.

## 3. *The Range of Penalties*

Some offences sent to the magistrates involved multiple charges, such
as dangerous driving, driving without a licence and using a car
without insurance. In describing the sentences passed the variations
for the main charge will be dealt with first; for example, in this case
dangerous driving. At the end of this section there is a discussion of
disparities in the total penalties imposed in multiple-charge cases.

With the exception of the offences of driving while disqualified,
where imprisonment was given, it was very rare for the maximum
penalty to be used.[1] Indeed in cases of dangerous and drunken driving no more than 4 per cent gave *over* half the maximum fine (£50)
for the main charge. In one case of careless driving 6 per cent
gave over £50. Thus, fines are ranged mainly in the lower half of the
possible distribution. It could, of course, be argued that this was
because the cases given to magistrates were not really very serious.
But if we consider an offence of drunken driving which was ranked
as 'very serious of its kind' by 53 per cent of the magistrates and
'serious' by the rest, we find that 38 per cent fined £50, but only
three fined more.[2] Similarly, taking the most serious offence of
dangerous driving (which 43 per cent rated 'very serious' and 50 per
cent 'serious'), seventeen gave £50 and only four more than this.[3]
Moreover, these figures reflect the level of average fine, which can be
computed from the national statistics.[4]

---

[1] The maximum penalties in operation at the time of the fieldwork are listed
in a chart in Appendix IV.

[2] In this case the defendant was earning £17 per week (1967), had been a
provisional licence holder for 5½ years, and had failed the test 9 times.

[3] In this case the defendant's income was not known.

[4] See *Offences relating to motor vehicles*, H.M.S.O. (annually). Over the years
covered by this research—roughly 1964 to 1968, average fines for most offences
increased. The size varied from only 8 per cent for dangerous driving, where the
1964 average was £20, to bigger increases where the average was lower—15 per
cent for careless driving (from £10 1s. to £11 6s.) and 28 per cent for speeding, 30
per cent for driving uninsured and 35 per cent for neglect of pedestrian-crossing

The variations in penalty were largest for the more grave offences —driving while disqualified, drunken and dangerous driving— although there was considerable difference of opinion on whether or not to disqualify those found guilty of failing to insure. Within each *kind* of offence there were some cases which led to much more disagreement than others. These involved either some special circumstance in the offence, such as a serious accident or evidence of deliberate intent, or offenders who had previously been convicted. Conversely, as one would expect, there was least variation where the offence seemed to be of a 'technical' nature. Thus, the more the offence corresponded to the accepted definition of a crime in producing definite harm, or the offender showed himself to be relatively anti-social, the greater the disparity in sentencing. This finding reflects two of the points made earlier. First, there was lack of consensus on whether motoring offenders could be considered as 'criminals'. Secondly, the decision-making game showed wide variation in the impact on the sentence of factors such as injury or previous convictions. Furthermore, it suggests that attempts to establish some basic 'starting points' have been much more successful where cases display some usual or ordinary or average circumstances than where there are complications, the seriousness of which needs careful interpretation. For it is clear that there is nothing like a consensus of opinion on the weight that should be attached to previous convictions, to name only one factor. It is certainly interesting that, in general, magistrates felt less confident that 'all would agree' with them when making their decisions in the more serious cases than they did with the minor ones. For example, in 14 of the 15 cases of dangerous and drunken driving and driving while disqualified no more than a quarter of the magistrates said 'all would agree' with them. In some cases as many as 20 per cent said only 'some' would agree, thus indicating a lower confidence that their decision would be accepted in a group decision-making situation. On the other hand, in a case of careless driving as many as 43 per cent said all would agree with them, and the figures for some speeding and pedestrian-crossing offences rose to 71 and 61 per cent respectively.

---

regulations—but of course any increase on such a small amount as £3 7s. (the average for 1964 for this offence) will look proportionately large.

On the other hand there was a 12 per cent drop in the average fine for drunken driving, where the proportion convicted at magistrates' courts (rather than at Quarter Sessions) rose from 89 to 97 per cent, and the number increased dramatically from 5,637 to 17,615; both facts being largely due to the introduction of the breathalyser after the Road Safety Act, 1967.

Tables 3, 4 and 5 of Appendix IV set out the average fines, the proportion using imprisonment (for driving while disqualified) and disqualification, the range of penalties imposed, and the number of magistrates giving the same or a similar sentence.[1] The actual cases are reproduced in Appendix II or in Chapter 1. An inspection of Table 6 of Appendix IV will show that the cases producing the greatest variation correspond to those which a relatively high proportion of magistrates rated either as very serious, or serious, or

FIGURE 5

VARIATIONS IN THE FINES IMPOSED FOR A CASE OF DANGEROUS DRIVING

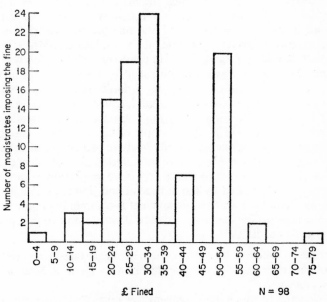

difficult, in terms of the other criteria discussed above. Here we shall just give brief details of these cases.

For *dangerous driving* the spread of fines and disqualifications were relatively wide for all offences, but especially in two cases, one where serious injuries were caused to the passenger in another vehicle through the offender overtaking at a relatively fast speed near the brow of a hill, and the other where a young man driving an old Jaguar motor car had driven fast across a major junction, gone

[1] As defined on pages 128–9 above.

the wrong side of a 'keep left' sign and narrowly missed an approaching vehicle. In addition he had previous convictions including a disqualification and a detention-centre sentence. For both offences about a fifth of the magistrates fined £25 and another fifth £50—one group being twice as severe as the other. This is illustrated in Figure 5. There was also a basic disagreement on whether to disqualify in the first case, and an extremely wide range of periods of disqualification in the second; while a quarter imposed one year, another fifth thought three or more years was appropriate.

In all cases of *drunken driving* between a fifth and a quarter chose fines of either £25 or £50; again, one group being twice as severe as the other. Disqualifications tended to be for the statutory minimum period, except for the case which the highest proportion of magistrates had rated 'very serious'. Here a man who was an 'L' driver, had failed his test nine times and had one previous conviction for speeding, drove through a junction into a bus. He denied the offence, claiming 'It was that 'bus driver. He came through the bloody lights at red.' The junction was not controlled by traffic lights. Furthermore, after being cautioned, he said, 'I don't know why you've got me. I'm making a stink about this, mind, Constable. I don't see why I pay £26 a year rates when they run you off the road.' In addition he declined to give the police a sample of urine. For this case only 39 magistrates chose one year, while 34 chose two and 17 three years.

*Driving while disqualified* is a rather different kind of offence from the rest. It has already been shown that more magistrates regard it as likely to be committed by the antisocial and 'criminals',[1] and it is the only offence for which imprisonment is commonly imposed. The five cases sent to the magistrates can be divided into two groups (see Table 4, Appendix IV):

(a) three in which a high proportion of magistrates sentenced the offender to prison or committed him to Quarter Sessions for sentence;

(b) two cases in which imprisonment was much less frequently used.

At the time of the fieldwork imprisonment could be imposed on all of them, but the 1967 Criminal Justice Act made it mandatory to suspend the sentence unless the offender had previously been in prison. The cases where magistrates frequently used imprisonment would still have been eligible *after* the Act, as the offenders all had prison records. The greatest amount of agreement was for a case which 83 per cent of magistrates rated 'very serious'. Here 71 imposed a prison sentence and 14 suggested committal to Quarter

[1] See pages 101–4.

Sessions so that a longer term could be imposed. But even so, only just over half the magistrates gave the same penalty of six months' imprisonment, and the periods of disqualification imposed varied enormously, ranging from none to 6 years: while 16 magistrates gave 12 months, 15 gave 24 and 22 over 3 years! These serious cases

FIGURE 6

VARIATIONS IN THE FINES GIVEN FOR A CASE OF CARELESS DRIVING
(This is the fine for the *main* charge; the range for the total fine in this multiple charge case was even wider.)

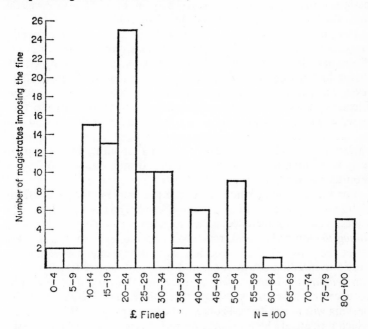

involved men with long records for motoring offences and dishonesty, their work patterns were poor and the offences all involved a substantial element of deceit and attempts to deny guilt. Two of the three were further complicated by long outstanding periods of disqualification. The cases which fewer magistrates imprisoned were less frequently rated 'very serious', but here the disparity could range from a £10 fine to 6 months in prison. For all driving-while-disqualified offences magisterial practice is particularly non-uniform.

In general the range of fines for *careless driving* was not particularly wide, although less than half of the magistrates gave the same penalty. Again a case involving an offender with a record produced substantial variation, which is illustrated in Figure 6. This driver collided with the back of a stationary car, reversed and drove off at speed. He was charged with failing to stop and report the accident as well as careless driving. His record showed 15 appearances in the previous 11 years, all for traffic offences. But within the previous four years he had kept out of trouble and started to run a one-man demolition business. Although he made a strong plea, through his solicitor, to be allowed to keep his licence so that he could continue work, about half the magistrates decided to disqualify and chose periods ranging up to five years. Once again, by all criteria it was the most difficult case that produced the greatest disparity.[1]

For *failing to insure* cases the variation in fines was not especially large, but there was considerable disagreement on whether or not to disqualify. Two relatively technical offences, in one of which the driver had reason to believe he was insured, were disqualified by fewer magistrates than the offences for which there was no excuse. Clearly magistrates disagree a great deal on whether to use their powers to disqualify those who do not insure their vehicles, and also on the appropriate period of disqualification. There was a lot of variation in the choice between 3, 6, 9 or 12 months. This is particularly interesting in view of the fact that disqualification for twelve months was mandatory until 1956.

For the remaining kinds of offence the fines imposed were fairly similar and disqualification was rarely used. The cases producing the widest variations included either an element of deliberateness (in *failing to stop and report*), repetition of the offence (in the *speeding* cases the most marked variation was for an offender with three previous speeding convictions) and potential danger (the sentences for *pedestrian-crossing offences* involving the failure to give precedence to those on crossings were more varied than those for parking within a restricted zone). Yet again, they were those offences which a relatively high proportion rated as serious, wished to retire to consider the decision, have more information before passing sentence, and for which a relatively low percentage thought their colleagues would agree with what they did.

Scattered among the cases sent to magistrates were some in which the offender had been charged with more than one offence. It was invariably so for driving while disqualified and other examples have

[1] See Table 6, Appendix IV. The only other case to raise disagreement was that of a man aged 62 who made a bad error of judgement in overtaking a long trailer. He said he would not drive again. Thirty magistrates disqualified him (eleven until a test), the rest did not.

been mentioned above. The decisions summarized in Table 3 of Appendix IV refer only to the penalty given to the main charge. It could be argued that the disparities exist because penalties are divided up rather haphazardly between various offences in a list of multiple charges and that the *totals* would be much the same. This was most certainly not true. In every example the range of penalty or disqualification noted for the main charge was compounded into even greater disparity in the total sentence for all charges in a list. For example, in the case of careless driving and failing to stop and report mentioned above (page 134), the range of fines for all offences combined was from £20 to £200: while 41 magistrates fined £30, £35 or £40 another 20 of their colleagues fined £60 or more. Similarly, in one of the cases of driving while disqualified 77 magistrates had imposed a fine ranging from £10 to £50, with a standard deviation of £10. For the case as a whole, which included additional charges of careless driving, no insurance and failing to report an accident the fines imposed varied from £27 to £162 with an average (mean) of £76 and a standard deviation of £30.

Taking into account that magistrates received *identical* facts, and that the permissible range of sentences is restricted by law and convention (we saw how only the bottom half of the permitted scale is usually used), variation in practice may be regarded as quite considerable. Its importance to the offender is, of course, greater in the more serious kinds of offence, where there can be differences of £25 between fines. Some may even regard the variations for the 'minor' offences relating to speeding and pedestrian-crossing regulations as at least irritating and conducive to ill-feeling towards the courts and the police—in fact this is one of the arguments for 'de-criminalized' traffic courts.[1] Where disqualification is commonly imposed there is, in general, much wider discrepancy, both in the decision whether or not to disqualify and in the length of the order chosen, than there is in the amount of fine imposed. The importance of this to the offender is obvious; fines may hurt, but disqualification sometimes affects livelihood and, at the least, seriously curtails a variety of activities. Of course, that is what it is meant to do; but when penalties are perceived as severe, dissatisfaction with a system which seems to some extent arbitrary will be even greater.

It seems, then, that there is greater agreement among magistrates for the 'easier-to-price' regulatory kind of offences than for those which more of them see as akin to crime in their seriousness. Among these serious offences the variations are especially striking where they are complicated by accidents and previous convictions, because the

[1] See Chapter 5 pages 105–7.

weight to be given these items is obviously difficult to determine. Nevertheless there is much greater unanimity in deciding the fine than in fixing periods of disqualification. The reasons for this have already been explored. While there are still some quite fundamental differences of view about the way to arrive at an appropriate fine, they pale into insignificance when compared with the very strong differences of opinion (or even lack of clear opinion) on the function of disqualification.

## 4. *Consistency in Relative Severity*

Before considering the relationship between magisterial backgrounds and attitudes and relative severity in sentencing it is important to consider whether magistrates are *consistently* relatively severe when going from one kind of offence to another. For example, do those who give higher than average fines for drunken driving also give higher than average fines for other offences? If they do not then it will be essential to discuss each offence in its own right. If they do it will be permissible to see whether there were any characteristics related to being relatively severe with a variety of cases.

The fines given for each offence were ranked in order of severity and correlated. The same process was repeated for lengths of disqualification imposed.[1] We compared the relative severity of fining for *all* offences; for dangerous and careless driving, and speeding, which were the three 'moving offences'; and for driving while disqualified and with no insurance, which are often regarded as two 'dishonest offences'.[2] The results showed conclusively[3] that it is permissible to talk of magistrates who are 'generally relatively severe' or 'relatively lenient' in the fines they impose. The same was not true

[1] Only the main offences were compared, because obviously it would have been nonsense to compare a fine given for a multiple charge with one given for a single charge. Each of the five groups of magistrates was treated separately. Where the comparison involves more than two cases the measure of association used was the *co-efficient of concordance* (Kendall's W); where only two offences were being compared the rank correlation coefficient was computed.

[2] See D. J. Steer and Carr Hill (1967), 'The motoring offender—who is he?' *Crim. L.R.*, 214–24.

[3] For *all* offences the co-efficients of concordance of about $0.3$ was statistically significant, $p < 0.05$; for four of the five comparisons of dangerous and careless driving the coefficients were $0.45$, $p < 0.05$ (the other group was almost significant at the 5 per cent level); for the comparison between driving while disqualified and no insurance (for the two groups which had fined a high proportion of the former cases), rank correlation coefficients of $0.29$ and $0.36$ were significant, $p < 0.05$.

for disqualifications. Although many combinations were examined[1] there was no overall consistency in results. It seems safest to conclude that, in general, magistrates are likely to vary in their relative severity when they disqualify as they move from one kind of case to another.

Again, the evidence supports the view that it has been far easier for magistrates to decide on their general level of fining than it has been to find a policy for disqualification.

[1] The analysis here is so complex, different offences having to be combined in each of the five groups, that it is easier to give a general summary. (1) Taking *all* offences in which a considerable proportion of magistrates disqualified offenders, only *two* of the five groups showed consistency. (2) Comparing driving while disqualified and no insurance, again only two groups showed a significant correlation, one being *negative*. (3) In two groups substantial proportions of both dangerous and careless driving cases had been disqualified. In only one was the correlation significant. (4) Only one *group* of magistrates showed consistency in their disqualifying over all three of the comparisons made. This may have been because of the cases they received, but inspection of them, and a comparison with the cases sent to the other groups, does not suggest that this is the reason.

# CHAPTER 8

# Towards an Explanation of Disparity

IT IS now clear that fines vary most for the more serious kind of offence and that there is greater disparity in deciding on disqualification than on the appropriate fine. Earlier it was suggested that these differences in practice may be accounted for partly by differences in magistrates' personal and social backgrounds and their varying approaches towards, and perceptions of, the problem posed by the motoring offender, and partly by whole benches tending to develop rather special policies, either through the informal influences of the chairman, senior magistrates and clerk, or through the more rigid application of some system of 'starting points' or 'basic penalties' set out in a schedule and available as a guide whenever sentence is passed. It is now time to see to what extent variations in sentencing for motoring offences can be explained by these three sets of variables: namely, personal and social attributes; perceptions and attitudes; the bench.

## 1. *The Influence of Personal Attributes of Magistrates*

(a) *Outline of the analysis.* The analysis is so complicated by detail that only the main statistical procedures and results are explained in the text.[1] We have simply tried to set out those findings which have some general theoretical interest or practical implication.

The basic purpose of the analysis was to discover which factors were associated with the imposition of *relatively* severe sentences. Each offence had been sentenced by about a hundred magistrates and it was possible to distinguish[2]:

(a) those who used imprisonment from those who did not;
(b) those who gave more than the 'average' (median) length of imprisonment from those who gave less;

[1] The details of statistical techniques and processes are fully explained, with reasons why they were chosen, in Appendix III.

[2] The analysis relating to imprisonment was only concerned with offences of driving while disqualified. The decision to disqualify or not was examined in all

138

(c) those who ordered disqualification and those who did not;
(d) those who gave longer than the median period of disqualification from those who gave shorter periods;
(e) those who imposed more than the median fine from those who gave a lighter penalty.

Thus, the distinction is made simply between those who give *relatively* high or low fines or *relatively* long or short periods of imprisonment or disqualification. It should be clear, therefore, that the term 'relative' has only a statistical meaning and does not imply that relatively heavy sentences are any better or any worse than more lenient ones. The analysis is concerned with disparity, not with effectiveness or appropriateness.

Because it was possible that particular aspects of magistrates' backgrounds, attitudes and perceptions might be related to the sentence given in some types or kinds of cases but not in others, it was necessary first to examine separately the associations for all 40 cases.[1] Obviously when there are so many calculations some will appear as significant associations purely by chance, and have no explanatory meaning whatsoever.[2] Therefore only those which seemed to have some value in explaining the sentences passed on a variety of cases were considered in detail. A logistic regression analysis was carried out to see if variables which had been associated with the sentence passed by the magistrates dealing with only one or two types of case when considered separately (e.g., one or two of the five cases of dangerous driving) were associated with the sentences

cases except where very few disqualified or almost all disqualified: the cases analysed included all those of dangerous driving and no insurance, two of careless driving, and one of speeding: 13 cases in all. The length of disqualification was analysed when enough magistrates disqualified to make the results meaningful: this included the drunken-driving and driving while-disqualified cases, making 23 overall (although it should be remembered that there was little variation for four of the five drunken-driving cases), Fines were analysed for all cases except the three of driving while disqualified where a large majority had imposed a prison sentence (37 cases in all).

[1] Obviously it was logically possible that within one kind of offence (say, dangerous driving) a characteristic of a magistrate could be positively associated with a high fine for one *type* of case and negatively associated for another type: so that if all the offences were lumped together the meaning of the association could be obscured. This kind of interaction effect is fairly common in criminological studies. See R. Hood and R. Sparks (1970), *Key issues in criminology*, Chapter 7.

[2] For example, approximately 1,800 tests of significance between 'background' attributes and the fine were performed. We would expect on average 90 of them to be significant at the 5 per cent level *by chance*. In fact we found 135 associations significant at this level.

passed by *all* (538) magistrates when variations in the cases they had received, and the effects of other variables, were controlled for.[1] This analysis, therefore, enabled us to check whether there was any *general* association between particular attributes or views of magistrates and the relative severity of the sentence they were likely to impose, whatever type of case of a particular kind (e.g., dangerous driving) they received.

(b) *The limited impact of personal factors.* One of the most important findings is a negative one. There were very few consistent associations over a variety of different types or kinds of offence between any of the attributes describing social, political, personal background, magisterial or motoring experience and relative severity in fining, imprisoning and disqualifying. Thus in this sample of magistrates disparity could not be accounted for simply by differences in their personal backgrounds.

Of course there were, for particular kinds of offence, some interesting findings. For example, the age of magistrates was related to the fine given in all five cases of dangerous driving; the older magistrates being relatively severe in two of the cases involving young, rather reckless drivers, and relatively lenient in the three cases in which offenders were older. The regression analysis showed that for *some* kinds of offence particular variables were statistically associated with the sentence imposed, but there was no clear pattern on which one could base generalizations about all cases. Only two factors affected the sentence in more than one kind of offence. Those who were more extravert in personality used imprisonment less frequently for those who drove while disqualified, and also disqualified fewer of those convicted of driving without insurance. Also, those who had been held responsible for an accident (only a minority of magistrates anyway) were less likely to imprison the driving-while-disqualified cases, and those who had been in one or more accidents were less likely to disqualify no-insurance cases. A list of the variables, which were included in this analysis, is given in Appendix III.

Thus, particular factors are associated with certain kinds of offence only. Also, personal and social factors taken together (in the regression analysis) were a relatively good predictor of the sentence for a few cases, but not for others. Obviously a magistrate's back-

---

[1] This analysis was only completed for those cases where either (a) there had been a substantial number of attributes associated with the sentence in the preliminary analysis, or (b) there was a relatively large variation in the sentences passed.

ground has an influence on the sentence he passes, but from this analysis it is impossible to ascribe any particular weight to the importance of any single attribute or group of related attributes over all kinds of case.

It is important also to note that whether magistrates came from the north, midlands or south, from urban or rural courts, or from large or small benches had no *consistent* effect on the size of the penalty.[1] Different practices cannot be explained therefore by these kinds of environmental factors.

## 2. *How serious is the case?—the importance of perception*

The connection between the perception of the seriousness of offences and severity in the punishment imposed is a complex one, but one point stands out. These variables were not significantly associated with the severity of the decision in absolutely every one of the cases, but they occurred so frequently—often at a one per cent level of significance—that it is reasonable to generalize about their effect on sentencing. The rating of an offence as 'serious of its kind' and the severity of punishment were statistically associated in just over half the cases dealt with. Also, we found that the other more general measures of seriousness—the relative ranking of a motoring offence in relation to 18 other offences, and the magistrates' stereotype of the kind of persons who commit offences—were both more frequently associated with the penalty than any background or personal attributes of magistrates. The seriousness with which the offence was generally viewed was particularly associated with relatively high fines for two offences: failing to stop after or report an accident, and neglect of pedestrian-crossing regulations.

There is, then, general support for an explanation of sentencing which sees differences in the way magistrates perceive and categorize offences as an important factor in producing disparate penalties. The caveats to this general conclusion are, however, extremely important. They are: first, that the association is strongest in relation to the decision to imprison or disqualify; is quite strong as regards the decision on the amount of fine; and hardly exists where the

[1] There were of course instances where these factors did have an effect. For example, in one of the five cases of dangerous driving more of those from large courts disqualified above the median, $p < 0.05$; in a case of drunken driving more of those from the north and midlands disqualified for periods above the median, $p < 0.01$; the same occurred for one of the cases of no insurance. On the other hand, in two cases of no insurance a higher proportion of magistrates from the south decided to disqualify.

relative *length* of disqualification is being considered. This is perhaps understandable, because once the serious step of deciding to disqualify has been made other factors come into play. And in fact we found that for those cases where a wide range of periods were imposed it was the magistrates' views on the 'optimum penalty' which distinguished the severe from the lenient. This finding indicates that it is more a question of differences in opinions on the effectiveness of different periods that matters rather than punishing the offence in relation to its perceived seriousness.[1]

Secondly, seriousness rating was *not* associated with the penalty imposed in just under half the cases, and therefore magistrates who *agreed* to rate an offence as 'very serious' or 'serious' gave different sentences for some other reason. Thirdly, as with background personal factors, seriousness ratings were associated with decisions in some kinds of case but not others. For example, in the three cases of driving while disqualified, where many magistrates passed a prison sentence, the rating of the offence as 'very serious' was significantly associated with making this decision.[2] But in all five cases of no insurance the decision on whether or not to disqualify was unaffected by how magistrates rated the relative seriousness of the cases. On the other hand, if one leaves aside these no-insurance cases, perception of seriousness was associated with the decision whether or not to disqualify in six of the seven cases where magistrates had been deeply divided in their use of this power.

It should be noted (in view of the findings reported in Chapter 7 that some types of case produced wider variation in sentence than others) that the seriousness rating of a case was not more frequently associated with the penalty in these 'complicated' cases than in those with a lesser spread in the penalties imposed. Thus magistrates not only vary in how seriously they rate *some* of the complicated cases, they also share no common equation between viewing a case as serious and fixing an appropriate fine.

Obviously, then, variation in the perception of the seriousness of cases is of importance, but (as with background variables) it is impossible to generalize about its influence as it is only one variable affecting the decision on which penalty to impose.

---

[1] The variable was actually the optimum disqualification for a *second* offender. In fact none of the cases given to magistrates involved an offender who had been convicted for a second time for the same offence, but attitudes towards second offenders discriminated between those who gave relatively long and short periods much more often than did attitudes towards first offenders. $r = 0.22$, $p < 10.0$; $r = 0.32$, $p < 0.001$; $r = 0.26$, $p < 0.001$; $r = 0.36$, $p < 0.001$.

[2] In one case $p < 0.001$, in another case $p < 0.01$, and the third $p < 0.05$.

We tried to see if there were any consistent associations between the attributes of magistrates who perceived the same circumstances differently: whether there was, for example, a relationship between political background or attitude and a tendency to consider cases as more or less serious. The analysis failed to find any consistent relationships between social, political, motoring, personality, magisterial experience or any other attributes of magistrates and both their perception of the seriousness of a case and the severity with which they sentenced it. This does not mean that no associations exist, only that we found none in this sample.

### 3. *The Pervasive Influence of the Bench*

(a) *Outline of the analysis.* The analysis dealing with the effect of the bench was simpler. It will be remembered (see page 34) that the cases sent to magistrates were grouped into five separate 'packages', each containing the eight different kinds of offence. They were sent in equal proportions to each of the 32 courts so that, for example, at a bench of 20 magistrates four would have received package A, four package B, etc., and at a bench of 30 magistrates, six would have dealt with the cases in A, six with those in B, etc. Thus in comparing the relative severity of sentences passed at different benches we knew that each had received the same proportion of each type of case. If belonging to a particular bench had no effect we would find that the relatively severe magistrates were distributed randomly between the different benches.[1] Conversely, if it were an important factor there would be a statistically significant association showing that the relatively severe or lenient magistrates were more frequently concentrated in particular benches than could occur by chance.

(b) *Bench membership and sentencing severity.* The bench a magistrate belonged to had a highly significant effect on the amount of fine imposed for all eight kinds of offence and on the decision whether or not to disqualify or to imprison.[2] It also had an effect on the length of disqualification given for dangerous driving but *not* for either drunken driving or driving while disqualified. There seem to be good reasons for this. In drunken-driving cases there is general agreement that disqualification will normally be for the statutory

[1] Only the 24 courts with ten or more members were included. At the other eight benches the numbers were too small to make the analysis meaningful.

[2] The decision to disqualify or not was analysed for cases of dangerous driving and no insurance. The numbers involved for careless driving and speeding were too small. The analysis of imprisonment was, of course, confined to driving while disqualified.

minimum period of 12 months. In four of the five cases sent to magistrates, two-thirds or more imposed this statutory minimum. At the nine courts with local starting points for this offence, six suggested 12 months, one simply said 'consider disqualification', and two recommended two years. The minimum seems to have become hardened into 'the usual', and this may of course be due to the increasing distrust of long periods of disqualification. We have already noted that the debate on the value of long disqualification had centred around the problem of dealing with those who drive while disqualified. There are wide differences of opinion about what is the best policy. In four of the five cases sentenced by our sample there were highly significant correlations between individual magistrates' views on the optimum period and the length actually imposed. Furthermore, bench guides or starting points generally suggest fines or imprisonment for this offence but make no recommendation about disqualification beyond mentioning the (former)[1] statutory need to impose a further twelve-month ban. It is significant that the only court that had a recommended period—of five years—had the highest proportion of magistrates of any bench giving a similar penalty; three-quarters gave more than the median period of disqualification. It is not surprising that the seriousness rating was only associated with length of disqualification for one of the five cases because it is more important for magistrates to take into account the impact of a long ban on the future driving and criminal behaviour of the offender and potential offenders. While courts remain so ignorant on these matters, different individual views will prevail.

Where all other offences are concerned, why does the local bench have such an important and pervasive effect on the size of the fine and on the use of disqualification? The association between bench membership and the sort of penalty given is all the more remarkable because it will be remembered that magistrates 'sentenced' the cases at home, and alone, and not in groups in the atmosphere of the court.

Obviously the variations are affected *partly* by the backgrounds of magistrates and their views on the relative seriousness of motoring offences and *partly* by the influence of local bench norms. But in this research, because of the way a variety of cases were distributed at each court, it is not possible to disentangle the weights which should be given to the individual perception and to bench 'constraints'. But there is a good deal of evidence to show how some local courts may reach a common practice. Before going further, though, we should warn the reader that we are *not* saying that all members of a bench

[1] Repealed by the Road Traffic Disqualification Act 1970, Sec. 1. See pages 84–5.

### TABLE 11

#### A COMPARISON OF THE RELATIVE SEVERITY OF FINES GIVEN FOR DRUNKEN DRIVING CASES AT 24 COURTS

| Court<br>S = South<br>M = Midlands<br>N = North | Number<br>on bench<br>dealing<br>with cases | % Fine<br>below<br>median* | % Fine<br>above<br>median* | % saying<br>they use<br>basic<br>penalty<br>in general | Courts<br>having<br>local lists<br>including<br>drunken<br>driving |
|---|---|---|---|---|---|
| S1 | 9 | 89 | 11 | 80 | Yes |
| S2 | 22 | 59 | 41 | 95 | Yes |
| S3 | 17 | 41 | 59 | 100 | Yes |
| S4 | 21 | 62 | 38 | 68 | No |
| S5 | 16 | 50 | 50 | 63 | No |
| S6 | 12 | 58 | 42 | 100 | Yes |
| S7 | 14 | 36 | 64 | 100 | Yes |
| S8 | 13 | 62 | 38 | 92 | No |
| S9 | 28 | 14 | 86 | 100 | Yes |
| S10 | 28 | 46 | 54 | 13 | No |
| S11 | 21 | 43 | 57 | 82 | Yes |
| S12 | 14 | 43 | 57 | 93 | No |
| M13 | 11 | 45 | 55 | 36 | No |
| M14 | 32 | 63 | 38 | 6 | No |
| M15 | 12 | 92 | 8 | 100 | Yes |
| M16 | 19 | 37 | 63 | 95 | Yes |
| M17 | 24 | 21 | 79 | 100 | Yes |
| M18 | 15 | 53 | 47 | 31 | No |
| M19 | 38 | 66 | 34 | 2 | No |
| N20 | 12 | 83 | 17 | 15 | No |
| N21 | 34 | 50 | 50 | 33 | No |
| N22 | 13 | 92 | 8 | 0 | No |
| N23 | 21 | 19 | 81 | 100 | Yes |
| N24 | 14 | 50 | 50 | 100 | Yes |
| Total | 460 | 50·4 | 49·7 | 66.8 | |

$\chi^2$ 71·62, 23df, p<0·001
* This is the median fine for the whole sample.

do the same thing, only that they are more *likely* to do something similar to their colleagues than we would expect by chance.[1]

In fact, as Table 11 shows for drunken driving, there was considerable variation in the extent of agreement at different courts. In

[1] Because only a few magistrates on any one bench would have dealt with the same package of cases it was not possible to compare the variations in decisions

eight courts, two-thirds or more of the magistrates agreed to fine either above or below the median (which usually meant choosing either around £25 or around £50), but in others the bench was split nearly fifty-fifty. Also within most courts there was considerable variation, often with over a third doing something quite different from their colleagues. This is perhaps due to the fact that some magistrates at all courts would have received those cases involving complicated circumstances which had produced a relatively wide range of sentences.[1]

Thus, while it is important to stress the highly significant association between bench membership and sentencing practice, it must not be interpreted as an iron rule that membership of a particular bench will *dictate* a magistrate's practice.

As Table 11 also shows, there was a very strong association between membership of a particular bench and the use of basic penalties or starting points.[2] The Magistrates' Association (with the support of the Lord Chancellor and Lord Chief Justice) does not print recommended penalties for dangerous or drunken driving, but twelve courts had their own lists which included these offences. However, there is only a slight indication that having a basic penalty system produces a higher level of agreement among the members of a bench.[3] What is more striking is that the benches where the magistrates are divided nearly fifty-fifty[4] are just as likely to have a basic penalty schedule as not to have one. It would seem therefore that the development of a common policy on a bench is a subtle process brought about through the influence of clerks and senior magistrates becoming embodied in a tradition. Where the conditions for this do not exist—for example in benches with a number of strong

---

found *within* a bench with those found *between* different benches. It was also not possible to add 'bench membership' to the regression analysis because this would have meant there were a further 24 (or 32) variables to hold constant. This would not have produced accurate results.

[1] See pages 129–31. Because of the way the cases were distributed too few magistrates at each court would have dealt with the 'complicated' cases to make within-court comparisons meaningful.

[2] $\chi^2 = 315.65$, df $= 23$, p $< 0.001$.

[3] For example, of the 12 benches with a basic penalty for drunken driving, 5 had two-thirds or more of their magistrates agreeing on the relative size of their fine. This compares with 3 of the 12 courts without a starting point. For careless driving the association is more marked; 7 out of the 13 courts with a schedule had two-thirds or more agreeing on the relative level of the fine, compared with 3 of the 9 without a schedule. Yet in speeding cases the reverse was true. Only 6 of the 15 courts with a list had high agreement compared with 6 of the 9 without a list.

[4] Nearly fifty-fifty is taken as between the limits of 60 and 40.

personalities with differing views, or in large courts with magistrates divided into 'rotas' which rarely change or where the clerk plays little part in trying to advise on sentencing[1]—the publication of a schedule may have little impact. In fact at two of the six courts without basic-penalty schedules the clerks claimed there was little disparity between rotas because at one 'the benches are shuffled around so that they all know what is a fair idea', and at the other 'the deputy chairman and chairman keep them steady'. At the remaining four these situations did not exist. They were the largest courts in our sample. One clerk said:

> Yes, very marked variations. One can tell (almost) by looking at the fines which day they were imposed. Tuesday and Thursday are lenient; Wednesday is the most severe; Friday is also fairly severe. Monday is mixed . . . the solicitors try to get adjournments to various days in order to get lenient sentences for their clients.

He then pointed out that two attempts to gain uniformity, one through a tariff list and the other through posting details of penalties given each week on the notice board, had both failed 'because the J.P.'s would not make comparisons . . . they never ask what the other days are doing, and even if they did one could not tell them because the variations are so large'. At another court the clerk pointed to difficulties due to particular personalities—a view which was echoed at both the other courts—'there are variations in average penalties according to the particular outlook or personality of the rota chairman'.

There was some evidence to suggest that certain assumptions about penal policy are shared by magistrates on the same bench. For example, we found that magistrates who said they would give the same fine in serious cases regardless of the income of the offender tended to be concentrated in particular benches. At ten out of the twenty-four larger courts 36 per cent or more of the magistrates shared this view, while at seven courts more than 80 per cent completely rejected it.[2] Similarly, the view that fines should not be affected by the costs in a case was associated with bench membership.[3] It is interesting to note that holding either of these views was

[1] It has already been noted on page 59 that most magistrates regarded the clerk as having an unobtrusive but certainly not an overbearing influence. But, as the *Justice of the Peace* noted, 'The High Court has placed on the clerk the duty of seeking the agreement of his justices within each division to some degree of uniformity of fines', *131* (1967), 36. Most clerks agreed that they used their influence to point out variations between rotas in an attempt to achieve some uniformity.

[2] $\chi^2 = 50.50$, 23 df, $p < 0.001$.

[3] Where costs were £10, $\chi^2 = 62.44$, 23 df, $p < 0.001$. Where costs were £20, $\chi^2 = 50.51$, 23 df, $p < 0.001$.

not confined to those benches without basic penalty schedules. At six courts more than 40 per cent of magistrates wanted to give a poor man convicted of a serious offence the same fine as a wealthy man. Three of these courts had schedules, three did not. This reinforces the conclusion that uniformity of *approach* cannot be achieved simply by adopting lists of 'starting points'. This is even more strikingly underlined when one examines the relationship between views on the seriousness of cases and membership of a particular bench. In only three of the eight kinds of offence in the study was there a significant association between how magistrates rated offences and bench membership. In other words, for five kinds of offence the bench to which a magistrate belonged affected the probability of his giving a particular fine, or imposing imprisonment for driving while disqualified, or disqualifying a dangerous driver, *even though* views on how serious these cases were varied between the members of the same bench. The exceptions were drunken-driving, no-insurance, and speeding cases, where magistrates on the same bench tended to share similar views of what constituted a serious case.

Altogether these findings strongly suggest that 'bench constraints' and individual differences in the perception of the seriousness of cases act independently in affecting the sentence. Indeed, they suggest that while there is such diversity of views among magistrates the problem of disparity should not be solved simply by imposing a system of tariffs.

IMPLICATIONS AND CONCLUSIONS

The results presented in Chapter 7 suggest that while benches may tend to agree in general on the appropriate fine, there is less agreement when cases present 'unusual' features. Our analysis seems to indicate that disparities in these cases may arise out of too great a reliance on systems to achieve uniformity in 'ordinary' cases. The Magistrates' Association has repeatedly denied that its list of 'suggested penalties' is a tariff, because that implies a rigid sentencing procedure. Yet in practice it must work rather like a tariff, for the vast majority of cases will be like the 'average' and the penalty will be the norm suggested or a slight variation on it. I am inclined to believe that disparities were due to lack of discussion about the principles which should be used in deciding what weight should be given to various aggravating circumstances in 'out of the ordinary' cases. This is supported by two findings—first, the lack of association in some of the complicated cases between their perceived seriousness and the size of the fine and, secondly, the variation in response to the introduction of 'complicating factors' in the information game. Leaving aside these 'complicated' cases, there is less cause for concern about fines, but there is a great deal of variation in the use of disqualification. Obviously here it is not a question of agreeing on a 'price' but of weighing up basic questions of penal philosophy.

The pervasiveness of an approach to fining which was basically aimed at finding the right 'price' for the offence was reflected throughout the research by a number of striking reactions to our questions. One of these was the inability of many magistrates to give coherent reasons for their decisions other than that it was at the right place on the tariff. Examples were:

> ' . . . this is a very serious case and should be dealt with as such' . . ; 'normal minimum on my bench for a first offence' . . . 'fair assessment . . 'defendant was contrite, first offence of this nature' . . . 'average penalty' . . . 'a certain amount of mitigating circumstances'.

and many more in similar vein. Others simply said something about the offence which indicated little beyond their grading of its seriousness. Examples were:

> ' . . . consequences could have been more serious' . . . 'serious—must be dealt with properly to save lives' . . . 'a menace to himself and others' [all drunken driving] . . . 'take a serious view of driving while disqualified' . . . 'serious offence committed within a short time of other offence' [both driving while disqualified] . . . 'very careless' . . . 'stupid and irresponsible action—record showed improvement' . . . 'error of judgement' . . . 'adjust speed according to road conditions' [all careless driving].

We were also struck by the large number who found the questions about the principles of fining and disqualification and about the relationship between motoring offences and criminality extremely difficult. Many were particularly disturbed by the request for reasons to justify their answers, and our overall subjective impression was that most had never really thought through their attitudes towards the motoring offender or had to justify what was simply 'common practice' in their courts. Some wrote especially saying that they had found the experience of answering the questions rewarding and stimulating. We had similar experiences at the sentencing conferences. One of my most vivid memories is of a meeting during the pilot stages for the conferences where magistrates discussed a case of driving while disqualified (see Case 6, Chapter 1). After reaching individual decisions they were sent in groups of three to reach their joint conclusion. We told them that they would have half an hour to record their decision in writing and received a unanimous response that such a long period was unnecessary as they dealt with such cases

F

quite regularly in five or, at the outside, ten minutes. After half an hour no group had reached a joint decision based on a commonly agreed set of reasons—and eventually a time limit had to be placed on the exercise. One woman magistrate said afterwards: 'I have been sitting with Mr —— for seven years and this is the first time I realized our views are diametrically opposed.'

This is not an isolated incident: the long periods spent clarifying and recording reasons for group decisions were a feature of the conferences at all six courts we visited—even though the two cases being dealt with were not especially complicated (see Appendix II (2), Cases 12 and 13).

The danger is that attempts to achieve uniformity in sentencing through booklets, scales or more informal methods (such as the steady influence of the clerk) may well inhibit change—whether it be adapting present methods, or experiments with new approaches towards disqualification or traffic attendance centres.[1] One of the prices of uniformity is stagnation, and it is certainly not clear that the courts are so correct in their solution to traffic offences that they can afford a standard approach rather than pursuing a more dynamic experimental policy. This would admittedly be less uniform but perhaps more in line with a modern penal philosophy based on individualization of punishment. Clearly many people would regard this as inappropriate because they believe that motoring offenders are unlike 'real criminals', and that therefore so-called treatment aimed at attitude change is inappropriate. The wealth of studies in recent years, including Willett's and Parry's, has done something to shatter this illusion, and it is clear from this research also that a considerable minority of magistrates now share the view that the problem is more complex. It would be a pity to stifle this new-found perspective, this concern to re-examine some basic assumptions about the problem posed by the dangerous, drunken or careless motorist (not to say the defiant one!) in too rigid a system of local or even national agreements on 'basic penalties'. The fears of 'computer justice' are a natural outcome of too great a reliance on tariff principles.[2]

At the same time, one must recognize that there is a complete absence of information about the impact of a fine on motorists' attitudes and driving performance and that magistrates do not, and

---

[1] *Non-custodial and semi-custodial penalties* (1970), paragraph 10, pages 35–8. The Committee, in particular, noted the lack of diversity in the sentences imposed for traffic offences, including the serious ones.

[2] Editorial, 'Consistency in sentencing', *Law Society Gazette*, 67 (6), June 1970, 366.

cannot, act in a vacuum. They are bound to reflect some of the common assumptions about the causes of driving behaviour and the view that, with certain exceptions, such offences are not properly classed as crime. Unless evidence changes the social evaluation of these offences, the fine will continue as the main type of sentence employed. But there is obviously a need to consider the principles underlying its use—whether as a 'penalty' or a deterrent punishment —and to evaluate critically the purposes of disqualification—especially in those cases which are clearly 'out of the ordinary'. Without much consideration there can be no common acceptable policy.

Of course, to some extent these problems are recognized. The Lord Chief Justice in particular has called for more liaison between magistrates from different benches within the same area or county:

> Surely it could be arranged that justices could sometimes sit on another bench and under a different chairman. For ten years I have been advocating this and am told that it is administratively difficult. Nevertheless it is done in a few counties and in my opinion should be done however difficult it may be.[1]

This liasion does, of course, already exist to some extent through the great increase in training courses which have been organized for magistrates at all levels since formal training for new magistrates was made mandatory in 1965.[2] Of particular importance is the enormous interest taken by many experienced magistrates in weekend courses which include 'sentencing exercises'. Undoubtedly this development has made many justices aware of different views. When the research began sentencing conferences were relatively new, although they had already shown that, faced with the same facts, different magistrates would recommend very different sentences. This did not escape the notice of the press: 'Thirty-five magistrates got together for a shattering experiment. They heard an imaginary motoring case and were asked what fine they would impose. Their scales of justice see-sawed wildly from £1 to £20.'[3]

The best of these exercises often deal at length with one or two

---

[1] Lord Parker of Waddington (1970), 'A team spirit', *The Magistrate*, *26*, 186–8. In 1967 the *Justice of the Peace* commented that 'the Lord Chief Justice has indicated that some degree of congruence is desirable between adjacent divisions', *131* (1967), 36.

[2] *The training of justices of the peace in England and Wales* (1965), Cmnd. 2856, H.M.S.O.

[3] *Sunday Mirror*, 2 February 1964. Originally reported in *The Guardian* and the *Daily Mirror*, 18 October 1962 on the basis of a letter to *The Magistrate*, *18* (1962), 139. See also *The Guardian*, 3 February 1964, which reported variations in fines for a 'mock case' of a rich speeding offender ranging from £20 to £50. Also, *The Yorkshire Post*, 21 November 1966.

cases and discuss in detail the reasons lying behind different view-points, but too many are still rather rapid affairs in which a large number of cases are quickly reviewed in order to get some idea of a 'common standard'. Of course, it is not possible to tell whether *any* of these exercises are efficient in changing attitudes.[1] But it is more likely that the first type of 'exercise' will (at least) allow different views to be exposed to critical analysis. In so far as magistrates have undergone this experience in considering serious motoring offences there may have been some movement towards the development of policy based upon a more coherent philosophy of punishment and a similar conception of the kind of information which should be con-sidered and the way it should be interpreted. Yet it must be remem-bered that not all justices attend these meetings.[2] It may be that those who are most obdurate in their views are those who stay away. Lastly, it must be recognized that some magistrates believe the situation in these training exercises is rather false, especially because no offenders are there in person and cases are sometimes too heavily edited. They therefore doubt whether the variations exposed on a Sunday afternoon accurately reflect what would happen in court. This is an important point on which the study sheds some light. Our evidence suggests that where full details are given, the range of sen-tence imposed in 'paper' cases does indeed mirror what happens in court.

Probably more use can be made of the 'sentencing exercise' method of teaching. It should, however, eschew as its aim simple attempts to get a meeting to agree by a majority or consensus on the penalty. Instead it should probe as deeply as possible into the com-plexities of the case, and analyse the assumptions being made by the magistrates about the information contained there—for it has been

---

[1] A pilot study on this subject, based on case-material rather similar to that used in this study, has recently been completed by Dr Lemmon at Sussex Uni-versity. It was not concerned with motoring cases, but the results suggest that training in general does affect sentencing behaviour, including a tendency to cite legal rather than personal factors in a case as being relevant to the decision. Lemmon's work also suggests the importance of personality variables in influ-encing the attitudes of magistrates and their perception of which factors are important in a case in respect of the appropriate sentence. Dr Lemmon suggests that it is only through detailed study of the way magistrates deal with similar case material that we shall improve our understanding of the relations between personality, information use, experience and sentencing. See N. F. Lemmon (1971), *The use of information by magistrates in sentencing, mimeo.* A report to the Nuffield Foundation.

[2] It would be interesting if a small-scale comparable inquiry could be carried out in a few courts before and after the introduction of such training exercises to see if they do affect attitudes, information use and the sentences imposed.

shown that they do not always agree on the relevance of previous convictions or the result of an accident. Perhaps, also, a comparison could be made of the way magistrates interpret exactly the same information about an offender who has committed, say, a crime of violence and one who had driven while drunk. I suspect this would be extremely enlightening, for it would uncover some of the basic assumptions about the motivation of different kinds of behaviour. Certainly it will only be possible to conduct a rational discussion on the approach which should be taken towards the motoring offender when such assumptions have been exposed to critical scrutiny. This study has attempted to make a contribution towards such enlightenment.

As far as motoring offences are concerned, it appears that less attention needs to be paid to the question of 'balancing' appointments—for different backgrounds as such were not clearly associated with different sentencing practices or points of view.[1] Conversely, more attention should be given to the way in which magistrates learn their sentencing trade and local benches develop their policies. The organizational aspects, including the roles occupied by senior members, and clerks in particular, need to be studied in depth. There is sufficient evidence to suggest that research can as usefully concentrate on 'becoming a magistrate' as on 'becoming a marijuhana user'.[2] How one learns to interpret information, accommodate one's views to those of the group, and develop an understanding of those who present cases to the court from either a prosecution or a defence standpoint are all part of a socializing process, the study of which has been too long neglected. There is ample evidence from this research that magistrates and their clerks will co-operate with the detailed examination of the interactions between personal and social characteristics and sentencing behaviour, and that a method based on decision-making in simulated cases can provide a realistic assessment of how magistrates actually behave in court.

[1] Although of course this may have been due partly to the relative homogeneity of our sample. It is conceivable that a wider range of people on the bench would affect sentencing practices in these cases. And, of course, it may well be that different social backgrounds discriminate between sentences imposed for other types of offence.

[2] See the well-known article by Howard Becker (1963), *Outsiders*, The Free Press. Glencoe. There is, of course, a large literature on socialization into occupational groups. See, for example, Howard Becker (1970), *Sociological Work*, Allen Lane, the Penguin Press, Chs. 11–14.

# The Questionnaires

## 1. *The Interview Schedule*

STRICTLY CONFIDENTIAL                    For office use

| | | |
|---|---|---|
| | | |

*Research on Motoring Offenders*
*Sentenced in Magistrates' Courts*

Petty Sessional

Police District ...............................    Division ....................................

Interviewee ....................................    Date of Interview .......................

| 1. Sex | Male | 1 | | 3. Chairman | 1 |
|---|---|---|---|---|---|
| | Female | 2 | | Deputy Chairman | 2 |

2. Year of appointment ................

| Over 30 | 1 | 5–9 | 4 |
|---|---|---|---|
| 20–29 | 2 | 2–4 | 5 |
| 10–19 | 3 | Under 2 | 6 |

3. Chairman — 1
Deputy Chairman — 2
Chairman, Juvenile Court — 3
Sits in Juvenile Court — 4

4. If Chairman, record number   1   4
   of years since appointment   2   5
   to that position              3   6

I want to start with a number of questions about your personal background and experience as a Magistrate.

5. How old were you last birthday?

| 70–74 | 1 | 50–59 | 4 |
|---|---|---|---|
| 65–69 | 2 | 40–49 | 5 |
| 60–64 | 3 | 39 & under | 6 |

6. Are you married?

| Married | 1 | Widowed | 3 |
|---|---|---|---|
| Single | 2 | Divorced or Separated | 4 |

157

7. What is your present occupation?

...............................................

(If a woman, record her own occupation; if she has none, record her husband's)

*Women* Own occupation          1
        Husband's occupation     2

| Cl. I   | 1 | Cl. IV | 4 |
|---------|---|--------|---|
| Cl. II  | 2 | Cl. V  | 5 |
| Cl. III | 3 | Cl. VI | 6 |

Retired                           7
Self-Employed as ............     8   1

.....................................     9   2

Non-employed                      3
(i.e. Independent means)          4

...............................................

8. If Retired, ask

What was your former occupation?

*Women* Own occupation          1
        Husband's occupation     2

| Cl. I   | 1 | Cl. IV | 4 |
|---------|---|--------|---|
| Cl. II  | 2 | Cl. V  | 5 |
| Cl. III | 3 | Cl. VI | 6 |

Retired                           7
Self-employed as..............    8   1

.....................................     9   2

Non-employed                      3
(i.e. Independent means)          4

.....................................

9. What sort of secondary school did you attend?

| Elementary | 1 | Public | 4 |
|------------|---|--------|---|
| Grammar    | 2 | Modern | 5 |
| Technical  | 3 |        | 6 |
|            |   |        | 7 |
|            |   |        | 8 |

10. At what age did you finish full-time education *at school?*

| 14 | 1 | 16 | 3 | 18 | 5 | 20 | 7 |
|----|---|----|---|----|---|----|---|
| 15 | 2 | 17 | 4 | 19 | 6 |    |   |

11. Did you continue *full-time* education after leaving school?

Yes  1

If Yes, ask. Was it at:

| Technical Coll. | 2 | University | 5 |
|---|---|---|---|
| Teachers' T.C. | 3 |  | 6 |
|  | 4 |  | 7 |

What did you study?

| Law | 1 | Arts | 4 |
|---|---|---|---|
| Medicine | 2 | Pure Science | 5 |
|  | 3 |  | 6 |

Did you gain any qualifications from this study?

| Diploma | 1 | Professional certificate | 4 |
|---|---|---|---|
| Degree | 2 |  | 5 |
| None | 3 |  | 6 |

12. Since you completed your *full-time* education have you followed any *part-time* courses?  Yes  1

If Yes, ask: What type of course?

| Univ. Extra-Mural | 2 | Evening (night school) | 5 |
|---|---|---|---|
| Correspondence | 3 |  | 6 |
| Refresher | 4 |  | 7 |

What did you study?          1  3

..............................................  2  4

..............................................

Did you gain any qualifications from this study?

| Diploma | 1 | Professional certificate | 4 |
|---|---|---|---|
| Degree | 2 |  | 5 |
| None | 3 |  | 6 |

13. Do you ever take the Chair in the Adult Court?

| Regularly | 1 |
|---|---|
| Occasionally | 2 |
| Never | 3 |

14. Have you been, in the past, *officially* Chairman or Deputy Chairman of your Bench?  Yes  1

| Chairman | 1 | 2 |
|---|---|---|
| Deputy |  | 3 |

**15a.** In general, would you like to see magistrates reimbursed for income lost through attending court?

| | | | |
|---|---|---|---|
| Yes | 1 | Don't know | 3 |
| No | 2 | Other | 4 |
| | | | 5 |

**b.** Would you personally like to be reimbursed?    Yes    1

What reasons have you for your answer?    2  5

    3  6

    4  7

**16.** Are you a member of the Magistrates' Association?    Yes  1

If *NO*, ask: Why did you decide not to join?

| | |
|---|---|
| Too expensive | 1 |
| Ineffectual body | 2 |
| Waste of money | 3 |
| Other | 4 |
| | 5 |

**17.** Of which political party are you a *member*? If not a *member*, ask: Which party you would vote for in a general election?

| | M | Vote |
|---|---|---|
| Conservative | 1 | 7 |
| Labour | 2 | 8 |
| Liberal | 3 | 9 |
| Other | 4 | 1 |
| | 5 | 2 |
| None | 6 | 3 |

**18.** Do you hold any other public office besides being a magistrate?

| | | | |
|---|---|---|---|
| Councillor | 1 | | 5 |
| Alderman | 2 | | 6 |
| M.P. | 3 | | 7 |
| D.L. | 4 | None | 8 |

**19.** Are there any other forms of community service in which you take part?

    None    1

    2  5

    3  6

    4  7

Now I would like to go on to a few questions about what you read.

20. Which daily newspapers do you *read regularly* (emphasize)?

| Times | 1 | Mirror | 5 |
|---|---|---|---|
| Guardian | 2 | Mail | 6 |
| Telegraph | 3 | Sun | 7 |
| Express | 4 | | 8 |
| | | | 9 |

21. Which Sunday newspaper do you *read, regularly?*

| Observer | 1 | S. Express | 5 |
|---|---|---|---|
| S. Times | 2 | S. Mirror | 6 |
| S. Telegraph | 3 | News of World | 7 |
| | 4 | | 8 |

22. Do you subscribe to any journals dealing with magisterial or legal matters?

23. I am going to read out the name of a number of journals, and I want you to answer the following questions about each:

(a) Do you read it *regularly*, i.e. every issue
(b) Do you read it occasionally?
(c) Do you never read it?
(d) Do you know of it?
(e) Is it accessible to you?

| | Subscribe | Read | | | Know it | Accessible |
|---|---|---|---|---|---|---|
| | | Reg. | Occ. | Never | | |
| The Magistrate | 1 | 1 | 1 | 1 | 1 | 1 |
| Justice of the Peace | 2 | 2 | 2 | 2 | 2 | 2 |
| Criminal Law Review | 3 | 3 | 3 | 3 | 3 | 3 |
| Probation | 4 | 4 | 4 | 4 | 4 | 4 |
| British Journal of Criminology | 5 | 5 | 5 | 5 | 5 | 5 |
| Howard Journal | 6 | 6 | 6 | 6 | 6 | 6 |

24. Are there any *books* which you have purchased which are relevant to your work as a magistrate?

| | |
|---|---|
| No books | 1 |
| Legal books | 2 |
| Criminological books | 3 |
| Penological books | 4 |
| 1 or 2 books | 5 |
| 3–5 books | 6 |
| 5–10 books | 7 |
| 10 or more books | 8 |

25. Besides these, are there any such books which you have read in the last 2 years?

| | |
|---|---|
| No books | 1 |
| Legal | 2 |
| Criminological | 3 |
| Penological | 4 |
| 1 or 2 | 5 |
| 3–5 | 6 |
| 5–10 | 7 |
| 10 or more | 8 |

The next group of questions is about motoring.

26. Can you drive a car?     Yes 1

27. If yes, ask: How long have you been driving?

| | | | |
|---|---|---|---|
| Over 25 yrs | 2 | 2–4 | 5 |
| 10–24 yrs | 3 | under 2 | 6 |
| 5–9 yrs | 4 | | |

28. Do you own a car at present?
    Yes 1

29. How often *in a week* do you normally *drive* a car?

| | |
|---|---|
| Every day | 2 |
| At least 3 times | 3 |
| About once | 4 |
| Less frequently | 5 |

30. Can you give me an estimate of the mileage you covered in a car either as driver or passenger in the last 12 months?

| | | |
|---|---|---|
| 1 | 4 | 7 |
| 2 | 5 | 8 |
| 3 | 6 | 9 |

31. Do you subscribe to or read every week at least one motoring journal?
    Yes 1

32. How do you rate yourself as a driver?

| | |
|---|---|
| Better than average | 1 |
| About average | 2 |
| Not as good as most | 3 |

*Probe* membership of:

| | |
|---|---|
| I.A.M. | 4 |
| V.M. Assoc. | 5 |
| R.O.S.P.A. | 6 |
| A motor club | 7 |

33. Have you been involved in a road accident either as a driver or passenger?

                    Yes 1

If yes, ask: Can you give me brief details?

*Probe* Damage, injuries, responsibility.

|   |   |
|---|---|
| 2 | 6 |
| 3 | 7 |
| 4 | 8 |
| 5 | 9 |

---

34. Have you ever been prosecuted for a motoring offence?   Yes  1

If yes, ask:

(a) What was the offence?

| Dang. Dr. | 2 | Failure to stop etc. | 7 |
|---|---|---|---|
| Dr. Disq. | 3 | Speeding | 8 |
| Drunk Dr. | 4 | More than 1 conviction | 9 |
| Careless Dr. | 5 |  | 1 |
| No Insurance | 6 |  | 2 |

(b) When did it (the last one) occur?

| Over 20 yrs ago | 1 | 5–9 yrs | 3 |
|---|---|---|---|
| 10–20 yrs | 2 | Less than 5 yrs | 4 |

(c) What was the Court's decision?

| Fined | 1 |  | 4 |
|---|---|---|---|
| Disqualified | 2 |  | 5 |
| Licence Endorsed | 3 |  | 6 |

(d) How did you regard that decision?

| Fair and reasonable | 1 | Cannot remember | 5 |
|---|---|---|---|
| Unreasonable | 2 |  | 6 |
| Completely unjust | 3 |  | 7 |
| No opinion | 4 |  | 8 |

**35.** Have any of your *relatives* or *close friends* ever been *convicted* of a motoring offence?

Yes 1

(a) If yes; What was the offence (offences)?

| Dang. Dr. | 2 | Failure to stop etc. | 7 |
|---|---|---|---|
| Dr. Disq. | 3 | Speeding | 8 |
| Drunk Dr. | 4 | More than one con- viction | 9 |
| Careless Dr. | 5 | | 1 |
| No Insurance | 6 | | 2 |

(b) Taking the most serious case, ask: How did you regard the decision in that case?

| Fair and reasonable | 1 | Cannot remember | 5 |
|---|---|---|---|
| Unreasonable | 2 | | 6 |
| Completely unjust | 3 | | 7 |
| No opinion | 4 | | 8 |

I want now to ask you some questions about your views on how to deal with motoring offenders. I shall be using the term *serious* motoring offences in some of these questions. Here is a card (HAND CARD) which lists the offences we regard as serious in these questions. Please use the card as a reminder.

First I have some questions dealing with fines. You will be aware that when you decide to impose a fine there are two things you decide: firstly, the *amount of the penalty*; secondly, *how long* the offender may have to pay the fine.

I want to deal first with *fixing the amount of the penalty* (ensure that this is clear before proceeding).

36. Is there an acknowledged *basic fine* in your court for *serious* offences[1] (direct attention to card), which you then adjust to take into account the particular circumstances of the offence and offender?

|            |   |        |   |
|------------|---|--------|---|
| Yes        | 1 |        |   |
| No         | 2 | Unsure | 4 |
| Sometimes  | 3 |        | 5 |

..............................................................................................
..............................................................................................
..............................................................................................
..............................................................................................

37. If no, ask: Do you use the legal maximum fine as your starting point?

|            |   |        |   |
|------------|---|--------|---|
| Yes        | 3 |        |   |
| No         | 2 | Unsure | 4 |
| Sometimes  | 3 |        | 5 |

..............................................................................................
..............................................................................................
..............................................................................................
..............................................................................................

[1] The list of 'serious' motoring offences referred to in question 36 and others was:
1. Driving while disqualified
2. Drunken Driving
3. Dangerous Driving
4. Careless Driving
5 Failing to insure against Third Party Risks
6. Failing to stop after or report an accident.

38. If no, ask: How do you proceed then, to fix the penalty?

........................................................................ 1  6
                                                                         2  7
........................................................................ 3  8
                                                                         4  9
........................................................................ 5

39. I want you to listen very carefully to this example I am going to read out.

Imagine two motorists have had exactly the same accident and have been found guilty of the same offence arising out of it. Both have the same record of previous offences and both appeared apologetic in court.

*Motorist No. 1* earns £3,000 a year, say £60 per week, is a married man with his wife at home and two school-age children.

*Motorist No. 2* earns £15 per week with the same family circumstances, paying £2.10.0d. per week rent and £1 per week hire purchase.

*Summarize* They have committed the same offence in similar circumstances; have the same record, the same demeanour in court, and the same family circumstances. They differ only in their income.

Can you tell me:

Would you fine both these offenders the same *first*, if it was one of the serious offences listed on the card

                    Yes          1
                    No           2
                    Don't know   3

*second*, if it was not so serious an offence, say speeding or a pedestrian-crossing offence?

                    Yes          1
                    No           2
                    Don't know   3

What reasons have you for your answers?

........................................................................ 1  5
                                                                         2  6
........................................................................ 3  7
                                                                         4  8
........................................................................    9

40. Imagine another set of circumstances. Two men had committed the same serious offence in very similar circumstances and had similar records, family responsibilities and demeanour in court.

Yet, *Motorist No. 1* was very wealthy (say £5,000 per year plus) and *Motorist No. 2* was comfortably well off, say £1,800 per year.

Can you tell me: Would you fine the men the same
amount?

| | | |
|---|---|---|
| Yes | 1 | |
| No | 2 | |
| Don't know | 3 | |

What reasons have you for your answer?        1   5   9

................................................................................   2   6

                             3   7

................................................................................   4   8

..................................................................... .

---

41. Now I want to give you an example of the sort of situation you might face in court.

An offender has been convicted of the following four offences:

| | |
|---|---|
| 1. Careless driving | 2. No insurance |
| 3. No driving licence | 4. No excise licence. |

There are two ways in which you might reach the *total amount* of the penalty you will impose. I will read out both ways and I want you to tell me which method you use.

1. You might decide on the fine for each of the four offences separately and then add them up to get the total penalty.

2. On the other hand you might decide on the total amount first, and then divide it up appropriately between the four offences.

...............................................................................................

...............................................................................................

...............................................................................................

Which method do you use?

| | | | |
|---|---|---|---|
| Method 1 | 1 | A combination (detail) | 4 |
| Method 2 | 2 | | 5 |
| Sometimes 1, sometimes 2 | 3 | | 6 |

---

I am going to ask you now about granting *time to pay* fines.

---

42. Some people consider that the almost automatic practice of granting time to pay fines reduces the effectiveness of the sentence.

| | | |
|---|---|---|
| Do you agree with this? | Agree | 1 |
| | Disagree | 2 |

................................................................................   3   5

................................................................................   4   6

The next question is about costs awarded against the defendant.

43. Two men have committed the same serious motoring offence in similar circumstances, have the same record, income, family responsibilities and demeanour in court.

In *case 1* there are no prosecution costs
In *case 2* prosecution costs amount to £10

Can you tell me: Would you *fine* both cases the same amount?

| | | | |
|---|---|---|---|
| Yes | 1 | .................................. 4 | |
| No | 2 | .................................. 5 | |
| Don't know | 3 | | |

What are your reasons for this decision?

..............................................................................  1  4  7
                                                                              2  5  8
..............................................................................  3  6  9

..............................................................................

44. If prosecution costs in case 2 had been £*20* would you fine them the same amount?

| | | | |
|---|---|---|---|
| Yes | 1 | .................................. 4 | |
| No | 2 | .................................. 5 | |
| Don't know | 3 | | |

What are your reasons for this decision?

..............................................................................  1  4  7
                                                                              2  5  8
..............................................................................  3  6  9

..............................................................................

..............................................................................

..............................................................................

..............................................................................

..............................................................................

45. Do you think motorists who plead guilty by post under the M.C.A. should be made to state their income and financial commitments?        Yes 1

Can you say why?

..............................................................................  2  5  8

..............................................................................  3  6  9

..............................................................................  4  7

46. Leaving aside the M.C.A. procedure, you will know that motorists may plead guilty by letter to careless driving and failing to stop after an accident.

(a) What are your views on this practice?

| | |
|---|---|
| It's all right | 1 |
| Should stop | 2 |
| | 3 |
| | 4 |

(b) Would you like to see any alterations in this procedure?

| | |
|---|---|
| Should stop | 5 |
| Allow previous conviction to be made known | 6 |
| No, it's all right as it is | 7 |
| | 8 |
| | 9 |

---

47. When a *serious* motoring offender (direct attention to card) has been found guilty, what information do you think should be known about the *offender* (not the offence) before deciding on the sentence?

After interviewee has finished mentioning items spontaneously, say:

I will read some other things out; will you tell me whether you think they are in general relevant to the sentence in a *serious* motoring case?

| | Mentioned Spontaneously | Agreed Important | | |
|---|---|---|---|---|
| | | *Yes* | *No* | *Some-times* |
| All previous convictions | X | 6 | 2 | X |
| Serious motoring convictions | Y | 7 | 3 | Y |
| All previous motoring convictions | 0 | 8 | 4 | 0 |
| Previous indictable convictions | 1 | 9 | 5 | 1 |
| Previous non-indictable convictions | 2 | X | 6 | 2 |
| Occupation | 3 | Y | 7 | 3 |
| Income | 4 | 0 | 8 | 4 |
| Outgoings—financial | 5 | 1 | 9 | 5 |
| Commitments | | | | |
| Marital state | 6 | 2 | X | 6 |
| Number of children | 7 | 3 | Y | 7 |
| Employment record | 8 | 4 | 0 | 8 |
| Attitude of the offender to the offence | 9 | 5 | 1 | 9 |
| Family relationships | X | 6 | 2 | X |
| Physical health | Y | 7 | 3 | Y |
| Mental health | 0 | 8 | 4 | 0 |
| Other (specify) | 1 | 9 | 5 | 1 |
| | 2 | X | 6 | 2 |
| | 3 | Y | 7 | 3 |
| | 4 | 0 | 8 | 4 |
| | 5 | 1 | 9 | 5 |

48. How would you get the information you need?

    *First*, about an offender present in court?

    | | |
    |---|---|
    | Ask him | 1 |
    | Stand the case down for a while | 2 |
    | Remand for inquiries | 3 |
    | | 4 |
    | | 5 |

    *Second*   About an offender not present in court?

    | | |
    |---|---|
    | Ask police | 1 |
    | Remand case | 2 |
    | | 3 |
    | | 4 |

---

49. In *criminal cases* it is sometimes, or may be frequently, the practice to adjourn or remand cases for enquiries to be made into the circumstances of the offender before sentence is passed.

    I shall read out each of the list of serious motoring offences in turn and I want you to say whether this practice would be useful—never, very occasionally, occasionally, frequently, usually or always.

    | | Dr. Disq. | Drkn. Dr. | Dang. Dr. | C.D. | N. In. | Fail to stop |
    |---|---|---|---|---|---|---|
    | Never | 1 | 1 | 1 | 1 | 1 | 1 |
    | Very Occasionally | 2 | 2 | 2 | 2 | 2 | 2 |
    | Occasionally | 3 | 3 | 3 | 3 | 3 | 3 |
    | Frequently | 4 | 4 | 4 | 4 | 4 | 4 |
    | Usually | 5 | 5 | 5 | 5 | 5 | 5 |
    | Always | 6 | 6 | 6 | 6 | 6 | 6 |

---

50. How frequently is this procedure [remanding for inquiries in serious motoring cases] used in your court?

    | | |
    |---|---|
    | Never | 1 |
    | 1 in 1,000 cases | 2 |
    | 1 in 100 | 3 |
    | 1 in 10 | 4 |
    | 5 in 10 | 5 |
    | 9 in 10 | 6 |
    | Always | 7 |

---

51. If less than 1 in 10, ask: Why do you think it is not used?

    ........................................................................................ 1   4

    ........................................................................................ 2   5

    ........................................................................................ 3   6

52. What proportion of *serious* (see CARD) motoring offenders who appear before you do you think have convictions for *criminal offences*? (Read out proportions.)

| Less than | | | Less than | |
|---|---|---|---|---|
| 1/100 | 1 | | 40/100 | 6 |
| 5/100 | 2 | | 50/100 | 7 |
| 10/100 | 3 | | | 8 |
| 20/100 | 4 | | | 9 |
| 30/100 | 5 | | | |

---

53. Some people say that motorists who commit serious motoring offences (see CARD) are 'criminals' in the same sense as those who steal, rob, commit violent or sexual offences.

(a) Do you think this is true for *any* serious motoring offences?    Yes 1

(b) For each of the following offences I want you to tell me whether you consider the *majority* of persons convicted of them to be criminals.

| | |
|---|---|
| *Drunken Driving* 1st offence | 1 |
| 2nd offence | 2 |
| *Dangerous Driving* 1st offence | 3 |
| 2nd offence | 4 |
| *Driving while disqualified* 1st offence | 5 |
| 2nd offence | 6 |
| *Careless Driving* 1st offence | 7 |
| 2nd offence | 8 |
| *Failing to stop after an accident* 1st offence | 9 |
| 2nd offence | 1 |
| *Failing to insure* 1st offence | 2 |
| 2nd offence | 3 |
| *Exceeding the speed limits* 1st offence | 4 |
| 2nd offence | 5 |

..............................................................................

..............................................................................

..............................................................................

..............................................................................

**54.** For each of the following types of offence do you consider that *in general* the offender should be made to take another driving test?

(a) dangerous driving—

First offence    1

Second or subsequent offence    2

What reasons have you for thinking this?

.................................. 3 6 9

.................................. 4 7

.................................. 5 8

(b) drunken driving    1

What reasons have you for thinking this?

.................................. 2 5

.................................. 3 6

.................................. 4 7

(c) Careless driving—

First offence    1

Second or subsequent offence    2

What reasons have you for thinking this?

.................................. 3 6 9

.................................. 4 7

.................................. 5 8

(d) Exceeding the speed limit    1
(second and subsequent convictions)

What reasons have you for thinking this?

.................................. 2 5 8

.................................. 3 6 9

.................................. 4 7

**55.** Since 29 May 1963 a driver has been convicted of careless driving and speeding and his licence endorsed on both occasions. He now appears before you on a charge of exceeding the speed limit.

What sorts of circumstances would you consider amount to special reasons justifying a decision not to disqualify him?

.................................................................. 1 4 7

.................................................................. 2 5 8

.................................................................. 3 6 9

**56.** Are you, in general, in favour of the system of disqualification following three endorsements?    Yes    1

What are your reasons for your answer?

.................................................................. 1 4

.................................................................. 2 5

.................................................................. 3 6

57. (a) Do you think any new methods of dealing with motoring offenders
    should be introduced?                                          Yes 1

    If yes, ask: What have you in mind?

    ......................................................................................   2   5   8

    ......................................................................................   3   6   9

    ......................................................................................   4   7

(b) I am going to mention to you four methods which have been suggested
    for dealing with motoring offenders either in this country or elsewhere.
    Will you tell me whether *you think* they would be effective ways of
    dealing with motoring offenders?

    (i) The idea of a traffic school (with probation or suspended fines)        1

        *Explain;* It is suggested that when an offender is convicted of a serious
        motoring offence and before he is sentenced, he should be directed,
        with his consent, to attend a traffic school, the aim of which would be
        to improve the general attitude and driving habits of the offender.
        After completion of the course a report would be sent by the school
        authorities to the magistrates, telling them what response the offender
        made to the course and its effect on him. The report would then be
        taken into consideration by the magistrates in deciding what penalty to
        impose for the offence of which the offender was convicted.

        *Comments* ........................................................................

        ......................................................................................

        ......................................................................................

    (ii) A wider use of probation in dealing with motoring offenders            2

        *Comments* ........................................................................

        ......................................................................................

        ......................................................................................

    (iii) The idea of penalty plates. It is suggested that a person convicted of a
        serious motoring offence, or maybe specified motoring offences, should
        be made to display on any vehicle he drives a 'P' plate, signifying that
        he has been convicted.                                                   3

        *Comments* ........................................................................

        ......................................................................................

        ......................................................................................

(iv) More severe sentences.

(a) High maximum penalties?              4

If yes, ask: For what sorts of offence?

| Dr. Disqualified | 5 | Failure to stop etc. | 1 |
| Drunken Driving | 6 | Other | 2 |
| Dangerous Driving | 7 | | 3 |
| Careless Driving | 8 | | 4 |
| No Insurance | 9 | | |

(b) A wider use of disqualification?          5

If yes, ask: For what sorts of offences?

| Dr. Disqualified | 6 | Failure to stop etc. | 2 |
| Drunken Driving | 7 | Other | 3 |
| Dangerous Driving | 8 | | 4 |
| Careless Driving | 9 | | 5 |
| No Insurance | 1 | | |

---

58. What do you consider, in general, to be the optimum (i.e. the most appropriate) period of disqualification to impose for a typical case of the following offences.

*After each period has been specified ask*: Why this length? *Probe*: What do you wish to achieve by this particular period?

*First*

Driving while disqualified.

(a) A first offender

| 6 months | 1 | 5 years | 6 |
| 1 year | 2 | 10 years | 7 |
| 18 months | 3 | 20 years | 8 |
| 2 years | 4 | Life | 9 |
| 3 years | 5 | | |

Why this length? ............   1   4

.....................................   2   5

.....................................   3   6

.....................................

.....................................

(b) A Second Offender

| 6 months | 1 | 5 years | 6 |
| 1 year | 2 | 10 years | 7 |
| 18 months | 3 | 20 years | 8 |
| 2 years | 4 | Life | 9 |
| 3 years | 5 | | |

Why this length? ............   1   4

.....................................   2   5

.....................................   3   6

.....................................

.....................................

.....................................

*Second*

Drunken Driving

(a) A First Offender

| 6 months | 1 | 5 years | 6 |
| 1 year | 2 | 10 years | 7 |
| 18 months | 3 | 20 years | 8 |
| 2 years | 4 | Life | 9 |
| 3 years | 5 | | |

Why this length? ............ 1  4

...................................... 2  5

...................................... 3  6

......................................

......................................

......................................

(b) A Second Offender

| 6 months | 1 | 5 years | 6 |
| 1 year | 2 | 10 years | 7 |
| 18 months | 3 | 20 years | 8 |
| 2 years | 4 | Life | 9 |
| 3 years | 5 | | |

Why this length? ............ 1  4

...................................... 2  5

...................................... 3  6

......................................

......................................

*Lastly*

Dangerous Driving. In this case,
a second offender

| 6 months | 1 | 5 years | 6 |
| 1 year | 2 | 10 years | 7 |
| 18 months | 3 | 20 years | 8 |
| 2 years | 4 | Life | 9 |
| 3 years | 5 | | |

Why this length? ............ 1  4

...................................... 2  5

...................................... 3  6

......................................

......................................

---

59. Do you think there is a case for a separate traffic court?          1

Why do you think so?...............................................................  2  5

..............................................................................................  3  6

..............................................................................................  4  7

If yes, ask: In your area?

..............................................................................................  8  1

..............................................................................................  9  2

---

60. Would you like to see a system of on-the-spot fines for some motoring offences instead of bringing offenders to court?                Yes 1

   If Yes, ask: For what offences?

   Parking                                                                      2
   Minor lighting infringements and Construction and Use
      Regulation offences                                                       3
   Speeding                                                                     4
   Careless driving                                                             5
   Others                                                                       6
                                                                                7

---

61. Could you tell me how influential your Chairman (of the Bench) is in formulating the sentencing policy of the Bench? (Re-phrase for Chairman.)

   Of no particular influence                          1
                                                       2
                                                       3

   *Probe*: Is he more or less influential than you would like him to be?

   More                                                1
   Less                                                2
   About right                                         3
                                                       4
                                                       5

---

62. Could you tell me how influential your Clerk is in formulating the sentencing policy of the Bench? (Re-phrase for Clerk.)

   Of no particular influence                          1
                                                       2
                                                       3

   *Probe*: Is he more or less influential than you would like him to be?

   More                                                1
   Less                                                2
   About right                                         3

---

63. It has recently been decided that magistrates should be trained. What are your views about this?

   ........................................................................................   1   3

   ........................................................................................   2   4

   ........................................................................................

   If in agreement, ask:
   How do you think they should be trained, and in what subjects?

   ........................................................................................   1   4

   ........................................................................................   2   5

   ........................................................................................   3   6

## FOR CLERKS ONLY

64. Are there any marked variations between the penalties imposed for similar cases:

(a) between different petty sessions?

| | |
|---|---|
| Yes | 1 |
| No | 2 |
| In some but not others | 3 |
| Does not apply | 4 |
| | 5 |

(b) different rotas in the same petty session?

| | |
|---|---|
| Yes | 1 |
| No | 2 |
| In some but not others | 3 |
| | 4 |
| | 5 |

Please tell me about it and give your reasons *why* you think it occurs?

............................................................................... 1   4

............................................................................... 2   5

............................................................................... 3   6

65. Do you guide the magistrates over the question of sentencing in serious motoring cases?      Yes 1

If yes, ask: In what way?.................................................. 1   4

............................................................................... 2   5

............................................................................... 3   6

If no, ask: Why not?.......................................................... 1   4

............................................................................... 2   5

............................................................................... 3   6

## 2. *The Self-Completion Questionnaires*

### (a) *Comparative Seriousness of Offences*

*Please read these instructions carefully*

You may think some kinds of offence are *more serious* than others. To take an extreme example, nearly everyone would agree that robbery is more serious than a parking offence.

Below is a list of 19 offences arranged in alphabetical order. Will you try to imagine a typical case of each offence, and then arrange the offences in order of seriousness. Give the most serious offence the number 1, the next 2, and so on.

It may be that you are able to give each offence a separate number 1–19. On the other hand you may think a number of offences are *equally* serious. If so, these offences should be given the *same* number.

EXAMPLE: You have given five offences the numbers 1 to 5; you then find there are three offences you regard equally as the next most serious. All three offences should be given the number 6. You should then number the next most serious offence or offences *Not 7* but *9*: i.e., your numbering would read 1, 2, 3, 4, 5, 6, 6, 6, 9, etc.

Being in possession of an offensive weapon ...
Careless Driving ...
Causing grievous bodily harm ...
Common Assault ...
Drunk and Disorderly ...
Dangerous Driving ...
Driving under the Influence of Drink ...
Driving while Disqualified ...
Exceeding the Speed Limit ...
Failing to accord precedence on a Pedestrian Crossing ...
Failing to stop after an Accident ...
Housebreaking and Larceny ...
Indecent Assault on a female under 16 ...
Larceny as a Servant ...
No Third Party Insurance ...
Obtaining Money by False Pretences ...
Robbery with Violence ...
Shoplifting ...
Taking and driving away a Motor Vehicle without the
Owner's consent ...

### (b) *Types of Offenders*

The Questionnaire is reproduced as Table 8 on page 102.

The instructions were as follows:

'One realizes that, in some ways, every offence is unique, but it may also be true that people committing motoring offences fall into certain broad types.

On the inside of this sheet, four types of offender are suggested. There is space for you to suggest other types yourself if you consider this necessary.

Under each of the offences listed along the top of the page write in how many out of every ten people convicted of that offence you think fall into each of the types. Please make sure that the numbers in each column total 10.

You may think that some of the types apply to none of the people who commit these offences. If you do, please write "NONE" in the appropriate space.'

## (c) *The Social Attitudes Questionnaire*

The instructions and questions were:

Below are 24 statements which represent widely-held opinions on various social questions selected from speeches, books, newspapers, and other sources. They were chosen in such a way that most people are likely to agree with some and disagree with others. After each statement please record your completely confidential personal opinion regarding the statement, using the following system of marking:

+ + if you strongly agree with the statement
+ if you agree on the whole but not strongly
O if you cannot decide for or against or if you think the question is worded in such a way that you cannot give an answer
— if you disagree on the whole but not strongly
— — if you strongly disagree

|  | Your Opinion |
|---|---|
| *Attitude Statements* | |
| 1. Coloured people are innately inferior to white people | ... |
| 2. Present laws favour the rich as against the poor | ... |
| 3. War is inherent in human nature | ... |
| 4. We should give up punishing criminals and treat them instead | ... |
| 5. In the interests of peace, we must give up part of our national sovereignty | ... |
| 6. Sunday-observance is old-fashioned, and should cease to govern our behaviour | ... |
| 7. It is wrong that men should be permitted greater sexual freedom than women by society | ... |
| 8. Unrestricted freedom of discussion on every topic is desirable in the press, in literature, on the stage, etc. | ... |
| 9. Ultimately, private property should be abolished, and complete socialism introduced | ... |
| 10. Conscientious objectors are traitors to their country and should be treated accordingly | ... |
| 11. Only by going back to religion can civilization hope to survive | ... |

*Attitude Statements*

Your
Opinion

12. Marriage between white and coloured people should be strongly discouraged     ...
13. There should be far more controversial and political discussion over the radio     ...
14. Divorce laws should be altered to make divorce easier     ...
15. The nationalization of the great industries is likely to lead to inefficiency, bureaucracy and stagnation     ...
16. It is right and proper that religious education in schools should be compulsory     ...
17. Men and women have the right to find out whether they are sexually suited before marriage (i.e., by companionate marriage)     ...
18. The principle 'Spare the rod and spoil the child' has much truth in it and should govern our methods of bringing up children     ...
19. Women are not the equals of men in intelligence, organizing ability, etc.     ...
20. The Jews have too much power and influence in this country     ...
21. Differences in pay between men and women doing the same work should be abolished     ...
22. Abortion, where medically indicated, should be made legal     ...
23. The death penalty is barbaric and should be abolished     ...
24. Only people with a definite minimum of intelligence and education should be allowed to vote     ...

(d) *Eysenck Personality Inventory, Form A*

*Instructions*

Here are some questions regarding the way you behave, feel and act. After each question is a space for answering 'YES' or 'NO'.

Try to decide whether 'YES' or 'NO' represents your usual way of acting or feeling .Then put a cross under the column headed 'YES' or 'NO'. Work quickly and don't spend too much time over any question; we want your first reaction, not a long-drawn-out thought process. The whole questionnaire shouldn't take more than a few minutes. Be sure not to omit any questions.

Now turn the page over and go ahead. Work quickly and remember to answer every question. There are no right or wrong answers, and this isn't a test of intelligence or ability, but simply a measure of the way you behave.

Yes     No

1. Do you often long for excitement?
2. Do you often need understanding friends to cheer you up?

*Yes    No*

3. Are you usually carefree?
4. Do you find it very hard to take no for an answer?
5. Do you stop and think things over before doing anything?
6. If you say you will do something do you always keep your promise, no matter how inconvenient it might be to do so?
7. Does your mood often go up and down?
8. Do you generally do and say things quickly without stopping to think?
9. Do you ever feel 'just miserable' for no good reason?
10. Would you do almost anything for a dare?
11. Do you suddenly feel shy when you want to talk to an attractive stranger?
12. Once in a while do you lose your temper and get angry?
13. Do you often do things on the spur of the moment?
14. Do you often worry about things you should not have done or said?
15. Generally, do you prefer reading to meeting people?
16. Are your feelings rather easily hurt?
17. Do you like going out a lot?
18. Do you occasionally have thoughts and ideas that you would not like other people to know about?
19. Are you sometimes bubbling over with energy and sometimes very sluggish?
20. Do you prefer to have few but special friends?
21. Do you daydream a lot?
22. When people shout at you, do you shout back?
23. Are you often troubled about feelings of guilt?
24. Are *all* your habits good and desirable ones?
25. Can you usually let yourself go and enjoy yourself a lot at a gay party?
26. Would you call yourself tense or 'highly-strung'?
27. Do other people think of you as being very lively?
28. After you have done something important, do you often come away feeling you could have done better?
29. Are you mostly quiet when you are with other people?
30. Do you sometimes gossip?
31. Do ideas run through your head so that you cannot sleep?
32. If there is something you want to know about, would you rather look it up in a book than talk to someone about it?
33. Do you get palpitations or thumping in your heart?
34. Do you like the kind of work that you need to pay close attention to?

G

35. Do you get attacks of shaking or trembling?
36. Would you always declare *everything* at the customs, even if you knew that you could never be found out?
37. Do you hate being with a crowd who play jokes on one another?
38. Are you an irritable person?
39. Do you like doing things in which you have to act quickly?
40. Do you worry about awful things that might happen?
41. Are you slow and unhurried in the way you move?
42. Have you ever been late for an appointment or work?
43. Do you have many nightmares?
44. Do you like talking to people so much that you never miss a chance of talking to a stranger?
45. Are you troubled by aches and pains?
46. Would you be very unhappy if you could not see lots of people most of the time?
47. Would you call yourself a nervous person?
48. Of all the people you know, are there some whom you definitely do not like?
49. Would you say that you were fairly self-confident?
50. Are you easily hurt when people find fault with you or your work?
51. Do you find it hard to really enjoy yourself at a party?
52. Are you troubled with feelings of inferiority?
53. Can you easily get some life into a rather dull party?
54. Do you sometimes talk about things you know nothing about?
55. Do you worry about your health?
56. Do you like playing pranks on others?
57. Do you suffer from sleeplessness?

**Please check to see that you have answered all the questions.**

(e) *The questionnaire accompanying each case on which the sentence was recorded*

As the offender has been found guilty in this case, the following questions refer to the deciding of an appropriate sentence and not to deciding whether the case has been proved.

Please answer the following questions: tick in appropriate space.

1. (a) What penalty would you impose for:

| Charge | Penalty | Period of any disquali- fication | Licence endorsed | | Amount of fees and costs awarded against the defendant |
|---|---|---|---|---|---|
| | | | Yes | No | |
| (a) | | | | | |
| (b) | | | | | |
| (c) | | | | | |
| Others | | | | | |

(b) What are your reasons for reaching this decision?

..............................................................................................

(c) If you consider that there are 'special reasons' for NOT disqualifying a defendant or NOT endorsing his licence in a case where you would otherwise have done so, please say what those 'special reasons' are:

..............................................................................................

2. If you have imposed a financial penalty, would you allow   Yes ......
   the offender time to pay?                                   No  ......

   If your answer is 'yes', how much time would you allow?

..............................................................................................

3. (a) Would you have asked for any information *about the*     Yes ......
   *offender* additional to that which was available to the
   court in this case *before deciding on the penalty*?     No ......

   If your answer is 'yes', what additional information would you
   require?

..........................................................................................

..........................................................................................

..........................................................................................

..........................................................................................

  (b) From what source would you get this information?

..........................................................................................

..........................................................................................

..........................................................................................

4. Do you consider this is a case in which you would have     Yes ......
   suggested to your colleagues that you retire to consider the
   sentence?     No ......

5. (a) Do you think the colleagues with whom you normally sit would
   have agreed to the penalty on which *you* have decided?

| All would agree | Most would agree | Some would agree | None would agree | Don't know |
|---|---|---|---|---|
|  |  |  |  |  |

  (b) If your answer is that NONE would agree with you, say why not:

..........................................................................................

..........................................................................................

..........................................................................................

..........................................................................................

6. Of its kind, do you regard this particular case as:

                   A very serious case      ......

                   A serious case      ......

                   Not a serious case      ......

PLEASE MAKE SURE YOU HAVE COMPLETED EVERY
QUESTION.

(f) *Form for recording sentences passed in the information game at the 'sentencing conferences'* (See Chapter 6)

In view of the difficulty magistrates had in answering the straight question, 'What are your reasons for reaching this decision?' a revised set of questions was used for recording the decisions reached by the 'benches' (of two or three magistrates) at the six courts where conferences were held. It is set out below, and we believe it is a better way to approach the problem.

What do you aim to do by this sentence?

Put 1 against your principal aim and 2, 3, 4, 5 against other aims in order of priority, if any apply.

| Aims | Ordering of aims for: | |
|---|---|---|
| | Penalty | Disqualification |
| (i) Reform this individual | | |
| (ii) Deter this individual | | |
| (iii) Deter other potential offenders | | |
| (iv) Express society's disapproval of this behaviour | | |
| (v) Take away any opportunity for the offender to repeat his offence | | |

Why did you choose this *aim* for this offender?

Put 1 against your principal reason and 2, 3, 4, 5 against other reasons in order of priority, if any apply.

| | |
|---|---|
| (i) This type of offence is extremely dangerous | |
| (ii) These offences are too prevalent | |
| (iii) He is a first offender | |
| (iv) He needs help | |
| (v) He needs to be taught a lesson | |

(vi) Any other reason (please specify): ...........................................
............................................................................................
............................................................................................
............................................................................................

(g) *Method of recording changes in sentences at the conferences*

The following form was used by each 'bench' to indicate, when an item of information was changed, whether they would alter their penalty and, if so, in what way.

Please enter the decision reached by your BENCH.

| Penalty | Period of any disqualification | Licence endorsed | | Amount of any fees and costs awarded against the defendant |
|---|---|---|---|---|
| | | Yes | No | |
| | | | | |

| Item No. | No Change | NEW PENALTIES | | | | | Majority or Unanimous |
|---|---|---|---|---|---|---|---|
| | | Penalty | Period of any disqualification | Licence endorsed | | Fees or costs against defendant | |
| | | | | Yes | No | | |
| 1 | NC | | | | | | |
| 2 | NC | | | | | | |
| 3 | NC | | | | | | |

Continued up to 30 items

# APPENDIX II

# Cases

1. *Some of the cases on which magistrates were asked to reach decisions*

**Case 2 (Group E)**

DEFENDANT: H.O., 23 years, Mixer Man

APPLICATION:
A solicitor made application for legal aid on behalf of the defendant. He said he realized that it was an unusual request. Legal aid, he said, was not usually asked for in motoring cases as motorists could usually pay their way. The defendant was aged 23, married, with three children. His average wage when working was £14 a week, but the defendant had been off sick for three weeks and was not in a position to pay a fee.

The car the defendant was driving at the time of the offence had cost him £50 and he had sold it for £12.10.0. The solicitor asked the court not to regard the defendant as a moneyed motorist because he was driving a big motor car. The defendant also realized that he should have applied for legal aid before the hearing. He had not done so, said the solicitor, because someone had told him he could not have legal aid in a motoring case.

The magistrates granted legal aid.

CHARGE:
Driving a motor car in a manner dangerous to the public. Section 2 R.T.A. 1960.

PLEA:
The defendant appeared in person. He elected summary trial and pleaded not guilty to the charge. He was represented by a solicitor. A sketch plan was available (copy attached).

PROSECUTION CASE:
The prosecutor explained the sketch plan to the magistrates, saying the offence had taken place at the junction of a major road with a minor road in a built-up area on the outskirts of a city. The junction was a 'Y' junction where the major road made a sharp turn and was joined by a minor road at the apex of that turn.

At the junction there were three traffic islands with illuminated 'Keep Left' signs. It was alleged, said the prosecutor, that the defendant had driven his car on the wrong side of one of the islands, had skidded broad-side due to the speed at which he was travelling and that his car had followed the course of and caused the skid marks shown on the plan.

The incident had occurred at 10.25 p.m. on a Saturday in June. It was not completely dark, but was the kind of light when a motorist should have side-lights. It was a fine clear night and the road signs were illuminated. This was important, said the prosecutor, because it would affect the visibility of the four 'Keep Left' bollards on the traffic islands.

The prosecutor said he had two witnesses to call. The first, an independent witness, was Mr N., who had been standing at a bus stop which was not shown on the sketch plan. It was on the left-hand side of the minor road (looking north) about 100 yards from the junction and was in fact off the left-hand edge of the plan. The second witness was a police constable who had been standing on the right-hand side of the major road (looking north) some 300 yards from the junction at a point off the right-hand edge of the plan.

Mr N. would tell the court that the defendant was driving a Jaguar motor car along the minor road towards the junction. The car was showing side-lights. The witness would say that his attention was first drawn to the car because of its very high speed. When he saw the car it was passing him and overtaking another vehicle. It had its offside indicator flashing. The witness would tell the court that as soon as he saw the car he felt apprehensive. He realized it was approaching the first of the two traffic islands and he wondered what was going to happen. After overtaking the other vehicle the Jaguar car remained in the centre of the road and was approaching the junction at a speed which the witness estimated to be 50–60 m.p.h.

Mr N. would say, said the prosecutor, that he saw another motor car approaching the Jaguar car from the opposite direction. Because of the speed and position of the Jaguar, this car had to swing very sharply to the left to avoid a collision. The witness would say the Jaguar car went on, reached the first traffic island and went to the wrong side of it in the direction indicated by the skid marks shown on the plan. Then it swung hard to the left to avoid the second island, apparently hit the kerb and swung hard right to go between the kerb and the island. Finally, the car accelerated away along the major road to the north towards the constable. Mr N. would also say that throughout the manœuvres at the junction the car tyres were screeching.

The driver of the car travelling in the opposite direction to the Jaguar car was not available as a witness.

The police constable would tell the court that he was some 300 yards away from the junction. He heard the screeching of tyres and saw a car with side-lights on 'snaking' about the road near the junction. The constable would say that the car approached him at an estimated speed of 45–50 m.p.h. But, said the prosecutor, the court should bear in mind that the constable was rather far away from the junction and so they should not place too much weight on this estimate. However, the constable stopped the car, which was the Jaguar, driven by the defendant. He asked the defendant to explain his fast driving since he was in a built-up area restricted to 30 m.p.h. The defendant said that he was a stranger in the area and did not know the road. The constable would say that he warned him about fast driving and allowed him to go.

Before the defendant got away, said the prosecutor, Mr N. spoke to the constable and in consequence he stopped the defendant again. The constable would say that he put to the defendant what Mr N. had alleged: that the defendant had been going so fast that he had had to go on the wrong side of the traffic island. The constable would say that the defendant denied that this was so. Nevertheless the constable had cautioned the defendant and told him that the facts would be reported, and he was then allowed to go. The constable would also say that he went to the junction and inspected the skid marks and took measurements from which the sketch plan had been prepared. The defendant had not been present when these measurements were taken, said the prosecutor.

The prosecutor read to the bench and put in evidence a statement made by the defendant at a police station at noon on the following Sunday. The defendant's solicitor said he did not wish to challenge the statement and accepted it without formal proof (copy attached).

The prosecutor said that this was definitely dangerous driving, arising largely from the speed at which the defendant had driven. The skid marks were, in the submission of the prosecution, inordinately long for a flat road, especially when the incident happened in a restricted area and following an advance warning sign of the junction. The prosecution would contend that having regard to the vehicles and pedestrians about at the time and the nature of the road itself the whole manner of the defendant's driving was dangerous.

The prosecutor then called the evidence.

Mr N. said he was a sales representative. At the time this incident began, he was standing with his mother at a bus stop. It was a clear night, the roads were dry, dusk was coming down and the street lights were just coming on.

He said his attention was attracted to a Jaguar saloon motor car which was going north along the minor road towards the junction. It was travelling very fast at what he estimated to be 50 to 60 miles an hour. He felt confident of his estimate, he said, because he was a car-driver himself. The Jaguar was showing side-lights and its off-side trafficator was flashing. When the Jaguar was level with him at the bus stand, said Mr N., it was overtaking another car. It was, he said, right in the middle of the road going straight for the traffic island at the junction. When the car had almost reached the island there was a tremendous screeching and the Jaguar swung to the right of the traffic island, narrowly missing a car coming in the opposite direction. The Jaguar swung to the left between the two islands and then to the right again to pass the second island on the left side. Throughout these manœuvres, said Mr N., there was a tremendous screeching of brakes.

Mr N. said the car travelling in the opposite direction to the Jaguar stopped. After he had watched the Jaguar accelerate away from the junction along the major road, he went across the road to the other car. The driver was upset at what had happened. Mr N. said he got into his own car, which was nearby, and drove after the Jaguar. He saw the car had been stopped by a policeman. He spoke to the policeman about what he had seen and the policeman stopped the car a second time as it came along a side street.

Mr N. said he had not noticed whether the 'Keep Left' bollards on the island were lit up when the incident occurred. It appeared to him, he said, that there were five people in the Jaguar car.

Cross-examined, the witness said he would agree that he was a driver of some experience and that he found dusk was *one* of the most difficult times of the day for driving.

Mr N. said that there was a crossroads just off the left-hand edge of the plan. There was a 'Slow Major Road Ahead' sign between the cross-roads and the junction. The bus stop at which he was standing, said Mr N., was beyond the crossroads to the south, about 100 yards from the main junction. There was a crossroads sign and a bus stop sign near to the bus stop, and there was also a road information sign. He agreed with the defending solicitor that there was rather a multiplicity of signs for a driver going north to note.

The defending solicitor said that he would submit to the magistrates that with five occupants the Jaguar car could not have been doing 50 to 60 miles an hour, although in fairness to the witness it had to be remembered that it was dusk at the time, thus making accurate assessment difficult. Mr N. said it was a Mark 7 Jaguar, a powerful car, although rather an old type.

He agreed that the idea of the traffic islands was to slow traffic down so he would expect vehicles to brake as they came up to the junction. When he said there was a screeching of brakes what he really meant, he said, was that there was a screeching of tyres. He could still see the Jaguar car when he heard the tyres screeching. It was 'broadsiding'. Questioned on this point, he insisted that the car was 'broadsiding' when it swung to the right and then sharp back to the left again. He could not see why the four marks shown on the plan could not have been made by four different wheels of the Jaguar. The car must have been going along at an angle to its line of travel. The Jaguar had almost collided with the kerb outside the pork shop and the car must have had a right-hand lock on or it would have gone through the pork shop. When the defending solicitor put it to the witness that two of the scrub marks shown on the plan may have been caused by the Jaguar but that it could not have caused all four, Mr N. said he did not agree.

Re-examined, the witness said he knew the road junction well as he travelled on this road every day. There were a number of signs. About 50 yards south of the crossroads, off the left edge of the plan, there was first a sign indicating the crossroads then there was a road information sign giving directions for the crossroads. After that was a bus stop sign. After the crossroads there was a 'Slow Major Road Ahead' sign, which was not illuminated, and a road information sign both indicating the major road junction. He said he had watched the car from when he first saw it about 50 yards to the south of the bus stop until it was 300 or 400 yards away on his left to the north of the bus stop. As the car went by him he thought that the driver would have difficulty at the junction and he was puzzled about what the driver might do.

The constable said that at the time of this incident he was on duty about 300 yards to the north of the junction. He was standing on the right-hand side of the road. He heard a screeching noise as if a car was skidding and when he looked in the direction of the junction, he could see a car 'snaking' about the road. He watched the car as it approached him along the major road. It accelerated away from the junction at a speed which he estimated at 45–50 m.p.h. The constable said he crossed the major road and signalled to the driver to stop. The car turned sharp left into a side road at what he thought was a very fast speed, having regard to the sharpness of the corner. The car stopped, and he spoke to the defendant who was driving. He asked him why he was driving so fast in a built-up area and the defendant said he was a stranger in the district and did not know the road. He warned the defendant for driving fast in a restricted area and then allowed him to go. The defendant drove off along the side road and began to turn round to return to the major road.

After the defendant had driven away, said the constable, Mr N. came up to him and made a complaint about the defendant's driving at the junction. As a result of this, he stopped the defendant again as he came up to the major road after turning round. He cautioned him, and told him that it was alleged that he had driven on the wrong side of the traffic island at the junction. The constable said the defendant denied the allegation and said he had driven on the proper side of the bollard.

There were two other men and three women in the car. He had cautioned the defendant and told him that the facts would be reported with a view to prosecuting him for reckless, dangerous or careless driving, and had then let the defendant drive on.

After speaking to the defendant, said the constable, he went to the junction and inspected the road conditions. The weather was good, visibility was clear and the street lighting was on and gave a good light. The traffic bollards on the islands were lit and clear to see.

The constable said he saw there were some skid marks on the road. He took measurements of the marks and the road junction from which he prepared the plan. There were four skid marks on the road in the position shown on the plan. He said these marks had definitely been made by the defendant's car. The defendant's solicitor objected to this evidence on the ground that there was nothing to link the Jaguar car to the marks. The constable then said, in answer to the prosecutor, that the marks were fresh and of the same consistency, and again added that they were made by the defendant's car.

Cross-examined, the constable said there was no police inspector with him at the scene of the incident but there had been a police sergeant who had seen some of what had occurred. There was not the slightest suspicion on his part, said the constable, that the defendant had been drinking. He had stopped the defendant because he had been driving fast in a built-up area. The constable agreed that he had flagged the defendant down and asked him what the reason was for the tyre noises at the junction. It was true, he said, that the defendant was a stranger in the district, and at a later date the defendant had correctly produced his driving licence, insurance certificate and test certificate. He could not say exactly what sort of a car the defendant was driving. He decided to give the defendant a warning, had told him to be more careful about his driving and had let him go.

The constable said the sergeant had been with him when he first heard the tyre noises on the right-hand side of the road. The sergeant had been sitting in a car and he had been making his report to him. Then, said the constable, he heard the car noises, looked up and saw the car snaking about in the road and accelerating towards them. The sergeant had not seen this happen. The constable said he left the sergeant and went across the road to stop the car. After he had warned the defendant, and just as the defendant was driving away, the sergeant came across the road to join him. The sergeant had not spoken to the defendant about the traffic bollard, nor had the sergeant asked him to speak to the defendant about the bollard. The defendant did not say 'Yes, I had to go on the wrong side of the bollard to miss it.'

The constable said he had made up his mind to let the defendant go before the sergeant came up. Then Mr N. came up and spoke to him, but the defendant was not present. He said it was Mr N. who asked him to speak to the defendant about his driving, not the sergeant. The sergeant did not warn the defendant about the prosecution to be taken. He had done that himself, he said.

Re-examined, the constable said that when he signalled the defendant to stop he had turned off the major road into a side road on the left. The defendant had turned left very fast, he thought, having regard to the fact that he was making a sharp turn at a blind corner.

DEFENDANT'S CASE:

The defendant gave evidence. He said that he was 23 years of age, a mixer man when in employment. He had been off sick, he said, for three weeks. His average weekly wage was £14 and he was married and had three children. He said the Jaguar car was a 1953, Mark 7, model which he had had for four months and which he bought for £50. He did not think, he said, that the car was capable of doing 50 m.p.h. with five people in it unless it had a good run down a hill. He had not had a drink at all during the evening of this incident because he had been to a stock car-racing stadium and there was no bar there.

The defendant said he was a stranger in the district where the incident occurred. He had only been in the city once or twice and was not at all familiar with the road he was on. He said that usually when he was in the district he went along the by-pass but that he had taken a wrong turn and got himself lost. So far as he could recollect, he said, he had never been to this road junction before.

He could remember that shortly before he reached the island he over-took another car. At that time he estimated his speed was 35–40 miles an hour, certainly not more. He said he had heard the witnesses say that the 'Keep Left' bollards were illuminated. He did not think they were. He said he didn't see the bollards illuminated at all. He didn't know he was coming to an island and he was about twelve yards away from it when he first saw it. He said he realized he could not pull up and he could not pass to the left of the island. He considered it safer to pass on the right side and did so. Then he pulled to the left to go on the correct side of the second island. There was a screeching of tyres as he pulled back on to his own side of the road.

When he saw the constable signalling him to stop, he said, he turned left off the main road into a side road. He did this because he thought it was safer to pull off the major road into the side road than to park on the major road.

He said that had he not been a stranger in the district and had known the corner he would not have approached it at the speed he did. He recognized that had he paid more attention he might have seen the signs and to that extent he had been careless. It could be, he said, that he had driven without due care and attention on a road which he was unfamiliar with, but he did not think his driving was dangerous. He had gone to the right of the island because he thought it was the safe course and had got back to his own side as quickly as he could.

Cross-examined, the defendant said the Jaguar car was a 3½-litre six-cylinder model. When it was new it would be a very powerful car but it was now some twelve years old.

He said his home was in a town about 16 miles away from the city. He was not familiar with the city and had only visited it once or twice. He was much more familiar with a neighbouring borough, and having turned off the by-pass in the direction of the borough he thought he had reached the outskirts of that town. In fact, he said, he must have taken a wrong turning and had got into the outskirts of the city on to roads which were entirely new to him. He had been driving around for a long time and was lost. He was expecting to find his way into the borough but had not seen a road he recognized.

He said he did not see any signs indicating he was in a restricted area but agreed that he should have realized this. He was keeping a look out for road signs but was more concerned to notice direction signs than others because he was anxious to find out where he was. He said he was also paying attention to warning signs. They came naturally to him and if the light had been such that he could not read them he would have put his headlights on. Nevertheless, despite all this, he said, he had not seen any of the advance warning signs of the junction with the major road and was unaware he was approaching it until he was about 12 yards from the 'Keep Left' island.

He realized now, he said, that he overtook in a bad place but he did not think so on the night. He did not see the car coming towards him, he said, until he was overtaking the other car. Had he seen it he would not have overtaken. He was not travelling at 50 miles an hour as he overtook the car. He had been travelling, he said, about 35 miles an hour and increased his speed to 40 to overtake.

The defendant said he did not agree with the other witnesses that the bollards were lit up. If they were they must have been very dim.

He said he did not know the car travelling in the opposite direction had stopped. He realized that he must have embarrassed the driver by going to the right of the island but since he didn't know the other driver had stopped he never thought to do so himself.

He agreed that the road between the kerb and the second island was narrow but he got through all right. The marks on the road followed the route his car had taken but, he said, he could not say whether his car caused them. He would not accept, he said, that he was applying his brakes for all the distance of the scrub marks as shown on the plan. He realized that at 40 miles an hour he should have pulled up sooner than he did, but just before the second bollard he had to touch the accelerator so as to get through. He said he did not accept that the marks were consistent with a speed of 50 to 60 miles an hour. It could have been less. He had accelerated away from the junction by changing into third gear but he had not accelerated to 40 to 50 miles an hour. His car, he said, could not do that speed in third gear.

The defendant agreed that when the constable signalled him to stop he turned off the major road into a side road. He had done so because it would be safer to stop in the side road and he wanted to get off the main road as soon as possible. As soon as the constable told him about the allegation that he had gone on the wrong side of the island, he said, he admitted it and explained that he was a stranger in the district.

The defendant's solicitor addressed the court. He said at no time had the defendant pretended that there was not some negligence. If the magistrates were to exercise their power to reduce the charge from dangerous to careless driving, the defendant would plead guilty. But, he said, the defendant did not regard his driving as dangerous.

There were, said the solicitor, several points to be made which supported this view. Firstly, this was clearly not one of those cases where, due to drink, the driver drives dangerously leaving havoc behind him. The defendant had not had a drink all evening. Secondly, the defendant was a stranger in a strange land. He had got himself lost and did not know the district in, or the road on, which he was travelling. He could not, as could a person familiar with a road, anticipate hazards in the road.

Thirdly, one had only to look at the sketch plan, said the solicitor, to see that this was an unusual place to have a traffic island. True, it was the junction of what had formerly been a trunk road with a minor road. Nevertheless today there was little difference between them. They were almost the same width and it was very doubtful which carried the heavier volume of traffic. In addition, a stranger in the district, as was the defendant, could easily fall into the error of thinking that the old trunk road was the minor of the two, coming as it did into a straight stretch of road. Once having made that error one might well understand a driver being taken by surprise by finding the islands positioned as they were at this junction, and they might appear to be particularly dangerous at dusk.

The bollards on these islands, said the solicitor, were the illuminated type. There was a clear issue in this case as to whether they were lit. There was a clear conflict in the evidence. The prosecution evidence was that they were lit, but the defendant was equally sure they were not. It was a straightforward disagreement, one word against another, and it was for the magistrates to decide who was right.

Next, said the solicitor, there was a dispute about speed. The prosecution witness estimated the defendant's speed at 50–60 miles an hour as he approached the junction. The defendant had denied this and placed his estimate at 35–40 increasing to forty as he overtook the other car. Here again, it was for the magistrates to decide. It was not, however, very likely that any motorist on a strange road would drive at 60 miles an hour.

It was the defendant's case, said the solicitor, that at no time had he denied going to the wrong side of the island. He had explained this action by saying that he was surprised by the bollard and in the emergency went to the wrong side because it was the safest course to take. Apart from this slip he seemed to have had his wits about him. What better example, asked the solicitor, could one have of driving with care than turning off the main road to park as the defendant had done when signalled by the constable. It was only because he had done so that he was charged. The constable had warned the defendant and allowed him to go. He would have got clear away had it not been for his turning round to rejoin the major road.

The solicitor said that in all probability this was a clear case of driving without due care and attention. One could say that the defendant had been going too fast and was surprised by a bollard on a traffic island, which he should have been aware of either because it was illuminated or because of the signs warning of the junction. But it was not dangerous. There was the dispute about whether the speed was 50 m.p.h. or 35–40 m.p.h. This old car, said the solicitor, could not have gone so fast. The dispute was quite clear and there was nothing to corroborate one version or the other.

There was no doubt, said the solicitor, that the defendant went round the island on the wrong side but he had never sought to deny this. The magistrates could ignore what the constable said on this point, said the solicitor, because the defendant had admitted it in his voluntary statement and had repeated it in his evidence. Perhaps he did the wrong thing in going to the right of the island rather than the left, but this could not be regarded as criminal negligence. It was, he submitted, a clear case of careless driving but not of dangerous driving.

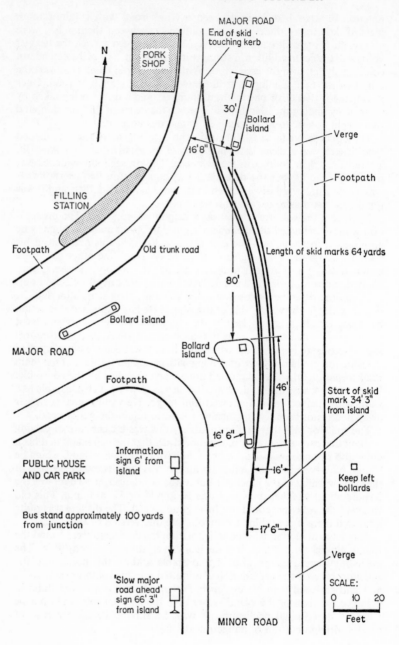

ADJUDICATION:
The magistrates found the defendant guilty of dangerous driving.

ANTECEDENTS:
The magistrates were informed of the following convictions recorded against the defendant:

| Time | Offence | Penalty |
|---|---|---|
| 3¼ years before present hearing | 1. Careless Driving | 1. Conditional discharge. Pay £12.12.0. Advocate's fee and £2.8.2 witness expenses |
| | 2. Failing to stop after an accident | 2. Fined £5 |
| | 3. No driving licence | 3. Fined £20. Disqualified for six months |
| 3½ years before present hearing | 1. No excise licence | 1. Fined £5. Pay 6/3 witness expenses |
| 3 years before present hearing | 1. Driving while disqualified | 1. Detention Centre for three months |
| | 2. No Insurance | 2. Fined £20. Disqualified for two years |

The prosecutor said there were also some offences of dishonesty included in the last conviction which he did not propose to put in. The prosecution costs included £4.0.3d witness expenses and an advocate's fee of £7.7.0.

*Defendant's Statement made under caution at 12 noon the following day, Sunday:*

About 10.20 p.m. Saturday night I was coming from the stock carracing with two of my mates. As we came round the round-about we thought we were lost when we saw the opening I thought I wanted so I turned into it. As I turned into it I saw the 'KEEP LEFT' sign and to miss it I had to go round the wrong side of it. I got round it alright then I was flagged down by a policeman. When I was going round the round-about I thought I was somewhere near the borough. I did not realize that I was in the city.

**Case 3 (Group A)**

DEFENDANT: H.K., 42 years, Boilermaker

CHARGE:
Driving a motor car while unfit through drink. Section 6(1) R.T.A. 1960.

PLEA:
The defendant appeared in person and elected summary trial. He pleaded guilty to the charge. He was not represented by a solicitor. He surrendered to bail allowed by the police after having been arrested at 8.50 p.m. the previous night.

PROSECUTION STATEMENT OF FACTS:

Two police constables saw the defendant driving a motor car on a minor road approaching a junction with a major road. The car was travelling at a fast speed. A public service vehicle, travelling on the major road, was also approaching the junction. The car did not slow down as it came to the junction. The public service vehicle driver braked hard to avoid a collision and so did the car driver but the car skidded and collided with the 'bus. There were no personal injuries and slight damage was caused to both vehicles. The car driver immediately reversed the car away from the scene of the accident. When the constables spoke to the defendant, the driver of the motor car, they saw that he was very unsteady on his feet. His speech was slurred and his breath smelled of drink. When asked to explain the accident the defendant said, 'It was that 'bus driver. He came through the bloody lights at red.' The junction was not controlled by traffic light signals. He was cautioned and told he would be arrested for driving while unfit through drink. He said, 'I don't know why you've got me. I'm making a stink about this, mind, Constable. I don't see why I pay £26 a year rates when they run you off the road.' He was taken to the police station. The station sergeant accepted the charge and called a doctor, offering the defendant the opportunity to have a doctor there on his behalf. He said one doctor would do. A doctor examined the defendant at 9.35 p.m. and when he concluded the examination at 9.55 p.m. he expressed the opinion that the defendant was unfit through drink to drive a motor car. When cautioned and charged the defendant made no reply. He declined to give the police a sample of urine.

DEFENDANT'S STATEMENT OF MITIGATION:

He said that most of what the prosecution had stated was correct. He did not at the time, or now, think he was drunk. He had only had two pints of beer all that day but he had not eaten since lunch time when he had eaten two sandwiches. He thought it was because he had not eaten rather than the amount of drink he had taken which had upset him.

ANTECEDENTS:

He was a provisional licence holder and had been driving for 5½ years. He had taken a test, he said, nine times and failed each time. He had not been to a driving school. He described himself as a boilermaker earning £17 a week. He was married with two daughters aged 10 and 9 years. His wife was not working.

The magistrates were told of the following conviction recorded against the defendant:

| Time before present hearing | Offence | Penalty |
|---|---|---|
| 2 years | Exceeding Speed Limit | Fined £3. Licence endorsed |
| | Provisional Licence Holder not displaying 'L' plates | Fined £2. Licence endorsed |

| *Offence* | *Penalty* |
|---|---|
| Provisional Licence Holder driving unaccompanied | Fined £5. Disqualified 3 months |

Prosecution costs amounted to £4.4.0.

## Case 4 (Group B)

DEFENDANT: H.E.N., 45 years, Company Secretary

CHARGE:
Driving a motor car when unfit through drink. Section 6(1) R.T.A. 1960.

PLEA:
The defendant appeared in person. He elected summary trial and pleaded guilty to the charge. He was not legally represented.

PROSECUTION STATEMENT OF FACTS:
The prosecutor said that at 11.6 p.m. on a Sunday in December, a police constable saw the defendant in a motor car on the car park of a hotel. The constable's attention was drawn to the car because the engine was revving very hard and the car was stationary. He saw the defendant drive the car from the hotel car park on to the adjoining road. The engine stalled and the defendant slumped over the steering wheel of the car. The constable went to the car and spoke to the defendant about the way he was driving. The defendant said, 'Have you been waiting for me?' The constable noticed that the defendant smelled strongly of alcohol. When he got out of the car he was unsteady on his feet and supported himself by leaning against it. The constable cautioned the defendant and told him that he would be arrested for driving a car while unfit through drink.

The defendant was taken to a police station in a police car. On arrival at the station, the defendant was asked to get out of the car and he said to the constable, 'Help me please, I'm not too steady on my feet.'

In the presence of the defendant, the constable told the station sergeant what had happened and the defendant said, 'I agree with what the officer says.' He was examined by a police surgeon who certified him unfit to drive a motor car because of drink. The defendant declined the opportunity of having a doctor present on his behalf and gave the police doctor a sample of urine. At the conclusion of the examination the police surgeon explained to the defendant that in his opinion he, the defendant, was unfit through drink to drive a motor car. The defendant said, 'You're kidding Doc.'

When he was cautioned and charged at 5.25 a.m. the following morning, the defendant said, 'All right'.

The sample of urine had been sent for forensic analysis and it showed that the defendant had consumed the equivalent of 9 pints of ordinary beer, 7 pints of best beer, or 13 to 14 fluid ounces of spirits.

DEFENDANT'S STATEMENT OF MITIGATION:
The defendant said that he did not dispute the facts as outlined by the
prosecutor. He had no witnesses he wished to call. He said that at the time
of the offence he had been severely distressed. The business of which he
was a director was being wound up. It was a family business and the man
on whom he had been relying to take over part of the business had backed
out on the day of the offence. There was a severe family quarrel over this,
which had depressed the defendant considerably and he had gone out on
his own in the evening.

He had been driving for 28 years and had never been convicted nor
had an accident. The defendant asked the magistrates not to disqualify
him. He was now virtually unemployed and it would severely limit his
chances of obtaining suitable employment if he could not drive a car.

He told the magistrates that his wife had a small private income, there
were three children in his family, one 9, one 7½ and the other 14. He was
now virtually without a job.

The Clerk explained to the defendant that, for the offence with which
he was charged, the magistrates had no discretion in the matter of disqualification unless there were some 'special reasons'.

The defendant then said that there was nothing more he wished to say.

ANTECEDENTS:
The prosecutor said that there was nothing known against the defendant.
The prosecution costs were £11. 4. 6d. for medical fees. The doctor had
attended court because it had not been possible to warn him of the
defendant's plea of guilty in time to stop him attending.

## Case 5 (Group C)

DEFENDANT: F.F., 48 years, Catering Officer

CHARGES:
(a) Driving a Mini van while unfit through drink. Section 6(1) R.T.A.
1960.
(b) Driving a Mini van in a manner dangerous to the public. Section 2
R.T.A. 1960.

PLEA:
The defendant appeared in person and elected summary trial. He pleaded
guilty to both offences. He was not legally represented.

PROSECUTION STATEMENT OF FACTS:
The proceedings arose out of a minor collision between two Mini motor
vans on a service road connecting airport buildings with a public highway.
The service road was a properly made road with street lamps and the
public had access to it.

About 9.15 p.m. on Christmas Eve a witness was sitting in the driving

seat of his Austin van talking to a woman who was in the passenger seat.
The van was parked under a lighted street lamp and was showing side-
lights and rear lights. It was about 40 yards from the airport restaurant
forecourt. Both these witnesses would have told the magistrates they saw a
Mini van coming towards them from the direction of the main road and
going towards the airport buildings. It was swerving about the road.
When it was about 50 yards from the front of the van it swerved on to their
side of the road and was heading directly towards them. The male witness
would have said that realizing there was likely to be an accident he switched
on his head lights to indicate his position to the oncoming van. The other
vehicle then swerved back to its near side but failed to get clear of the
parked van in time, and there was a collision between the front off side of
the two vans. The defendant's van then drove on for some distance before
it stopped. The male witness would have said he went to the van and saw
it was an Austin Mini van and that it was driven by the defendant. He saw
the windscreen was iced up. He spoke to the defendant and noticed he
smelled of drink. The witness told the defendant he proposed to call the
police. The defendant then said the headlights of the van had dazzled him
when the witness had suddenly switched them on.

At 9.40 p.m. a police constable arrived. He found that the defendant
smelled strongly of drink and his speech was hesitant. He asked the
defendant to explain what had happened, and he said, 'That car came out
of the airport entrance towards me with blazing headlights.' The constable
asked him to point out exactly where this had happened, and the defendant
walked unsteadily across the road and stood holding one of the fence
posts bounding the road. He would not move away from the fence.

The constable cautioned the defendant and told him he would be
arrested for driving the vehicle when unfit to drive through drink. The
defendant was taken to a nearby police station where he was seen by a
station sergeant. The sergeant told the defendant why he had been arrested
and the defendant agreed to be examined by a police doctor. He was
examined by a doctor, who certificated that the defendant was unfit
through drink to drive a motor vehicle. During the examination the
defendant gave a urine sample which was subsequently sent for analysis.

The defendant was released on bail six hours after arrest.

The next week the defendant was seen again by the police and after
being cautioned he made a statement regarding the accident. He was also
told he would be prosecuted for dangerous driving arising out of the
accident. He did not make any reply.

The airport service road was 20′ 4″ wide at the scene of the accident.

The analysis of the urine sample showed 210 milligrammes of alcohol
per 100 millilitres of blood. This was equivalent to 7–8 pints of ordinary
beer, 5–6 pints of best beer, or 9–11 fluid ounces of spirits.

The prosecutor called a police sergeant who read the defendant's statement: 'On Christman Eve I had gone to the end of the airport service road.
I had not gone on to the high road. I had gone to meet my wife from the
bus. I turned round and waited for the bus but she wasn't on it, so I

went back to the airport. On the way back two men stepped from the pavement on my near side to allow a couple to pass them. That's when I cut over to miss them and that's when the headlights of a vehicle coming out of the airport hit me and blinded me and I went straight over and hit the front end of the parked van. I asked the young couple in the van if they were all right.'

DEFENDANT'S STATEMENT OF MITIGATION:
The defendant said there was very little he could add; he wished to apologize to the court for his conduct on the night of the offence. He had never been in trouble before and had no convictions. The arrest on Christmas Eve had been very upsetting, particularly to his family, and the result had been that the family's Christmas had been ruined because of what he had done. Since then things had been pretty rough for him and there was still considerable worry for him about what was going to happen to his job. The local airport officials had been very good to him but whether or not he lost his job was a matter for headquarters and they were waiting for the outcome of the case.

He understood his employers had written to the bench on his behalf (copy of letter attached). He would like to add that he had not driven on the road. It had all happened on the airport forecourt. He at present had a clean licence and he needed a driving licence to drive the airport mini-van, which was used mainly for carrying food to airplanes on the airport. What would happen to his job if he lost his licence he could not say—that would be up to headquarters. He was a married man with two daughters aged 17 years and 15½ years. He earned an average wage of £11 per week.

ANTECEDENTS:
The prosecutor confirmed that there were no previous convictions recorded against the defendant. There were £7.0.6d. costs for medical fees.

Dear Sirs,

F.F.

May I refer to the above employee who we understand appears before you on Wednesday, on a charge relating to an accident on December 24th.

We should be grateful if you would take into consideration that he has always been, in our experience, a satisfactory employee and that whilst he is not employed by us as a driver he does require a driving licence to carry out his duties as a catering assistant on the airport.

We are, of course, taking our own disciplinary action regarding the incident on Christmas Eve but we would wish to commend the defendant to you under the circumstances which he will himself quote.

Yours faithfully,

**Case 7 (Group E)**

DEFENDANT: H.G.N., 21 years, Decorator

CHARGES:
(a) Taking a motor vehicle without the consent of the owner. Section 217 R.T.A. 1960.
(b) Driving a motor car while disqualified for driving. Section 110 R.T.A. 1960.
(c) Using a motor car without third party insurance. Section 201 R.T.A. 1960. •

PLEA:
The defendant appeared in person and elected summary trial. He pleaded guilty to each of the charges. He was not legally represented. He appeared in custody by Home Office order while serving a sentence of imprisonment imposed for another offence.

PROSECUTION CASE:
The defendant was charged with taking a motor car from the garage of an ice-cream merchant for whom he was doing a job. The car was owned by a friend of the merchant and both the merchant and the car owner were spending a week-end away from home at the time the offences were committed.

The prosecution's first witness was the ice-cream merchant. He said he knew the defendant, having met him while visiting Manchester two months ago on business. During their first conversation the defendant had said he was a decorator and had promised to decorate a house which the witness had recently bought. A short time after this meeting in Manchester, the defendant went to stay at the home of the witness to do the decorating. When the defendant had been there for three or four days, it was necessary for the ice-cream merchant and a friend to spend a week-end away from home on business. The witness asked the defendant if, during the week-end, he would attend to the ice-cream freezers and gave him the keys to his garage so that the defendant could get into the business premises. The ice-cream merchant's friend came to the garage in his own car, put his car in the garage, and the two men went away in the ice-cream merchant's car. Neither the witness nor, so far as he knew, his friend, had given anyone permission to use the car during the week-end. When they returned late on Sunday evening the friend drew attention to the fact that his car was wet and appeared to have been used. They examined the car and in consequence of what they found they went, the following Monday evening, to see the defendant at a restaurant where he was having a meal. The friend asked the defendant if he had used the car during the week-end and the defendant replied 'Yes, but I can explain.' He produced a note, purporting to have been written by the ice-cream man, addressed to the defendant and saying he could use the car while they were away. The witness identified the note and said he had not given the defendant permission to use the car nor had he written the note. When the defendant produced the note to them, both the witness and his friend told the defendant it was false and said he had better come along with them to the police station. The defendant then ran away and was not seen again by the two men until he appeared in court.

Cross-examined, the witness denied that the defendant had told him at the restaurant that he did not take the car during the week-end but that he had been in it.

The ice-cream merchant's friend was the next witness. He said he left the car in his friend's garage and went away with him for the week-end. When they got back late on Sunday night, he saw that his car had been used while he had been away. There were some 200 extra miles on the speedometer clock; the car was wet, which it had not been when he put it away. He found an empty beer bottle in the back seat and a packet of Player's Gold Leaf cigarettes in the car, which had not been there when he left it. The mirror and driving seat had been moved. He told the ice-cream merchant what he had found and on the following Monday evening they went together to see the defendant. They found him at a restaurant where he was having a meal. He asked the defendant whether he had used the car during the week-end and the defendant said 'Yes' and showed him a note which the defendant said he had found on the car. He, the witness, did not recognize the note, nor had he left it on the car. The ice-cream merchant, by whom the note purported to be written, also said he knew nothing of the note. They got hold of the defendant, intending to take him to the police station. There was a bit of a struggle and the defendant ran away. The witness had not seen him since. The defendant did not cross-examine this witness.

The prosecution also called the step-father of the ice-cream merchant. He said that he remembered the defendant coming to stay at his stepson's house to do some decorating. Three or four days after he came his stepson and a friend went away on business for the week-end. On the Friday evening he went round to the garage and business premises and saw that his stepson's friend had left a car parked in the garage. He knew this car quite well. On Saturday night, just after nine o'clock, the defendant called at his house to collect a book and some sketches. It was raining very heavily and the defendant was not wearing a jacket. There was some conversation about this and the defendant said he would not get wet because he had a car with him. When the defendant had got the book and the sketches, the witness went to the door with him and saw that the car which was parked in the road was the one from the garage. There was a young woman in the car. She was sitting in the passenger seat. The witness's wife, who was also with them at the door, asked the defendant who owned the car and the defendant said it was owned by one of 'Johnny's friends' (Johnny being the witness's stepson).

Cross-examined, the witness said he was sure the defendant had said the car belonged to one of 'Johnny's friends'. He was sure the defendant did not say 'a friend's car'.

A police constable gave evidence that four months earlier, the defendant was disqualified for driving for twelve months, fined £10, and his driving licence endorsed, for using a motor vehicle without insurance. This witness was not cross-examined.

When interviewed by the police and told that he was being reported for the offences charged, the defendant did not reply.

DEFENDANT'S CASE:
The defendant elected to give evidence and said the ice-cream merchant asked him to decorate a house and to do so he went to stay at the home of the ice-cream man. Three or four days later, the ice-cream man asked the defendant if he would attend to the freezers during the week-end because he and a friend were going away on business. The ice-cream merchant gave the defendant the keys to the garage so that he could get into the premises. On Saturday evening, early on, he went into a nearby city for a night out. He travelled by 'bus and while on the 'bus met a young man. In conversation with the young man he asked where it was possible to have a good night out and together they went to a public house on the outskirts of the city. At the public house the two men met a girl and after a drink or two together the young man left the defendant alone with the girl. She asked him to tell her something about himself. He told her that he owned an ice-cream business in a nearby town and that he would soon have to leave her to visit his business premises, because he must switch the freezers on. She asked him if he needed to leave so soon and he said he had to go because he was travelling by 'bus. She said she had a car and would drive him to his business premises. This conversation occurred between half-past eight and nine o'clock. She drove him to the business premises and on the way there, he called at the house of the ice-cream merchant's step-father, to collect a book and some sketches to show the girl. It was raining heavily when they got to the house and he had no jacket on. He went into the house, collected the book and sketches, and when comment was made about his having no jacket, he told the step-father that it was all right, he had a girl-friend's car. The witnesses were wrong to say he told them that the car belonged to one of 'Johnny's friends'. The girl was sitting in the passenger seat because the driver's door was nearest to the house door. He ran down to the car and got into the driver's seat in order to avoid getting wet. Then they changed over and the girl drove the car to the garage. They both went into the garage where the girl saw the parked car and commented on how similar in appearance it was to her own. She asked whose car it was and, because he had told her that the ice-cream business was his, he let her believe that the car also belonged to him. She said she would like to try it and got into the car. They both sat in the car and had a cigarette and he remembered a bottle of beer which he had bought earlier and they shared this. He was very uneasy when they were sitting in the car because he did not want her to do any damage to it. He eventually got her out by suggesting that they should visit the house which he told her he was decorating. They then left the garage without having driven the car and

went to the house where they stayed for the rest of the evening. When she left he arranged to meet her on the Sunday night, anticipating that by that time the ice-cream merchant would have returned and would be prepared to go with him on the date, as a foursome, using the ice-cream merchant's car. He did not keep the date because the ice-cream merchant and his friend did not return until late on the Sunday evening. He did not know who the girl was or where she could be traced.

On the Monday evening after working on the house, he went to a restaurant for a meal. While there the ice-cream merchant and his friend came in and accused him of having used the friend's car which had been parked in the garage during the week-end. He did not admit having driven the car. What he did say was that he had been in the car and could explain how this had happened. They would not allow him to give his explanation and became very threatening. They got hold of him but he broke away from them and ran. He had not seen them since but had telephoned the ice-cream merchant's fiancée and she had told him that the matter of the car had been reported to the police and that he was to be charged. He was quite sure that he had driven neither the car from the garage or the car belonging to the girl from the public house.

Cross-examined, he said that he had visited the step-father's house on the Saturday evening and that he had gone there in a car. It was the girl-friend's car and he was sure he said this to the step-father when he asked who owned the car. He had got into the driving seat of the car when he left the house but the step-father was wrong when he said the defendant drove the car away. He did not drive the car. He got into the driver's seat to avoid the rain, but once inside the car he and the girl changed over. Neither of them had to get out of the car to do this; it was a bench seat and the girl climbed over his knee.

On the Monday night, when he was in the restaurant, the two men came to him and accused him of using the car from the garage. He did not say that he had driven the car. He did say that he had been in the car. He was not given time to explain more than this before they got threatening and there was a struggle. He ran away to avoid further trouble. He did not know who the girl was and he had not asked for her to be traced, because he did not think that he could provide sufficient information for her to be located.

The defendant said that he had no witnesses to call. If the magistrates thought that the girl could be traced he would like an opportunity to make arrangements for her to be found and to give evidence. The Chairman asked the defendant to describe the 'bus journey which he took on the Saturday evening, paying particular attention to any changes of 'bus service which he made to reach the public house. The defendant said that 'bus services mystified him, he did not think that he could help the magistrates in this respect except to say that he knew they made at least one change, although he could not say where.

ADJUDICATION AND ANTECEDENTS:
The bench found the defendant guilty and the magistrates were then
informed of the following convictions recorded against the defendant:

| Time | Offence | Sentence |
|---|---|---|
| 5 months before present hearing | 1. No insurance | Fined £5. L.E. |
| | 2. No driving licence | Fined £5. L.E. |
| 4 months before present hearing | 1. No insurance | Fined £3. L.E. |
| | 2. Failing to give name and address | Fined £5. L.E. |
| | 3. Motor vehicle in dangerous condition | Fined £2 |
| 4 months before present hearing | 1. No insurance | Fined £10. L.E. Disqualified 12 months |
| | 2. No insurance | Fined £1. L.E. |
| | 3. No test certificate | Fined £5 |
| | 4. No test certificate | Fined £1 |
| | 5. Provisional licence holder driving unaccompanied | Fined £2. L.E. Disqualified 6 months |
| | 6. —do— | Fined £1 |
| | 7. Provisional licence holder, no 'L' plates | Fined £2. L.E. |
| | 8. —do— | Fined £1. L.E. |
| | 9. No Road Rund Licence | Fined £5 |
| | 10. No Road Fund Licence | Fined £1 |
| 1 month before present hearing | 1. 'L' driver not accompanied | Fined £2 or 7 days |
| | 2. 'L' driver no 'L' plates | Fined £2 or 7 days |
| | 3. No Road Fund Licence | Fined £1 or 5 days |
| | 4. No insurance | 3 months imprisonment. L.E. |
| | 5. No test certificate | Fined £5 or 1 month |
| | 6. Failing to stop for P.C. | Fined £5 or 1 month |
| | 7. No lights | Fined £1 or 5 days |
| | 8. Sounding warning instrument in prohibited hours | Fined £1 or 5 days |
| | 9. No Road Fund Licence | Fined £5 or 1 month |
| | 10. No test certificate | 7 days imprisonment, L.E. |
| | 11. No insurance | Fined £1 or 5 days |
| | 12. No lights | Fined £2 or 7 days. L.E. |
| | 13. 'L' driver not accompanied | Fined £2 or 7 days. L.E. |
| | 14. Failing to display 'L' plates | Fined £2 or 7 days. L.E. |
| | 15. No Test Certificate | Fined £5 or 1 month |
| | 16. No Road Fund Licence | Fined £10 or 2 months |
| | 17. No insurance | 3 months imprisonment consecutive. Disqualified 4 years consecutive to disqualification imposed four months previously. |

**Case 9 (Group E)**

DEFENDANT: H.C.S., 62 years, Retired Engineer

CHARGE:
Driving a motor car without due care and attention. Section 3 R.T.A. 1960.

PLEA:
The defendant did not appear in person. The case was disposed of by the procedure under the Magistrates' Courts Act, 1957, a plea of guilty having been received from the defendant.

PROSECUTION STATEMENT OF FACTS:
The prosecutor said that the proceedings were the result of an accident which occurred on a busy trunk road at 2.25 p.m. on a Tuesday, in December. At the scene of the accident, the trunk road was 30 ft. 6 ins. wide, it curved gradually and the view ahead was slightly restricted. Nearby where the accident occurred, there were three minor road junctions entering the major road.

A large unusual load was travelling south on the trunk road. Its speed was restricted to 4 m.p.h. There were two light locomotives coupled together towing a long trailer. The overall length of the vehicle and its load was 89 ft. and it was 14 ft wide. The vehicle and load weighed 19 tons. A police patrol car was escorting the load, to mitigate, as far as possible, obstruction and inconvenience to other traffic.

There were several vehicles following the load, one of which was the car driven by the defendant. There were several vehicles between the defendant's car and the load. The defendant drew out from the line of vehicles and began to overtake the other vehicles and the wide load.

The driver of the leading tractor, seeing the defendant's car overtaking, and seeing also that there was a lorry approaching from the opposite direction, braked his vehicle to try to let the defendant pass him in time to avoid the lorry. Because of the weight of the vehicles, the coupling bar between the two tractor vehicles crumpled and broke, and the second towing vehicle ran into the rear of the first and went on to the nearside footpath. In an effort to give the lorry sufficient room to pass on the off side of his car, the defendant drove his vehicle as close to the load as he could and in so doing collided with the front off side of the trailer of the wide load.

The police constable escorting the load asked the defendant to explain what had happened, and he said, 'I am afraid it was my fault'.

After being cautioned, the defendant made the following statement: 'On Tuesday I was driving my car behind the wide load. I was about four vehicles behind the load. I saw that the road in front was clear of oncoming traffic so I overtook the preceding cars and drew alongside the wide load. When I was alongside it, I saw some traffic coming towards me in the opposite direction, so I moved nearer in to the load. That traffic went past me, then I saw a lorry coming towards me and I realized that it would not have room to get through and as it was coming fairly fast, I moved even closer to the load and the nearside front of my car struck the front off side of the trailer of the load. Because I was in the wrong traffic lane I turned right into a road junction to clear the road and then I went back to the police car which was with the load. I consider the accident was due to a misjudgement on my part.'

DEFENDANT'S STATEMENT OF MITIGATION:
A statement of mitigation was received from the defendant in which he said, 'I am glad no one suffered injury due to my unfortunate misjudgement. I have held a driving licence for 33 years, and this is my first offence. I have a clean record, both for driving and insurance. I am very sorry this should have happened. So much so, that I have disposed of my car and even though I do not feel old at 62 have decided that I should not drive again.'

ANTECEDENTS:
The magistrates were not informed of any convictions recorded against the defendant. The prosecutor said that the prosecution had not incurred any costs.

## Case 10 (Group C)

DEFENDANT: W.G., 31 years, Steel Erector

CHARGES:
(a) Using motor car without insurance. Section 201 R.T.A. 1960.
(b) Using motor car without excise licence. Section 7 Vehicles Excise Act, 1962.
(c) Failing to inform registration authority and return registration book of a vehicle which was being broken up. Regulation 11, Registration and Licensing Regulations, 1955.
(d) Fraudulently using an excise licence on a motor car. Section 17(1) Vehicles Excise Act, 1962.
(e) Being the new owner of a motor car did fail to enter name and address in the registration book and deliver it to the registration authorities. Section 17(3) Vehicles Excise Act, 1962.

PLEA:
The defendant appeared in person and pleaded guilty to each offence. He was not legally represented.

PROSECUTION STATEMENT OF FACTS:
At 4.50 a.m. on a Sunday in May, the defendant was seen, by a police constable, sitting in a parked motor car. The constable noticed that the registration number on the excise licence displayed in the vehicle did not correspond with the registration number of the vehicle. The defendant explained this by saying that he had scrapped another motor car the previous Monday and had put the excise licence from that vehicle on to the

vehicle which he was using, thinking that would be in order. The licence was current. The constable then asked if there was an excise licence in force in respect of the vehicle being used. The defendant said there was not. He was asked if he had notified the registration authority of his being the new owner of the car in use by filling in his name and address in the registration book and sending it to the registration authority. He said he had owned the vehicle only a short time and had not had time to do so. He was then asked if he had notified the registration authority and returned the registration book of the vehicle which had been scrapped. He said he had not. The defendant was asked to produce a certificate of insurance in respect of the vehicle in use. He did not do so and was then asked to produce it at the local police station within five days; he did not do so and was interviewed again when he produced a valid certificate of insurance in respect of the scrapped vehicle. He was told that this did not cover use of the other vehicle. He insisted that it did and said that he would see his insurance company and get a certificate. He was seen again later and then said that his insurance company had told him that he was not covered by the company when he was seen using the car.

DEFENDANT'S STATEMENT OF MITIGATION:
He said he was a plant-hire driver and required a car for his work. He had recently scrapped one vehicle and had fitted the gear box of that car into the car he was seen using. He had been anxious to test the repaired vehicle and had taken it out to do that. He thought it would be all right to use the excise licence from the scrapped vehicle for which tax had been paid and he believed that the insurance cover for that car would also cover the repaired car he used. He had seen the insurance company about this after he was spoken to by the police constable and had been told that technically he was not covered while using a car other than the scrapped vehicle. He did not know anything about having to tell the registration authority about the car he had scrapped. He had filled his name and address in on the registration book of the repaired car, intending to take it to the registration authority, but he had owned the vehicle only three weeks and had not had time to do so.

ANTECEDENTS:
He was the holder of a full driving licence on which there were no endorsements. He had been out of work for over six months but had started work four days before the hearing as a labourer in a factory, earning about £11 a week. He had not, at the time of the hearing, received any wages. He was a married man with five children. He had been driving for 13 years.

The magistrates were told of two convictions:

| Time | Offence | Penalty |
|---|---|---|
| 5 years before present hearing | 1. Aiding and abetting the taking of a motor vehicle without owner's consent | Fined £2 |
| | 2. Aiding and abetting the use of motor vehicle without insurance | Fined £2 |
| | 3. Getting on to a moving vehicle | Fined 10/– |

| Time | Offence | Penalty |
|---|---|---|
| 6 months before present hearing | 1. Failing to produce a driving licence | Fined £1 |
| | 2. Failing to produce certificate of insurance | Fined £1 |
| | 3. Using a motor vehicle without test certificate | Fined £2 |

**Case 11 (Group C)**

DEFENDANT: O.M.A., 23 years

CHARGES:
(a) Failing to stop after an accident. Section 77 R.T.A. 1960.
(b) Failing to report an accident. Section 77 R.T.A. 1960.

PLEA:
The defendant appeared in person. He pleaded guilty to both charges.
He was not legally represented.

PROSECUTION STATEMENT OF FACTS:
The prosecutor began by saying that the police were getting quite a number
of accidents late at night in which motorists were not stopping at the
scene of accidents and were subsequently failing to report them to the
police. It was the feeling of the police, said the prosecutor, that this was
done in order to avoid being interviewed by the police and to evade more
serious charges which might arise from the accident.

The prosecutor went on to say that the facts of the present case were
that at 12 midnight on a Saturday in January, an accident occurred when a
Morris Oxford motor car, driven by the defendant, collided with a Commer
shooting brake which was parked outside the house of the owner in a
street in a large town.

Just before the accident, the owner of the Commer had gone to bed. He
heard a crash outside his house. He got out of bed and looked out of the
window. He saw a grey Morris Oxford motor car parked at an acute angle
to the kerb and immediately in front of his car. He went downstairs and
into the street. He then saw that the Morris car has been moved and was
parked some way along the street. He also saw that the front end of his car
had been damaged. The front bumper bar and number plate were slightly
buckled. He went to the Morris car and spoke to the driver, a youth of
about 20 years old. There were three other people in the car. He asked the
driver of the Morris car, who was the defendant, to return to the Commer
shooting brake to examine the damage which had been caused in the
collision. The defendant said, 'I can't be bothered to come and see the
damage to your car.' The owner of the Commer then asked the defendant
to wait where he was until the police arrived. He then went to inform the
police but before he had reached his house, the Morris car had driven off.
He went outside, got into the Commer and chased the defendant's car to
try to stop it, but he was unable to do so.

Another witness had obtained the registration number of the car and reported the incident to the police. As a result of police enquiries, the defendant was interviewed a week after the accident. He was told that enquiries were being made about the accident, and he said, 'I don't know about the time but I was up there that night.' He was told there was evidence that his car had collided with and damaged a Commer shooting brake. He said, 'No, I had to manœuvre to pass two cars, but I didn't hit either car.'

When told he had been seen by two witnesses, he said, 'They must be light sleepers, because I don't remember any crash.'

He was questioned again as to whether he had been involved in a collision that night, and he then said, 'Well, yes, I was.'

Asked if he had reported the accident or stopped to give particulars to anyone, he said, 'No, I didn't think any damage was caused.' He was told he would be reported for the two offences of failing to stop after the accident and failing to report it, and he said, 'All right.'

After being cautioned, the defendant made a statement in which he said, 'I came round the corner into the street and saw two vehicles parked. I was only doing 10 miles per hour. I pulled out to pass the vehicle on my left and was then on the wrong side of the road. I touched the brakes and slid forward on some ice. I came to a stop but I must just have touched the bumper bar of the second car. I had to reverse the car to get through, so I carried on along the street to drop off my mate.'

DEFENDANT'S STATEMENT OF MITIGATION:
The defendant said he thought there was no damage to the Commer shooting brake so he didn't go back. He was asked by the bench why he didn't go back when the owner informed him that the shooting brake had been damaged. The defendant did not reply.

ANTECEDENTS:
The prosecutor said that there were no convictions recorded against the defendant. His driving licence was before the court and bore no endorsements. The prosecutor said that his witnesses had attended court and the costs amounted to £22.11.0d.

2. *The cases used at the Sentencing Conference*

Case 12

DEFENDANT: E., 27 years, Process Worker

CHARGE:
Driving a motor car when unfit through drink. Section 6(1), R.T.A. 1960

PLEA:
The defendant appeared in person. He elected summary trial and pleaded guilty. He was not legally represented. The police laid the information and

were represented by a solicitor. The prosecutor read a statement of the facts.

STATEMENT OF FACTS:

At 11.20 p.m. on a Saturday in January two police officers in plain clothes were in a motor car, travelling along a busy main road in an urban area on the outskirts of a city. They saw a motor car travelling in the same direction in front of them. It was travelling at 5–10 m.p.h. and was swerving about the road. On two separate occasions it almost ran into parked cars, having to swerve sharply into the centre of the road to avoid colliding with them. In swerving to avoid these cars the vehicle narrowly missed colliding with vehicles moving in the road.

The police officers overtook the car, intending to stop it. Shortly after overtaking the car the police vehicle passed through a set of traffic lights, which were at green, and then pulled on to a lay-by preparatory to stopping the car. The officers got out and saw the car driven through the traffic lights while they were red. The car then accelerated to about 35 m.p.h. and drove past them without stopping. The officers followed the car and caught up with it when it stopped at the next set of traffic lights about half a mile further on.

One of the officers went to the car. He saw the defendant in the driving seat. He was alone. The constable asked the defendant to open the car door but he did not appear to comprehend what was said and the constable shouted to attract his attention. Even so the defendant did not seem to understand, so the constable opened the car door. There was a strong smell of alcohol. The police officer explained that he had followed the car, and described what he had seen. He asked the defendant if there was anything wrong to account for the way the car had been driven or if he was feeling unwell. The defendant said, 'I don't know, I have had a few, that might be it.' The constable asked the defendant how much he had had to drink and he replied, 'Ooh I don't know. At least I've had a couple too many.'

The constable told the defendant he would be arrested for driving the car while unfit through drink. He was asked to get out of the car, and did so. He was very unsteady on his feet. He was taken to a police station where the station sergeant asked him if he understood why he had been arrested. The defendant replied, 'Yes, I suppose so.'

The station sergeant told the defendant that he would be examined by a police surgeon and he was asked if he would like a doctor to attend on his behalf. The defendant said, 'I have a doctor but I don't know his name.' He was asked to nominate another doctor.

No doctor had been nominated by the time the police surgeon arrived and the examination went ahead. The police surgeon certified that the defendant was unfit through drink to drive a motor car.

The defendant gave a urine sample which had been analysed. The analysis showed 356 milligrammes of alcohol per 100 millilitres of urine which was equivalent to a blood alcohol content of 267 milligrammes of

H

alcohol per 100 millilitres of blood. It was a British Medical Association recommendation that rapid deterioration of control occurs at blood levels in excess of 100 milligrammes of alcohol per 100 millilitres of blood.

At 12.50 a.m. the defendant was cautioned and charged and he said, 'I don't want to say anything.'

DEFENDANT'S STATEMENT OF MITIGATION:
The defendant told the court that on the night of the offence he had been with friends and had some drinks. When he left them he did not realize that he was unfit to drive. He had not consumed a larger than usual number of drinks. He had, however, taken drink at lunch-time, which *was* unusual, and he felt that the amount must have built up to make him unfit.

He realized that what he had done was very serious. He had been very fortunate, for his behaviour could have resulted in someone being seriously injured. He was very sorry for his behaviour and apologized for the trouble and inconvenience he had caused. He promised to do all he could in the future to ensure that he did not get into such a situation again.

ANTECEDENT HISTORY:
A police officer told the court there were no convictions recorded against the defendant.

ADDITIONAL INFORMATION:
The prosecutor asked for costs of £5 5s. 0d. for medical fees. The defendant was a married man earning £20 per week.

**Case 13**

DEFENDANT: B., 20 years, Serving soldier

CHARGE:
Driving a motor car on a road in a manner which was dangerous to the public. Section 2(1), R.T.A. 1960.

PLEA:
The defendant appeared in person. He elected summary trial. He pleaded not guilty. He was not legally represented. A sketch plan was available to the Bench (copy attached). The information was laid by the police who were represented by a solicitor.

PROSECUTION CASE:
The case arose out of an incident which occurred at 11.10 p.m. on a Saturday, and in which three motor cars were involved, one driven by a prosecution witness, one a police patrol car, and the third driven by the defendant. There was no collision, no one was injured and none of the vehicles was damaged. The incident occurred on a minor road in a rural area, at a point where the road bends acutely. The prosecution alleged that the defendant's car overtook the other private motor car at a fast speed

on the bend and by so doing caused the police patrol driver, travelling in the opposite direction, to brake and stop in order to avoid colliding with the defendant's car.

The first witness said that he was driving his motor car, approaching a sharp left-hand bend. He saw the word 'Slow' painted on the road. He was driving at about 30 m.p.h. as he began to go round the bend. As he was taking the bend his car was overtaken by another motor car driven by the defendant. It was travelling at a fast speed and, as it overtook, there was a screech of tyres.

The witness also saw that there was a motor car coming in the opposite direction which had to brake and pull into the road-side to avoid a collision.

In cross-examining the witness, the defendant suggested that the witness's car was clear of the bend and on the straight when it was overtaken. He also suggested to the witness that the bend was not as acute as shown on the sketch plan. It was possible to see round the bend from a point near the second lamp post shown on the sketch plan. The witness said he was on the bend when he was overtaken and he could not say for sure just where one got a clear view of the road ahead from the bend.

Travelling in the opposite direction was a police patrol car, which contained two police officers. They gave evidence that as their car approached the sharp bend, which to them was a right-hand bend, a motor car came round the corner on the correct side of the road, travelling at a steady speed. This car was overtaken on the corner by another motor car, driven by the defendant. The police driver had to brake sharply and stop to avoid colliding with this car, which was travelling at a fast speed. The police car pursued the defendant's car and it eventually stopped outside a shop. The constables spoke to the defendant, who said he could not recall the incident. He was reminded of it and, when he remembered it, was told that he would be reported for dangerous driving. He replied, 'All right, but not dangerous driving.' At the time visibility was good, the weather was fine and the road dry.

Cross-examined, the officers said that the police car was about 40 yards from the bend when the two cars came round it. They were abreast when they were coming round the corner. Both constables were sure that the two cars came round the corner together, not one behind the other.

THE DEFENDANT'S CASE:
The defendant gave evidence that he was driving towards the sharp left-hand bend. He was not travelling fast and he saw the other car in front of him. He followed the car round the bend until he was able to see that the road in front was clear for him to overtake and then he overtook. He began to move out to overtake the car while they were still on the bend, but it was not until he could see the road ahead and the cars were clear of the bend that he actually overtook. He saw the other car coming towards him. It was a sufficient distance away for him to overtake safely at a normal speed. He did not know that the police car had braked and stopped

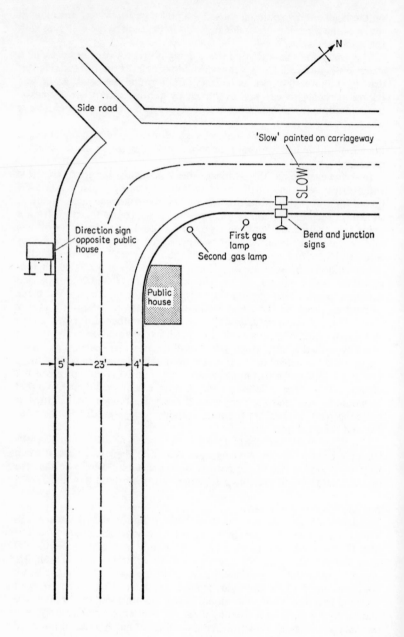

to let him through and he did not think this was necessary. When the policeman spoke to him he could not recall the incident because he remembered nothing out of the ordinary and did not believe that he had driven dangerously.

Cross-examined, he said he was quite sure that the cars were clear of the bend when they were overtaking. He thought it would be about opposite the road direction sign, outside the public house, when they were abreast.

VERDICT OF THE BENCH:
The defendant was found guilty.

ANTECEDENT HISTORY:
A police officer told the court there were no convictions recorded against the defendant.

ADDITIONAL INFORMATION:
The prosecutor asked the Bench to allow £10 15s. 8d. witness expenses and an advocate's fee of £5 5s. 0d.

# APPENDIX III

# Statistical Methods

1. *Statistical methods used in the analysis of factors associated with sentencing variations*

(a) *Introduction.* Non-parametric methods—i.e. methods involving no assumptions about the underlying distributions of the variables—were used throughout the analysis. This was because it cannot be assumed that the variables were from normal distributions. Many of them| were 'categorical', that is, magistrates were simply in one category or another, such as taking the chair regularly in the court or not doing so. Even the continuous variables could not be assumed to be normally distributed. The distribution of age, for example, was definitely skewed. Also, the values of the dependent variable—the fines or periods of disqualification—fall on neither a linear nor a log scale. Fines tend to take the following values in pounds (£s): 3, 5, 7, 8, 10, 12, 15, 20, 25, 30, 40, 50, 60, 75, 100; and disqualifications tend to take the following values in months, 3, 4, 6, 9, 12, 18, 24, 36, 60. Therefore, we decided to *rank* each magistrate's penalty in relation to the penalties given by the others (about 100) who dealt with the same case. (Obviously many magistrates will give the same fine and so there will be many 'tied ranks'. Of 100 magistrates dealing with a case three may fine the lowest amount. They would be ranked second equal. Nine more might fine the next highest amount; they would be ranked 7·5th equal, and so on.) Tests of significance were employed which used the rank of the penalty and not the value of the penalty itself.

Each of the 40 offences, 5 groups of 8 offences, was considered separately for most of the analysis to allow for interactions between the effects of any background variables on the penalties for different types of offences. Certain background variables might have different effects on the penalty given for different offences, including different cases of one kind of offence such as dangerous driving.

(b) *Measurement of associations amongst background variables.* Most of the variables were categorical. Those that were not were categorized into not more than four categories. Two-way tables were produced for each pair of attributes and the chi-square value calculated to detect significant associations between the variables. Also, a 'Dissimilarity score' consisting of the sum of the cross-products of the numbers in each cell was computed (omitting squares of numbers in cells) and used as a measure in a Cluster

218

Analysis computer program. This program measures different degrees of similarity between variables, and the results are shown in a dendogram (see Fig. 7.) The purpose of the analysis was to see whether there were distinct sub-groups of magistrates sharing particular attributes. If there were we should have examined whether their pattern of sentencing varied. In fact Figure 7 shows that almost no clustering occurred—except

FIGURE 7

DENDOGRAM DESCRIBING CLUSTERING OF BACKGROUND
ATTRIBUTES ON MAGISTRATES

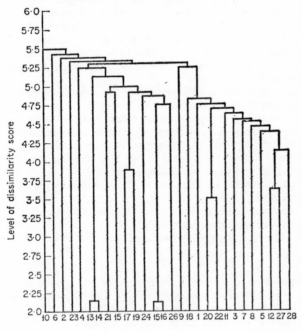

for some variables which obviously measured roughly the same thing—such as being a member of the Magistrates' Association and reading *The Magistrate*, (variables 13 and 14). The Cluster Analysis program was kindly made available by Dr Sibson of King's College, Cambridge. The method of analysis is described in reference 1.

(c) *Measurement of consistency of a magistrate's sentencing behaviour.* The consistency of a magistrate's sentencing behaviour over several offences was measured for each group of magistrates separately, and over the research offences only. Kendall's coefficient of concordance was used to test a magistrate's consistency in fining or disqualifying over various groups of offences, i.e., whether a magistrate was relatively severe over all the offences or relatively severe on some and relatively lenient on others. Offences were omitted for which not many or no magistrates had meted out the penalty (i.e. fine or disqualification) we were interested in. For a description of testing consistency using Kendall's coefficient of concordance see reference 2.

The association between the severity of penalties, relative to his group, given by a magistrate for each of the research offences he or she dealt with and corresponding multiple offences was measured for each group separately by Kendall's $\tau$ rank correlation coefficient. The association was measured for length of imprisonment, amount of fine and length of disqualification where appropriate. For a description of this test of association between two variables see reference 3.

The association between amount of fine and length of disqualification (or length of imprisonment and length of disqualification where appropriate) was measured for any particular research offence or multiple offence and for each group separately.

Kendall's $\tau$ rank correlation coefficient was also used to calculate this association.

(d) *Measurement of agreement amongst magistrates on relative seriousness of various offences.* This was measured by Kendall's coefficient of concordance, on the total sample of magistrates, both for the eight motoring offences and for the whole list of nineteen offences.

(e) *Measurement of the relationship between the sentencing behaviour of magistrates and their background variables* (*attributes and attitudes*). The model set up to describe the magistrates' sentencing behaviour in relation to their background was as follows:

For any offence,

1 (a) The decision to imprison or not is related to certain background attributes and attitudes.

(b) Given that the decision has been made to imprison, the length of imprisonment chosen is related to certain background attributes and attitudes which may be different from those in (a).

2 (a) Similarly, the decision to disqualify or not is related to the magistrates' background variables, and

(b) Given that the magistrate disqualifies, the length of disqualification is related to background not necessarily in the same way as in 2(a).

3 Given that a magistrate fines, the amount of fine is related to his background attributes and attitudes.

*No* attempt was made to combine fines and disqualification into one scale, nor fines or imprisonment. To do so would have been arbitrary. Is £20 and one year's disqualification less severe than a fine of over £20, as Rose suggested in a recent study? (Reference 4.) Rose admits that his classification is arbitrary. Another example is his placing of probation as a more severe sentence than a fine of over £20 plus disqualification. It cannot even be argued that imprisonment will always be more severe than a fine. For example, is a fine of £75 less severe than a short prison sentence for a man convicted of driving while disqualified who had already served many short terms in prison?

The preliminary investigation of associations between 'background' and sentencing behaviour was carried out using simple rank correlations and two-way tables. This was done because there were too many variables to put immediately into a logistic regression equation using Maximum Likelihood Methods of estimation. The preliminary analysis would enable us to select those variables where there was an association and leave aside those with no statistical association. Any alternative regression analysis using least squares methods would have involved assumptions about the normality of the distribution of the dependent variable (the penalties) which would not have been justified.

The following analysis was carried out for each group separately:

(i) Associations between whether a magistrate imprisoned or not and background, and whether a magistrate disqualified or not and background, were measured. If the background variable was categorical a chi-square test of significance on a two-way table was used. If the background variable was continuous the Mann-Whitney U-test was carried out to test the difference in the values of the variable between the two populations of those imprisoning and those not imprisoning, or of those disqualifying or not disqualifying. A description of the Mann-Whitney U-test can be found in reference 5.

(ii) Associations between length of imprisonment, or length of disqualification, or amount of fine and background variable were measured. If the background variable was continuous Kendall's $\tau$ rank correlation coefficient was applied to measure the association. If the background variable was categorical then for each type of penalty the magistrates were divided into two categories, those who gave a penalty below the median penalty for their group, and those who gave a penalty above the median penalty. Two-way tables of these categorized variables against background were computed and all chi squared tests of significance carried out on these tables. Some information is lost in categorizing penalties in this way, but since for most cases there was a high proportion of ties in the penalties given not much information was lost. Also this high proportion of ties can reduce the power of other methods of measuring these associations which do not involve categorizing the penalties, such as the Mann-Whitney U-test where the background variable has two categories, and the non-parametric analysis of variance where the background variable has more than two categories. The background variables are listed in the Annexe below.

(f) *Measurement of the association between how serious of its kind a magistrate regards an offence and his background.* The association was found to be significant or not by using chi-square tests of significance on two-way tables. Background variables which were continuous were categorized in the same way as for the cluster analysis.

(g) *Measurement of the effect of bench membership on penalty.* The penalty a magistrate gave was categorized in the way explained above. Two-way tables were drawn up for each of the eight kinds of offence comparing the fines, imprisonment and disqualifications given by the members of different benches, e.g.

*Dangerous driving*

|  | *Fine below median* | *Fine above median* | *Total* |
|---|---|---|---|
| Bench 1 | 7 | 1 | 8 |
| Bench 2 | 9 | 12 | 12 |
| Bench 3 | 5 | 9 | 14 |
| Bench 4 | 13 | 8 | 21 |
| etc. | | | |

The five groups of magistrates dealing with any kind of offence were combined so that the variety of cases were lumped together. Also only benches with ten or more members (although fewer may have actually sentenced any particular case) were included. This was done in order to avoid having too many small expected values in the cells of the table.

There was little danger of confounding the effect of bench membership with the effect of magistrates receiving particular types of any kind of offence because the cases were assigned to magistrates at each bench in random order, and so roughly equal numbers at each bench dealt with each case. The chi-squared test of significance was used in this analysis.

(h) *The measurement of the effect of bench on how serious a magistrate considers an offence of its kind.* This analysis was carried out by the same method as in the previous section. The three categories 'not serious', 'serious' and 'very serious' were combined to form two categories by taking the category with the least numbers in it (either the 'not serious' or 'very serious' category, depending on the offence) and combining it with the 'serious' category. This gives each magistrate a 'score' relative to his group. The three categories were collapsed into two in order not to let the expected values in each cell become too small.

(i) *Further analysis of the effect of background on penalty.* For each of the eight types of offence and each kind of penalty any variables which had an effect on the penalty in any group were included in a further analysis on the whole sample of the five groups of magistrates combined.

This analysis used the logistic regression model which is of the form

$$\log\left(\frac{p}{1-p}\right) = \alpha_1 x_1 + \alpha_2 x_2 + \ldots + \alpha_n x_n$$

where p = probability of some event and the n's are background variables (continuous or discrete). The coefficients $\alpha_i$, i = 1 to n are estimated from the data by the method of Maximum Likelihood. See reference 6 for a description of this method, which does not involve making any assumptions on the distributions of any of the variables.

In applying this model to the data on sentencing, for any offence p becomes the probability of a magistrate disqualifying, or the probability of a magistrate disqualifying below or above the median for his group, or the probability of a magistrate imprisoning, or the probability of a magistrate fining below or above the median fine for his group. The categorical background variables are dealt with by setting up dummy variables which are binary. See reference 6 for a description of this process.

In each analysis the coefficients $\alpha_i$, i = 1 to n which are estimated can be tested to see whether they are significantly greater than zero, in which case the corresponding variable has a significant effect on p. The fit of the model to the data can also be tested.

The group that the magistrate belonged to was always included as a background variable so that the effect of the individual case of any kind of offence could be controlled for.

REFERENCES

1. S. Jardine and R. Sibson (1968, 'A model for taxonomy', *Mathematical Biosciences*, 2, 465–82.
2. S. Siegel (1956), *Non-parametric statistics for the behavioral sciences*, New York, McGraw-Hill, 229–38.
3. Ibid., 213–23.
4. G. Rose (1965), 'An  experimental study of sentencing', *Brit. J. Criminol.*, 5, 314–19.
5. Siegel, op. cit., 116–27.
6. D. R. Cox (1970), *Analysis of binary data*, London, Methuen Statistical Monograph.
7. N. R. Draper and H. Smith (1966), *Applied regression analysis*, New York, Wiley, 134–41.

*Annexe to Notes on Statistical Methods; Variables Used in the Analysis*

*Variable relating to Personal Background* (the detailed questions are in the Questionnaire, Appendix I).
Bench, number of,
Geographical location of bench: north, midlands, south
Size of population served by bench
Bench membership sampled or not
Age
Sex
Years on bench
Chairman or deputy chairman/neither
Sits in juvenile court or not
Takes chair in adult court, regularly, occasionally, never
Retired/not
If female, whether has occupation or not
Occupational classification (Registrar General's)
Type of secondary school attended
Age left school
Full-time higher education or not
Member of Magistrates' Association or not
Reads *The Magistrate* regularly or not
Car-owner or not
Amount of driving
Reads motoring journal or not
Self-rating as a driver
Car-club member or not
Accident record
Responsible for an accident or not
Personal injuries involved in an accident or not
Attitude towards a court decision—fair or not


*Background attitude and personality measurements*
Member of a political party or not
Voting preference
Extraversion–introversion score
Neuroticism–stability score
Score on lie-scale
Radical–conservative attitude score
Tough–tender-mindedness score


*Attitudes towards penalties, motoring offences and offenders*
Use basic penalty
Use legal maximum as a basis for fining

Take income into account or not (serious offence)
Take income into account or not (minor offence)
Take income into account where one offender rich and the other 'comfortably off', or not
Use of adding-up method in multiple charges
Allow time to pay in general good or bad
Mitigate fine with costs £10 or not
Mitigate fine with costs £20 or not
Approve of Magistrates' Courts Act procedure or not
Attitude towards guilty pleas by letter for careless driving
Information on indictable previous convictions wanted or not
Estimate of proportion of serious motoring offences with previous convictions
Are serious motoring offenders 'criminals' or not?
Are majority convicted of each offence (listed) criminal—for a first offence, or a second offence—or not?
Should driver take a new test or not? (asked for each offence)
Should drivers be automatically disqualified after three endorsements in three years or not?
Circumstances justifying not disqualifying
In favour of higher maximum penalties or not
In favour of wider use of disqualification or not
In favour of separate traffic courts or not
In favour of on-the-spot fines for minor offences or not
Opinion on the optimum period of disqualification appropriate for each offence
Rank given to each of the nineteen offences on questionnaire
Proportion rated 'antisocial' on the 'types of offender' questionnaire
Rank given to the seriousness of each offence sentenced
Whether wanted more information in each case
Whether would retire in each case


## 2. *Analysing the Information Game*

The information game is described on pages 120 to 123. All 25 'benches' dealt with the same case but their initial penalty varied. Eleven started at £50, six at £40, three at £30 and one even at £15. Similarly some started at two years' disqualification, others at 18 months and the bulk at one year. We therefore had to find a way of comparing the size of increased fines and disqualifications given with each new item of information which would take into account the fact that the size of the increase would be related to the initial starting point. For example, an increase from £50 to £60 might be considered equivalent to an increase from £15 to £20. We decided to tackle the problem empirically. The 'jumps' in fine made by benches with different starting points were plotted and a value given to each jump. Although the system was bound to be arbitrary it reflected the

pattern or stages in amounts chosen. For example, those who began at
£50 usually went next to £60 and then to £75 and £100. The jump to £60
was given a score of 1, to £75, 2, to £100, 3; those who chose £70 got a
score of 1·5. Similarly, those who began at £30 went to £40, £50, £75 and
£100 in that order and were scored, 1, 2, 3 and 4. Thus a £100 fine for a
bench starting at £30 had a higher score than the same fine given by a
bench starting at £50. In the same way those who started at £25 had a
score of 4·5 when they reached £100. Exactly the same system was used
for analysing disqualifications.

| Bench | Change 1 | | Change 2 | |
|---|---|---|---|---|
| | Fine | Disq. | Fine | Disq. |
| 1 | 1·5 | 0 | 7 | 4 |
| 2 | 0 | 0 | 2·5 | 4 |
| 3 | 2·5 | 1 | 3·5 | 3 |
| 4 | 2 | 0 | 4 | 4 |
| 5 | 0 | 4 | 4 | 4 |
| 6 | 2 | 2 | 5·5 | 4 |
| 7 | 1 | 0 | 5·5 | 5 |
| 8 | 0 | 1 | 3 | 4 |
| 9 | 0 | 0 | 3·5 | 3 |
| 10 | 1 | 0 | 3·5 | 4 |
| 11 | 0 | 0 | 6 | 4·5 |
| 12 | 2·5 | 0·5 | 3 | 3·5 |
| 13 | 5 | 3 | 5 | 3 |
| 14 | 1 | 0 | 3 | 4 |
| 15 | 5·5 | 1 | 3 | 2·5 |
| 16 | 0 | 1 | 3 | 4 |
| 17 | 0 | 0 | 3 | 4 |
| 18 | 4·5 | 0 | 5·5 | 3 |
| 19 | 1·5 | 2 | 3 | 4 |
| 20 | 3 | 2 | 2 | 2 |
| 21 | 0 | 0 | 3 | 2·5 |
| 22 | 0 | 0 | 4·5 | 2·5 |
| 23 | 0 | 0·5 | 3 | 2·5 |
| 24 | 0 | 1·5 | 3 | 3·5 |
| 25 | 5 | 1 | 6 | 3 |

NOTE: The range of disqualification covered by one 'jump' is much wider than
a 'jump' in the fine.

For example, a jump of 2 from 12 months' disqualification would be an
increase from 1 year to 2, a jump of 4 would be from 1 year to 4. On the other
hand a jump in fine of 2 would be equivalent to an increase from £30–£50, and 4,
£30–£100.

Thus for each item put to magistrates they could record 'no change' and score '0', or a change in fine and/or disqualification and score according to the amount they 'jumped'. The sign test (see Siegel, pages 68–75) was used to compare the changes produced by the introduction of two different items of information. This test shows whether a change in a positive (or negative) direction is significant.

This system of scoring and the variability in response is illustrated by two examples below.

*Change* 1 was from 'no accident' to 'if on ignoring the red traffic lights the defendant had smashed into the side of a car travelling across the green lights and as a consequence the driver of that car was seriously injured so that he was detained in hospital for nine months and suffered permanent disablement, what would your decision be?'

*Change* 2 was from no previous convictions to:

2½ years ago Drunken driving Fined £75, Disqualified 2 years, plus costs.
6 months ago Careless driving Fined £30, Licence endorsed, plus costs.

# Tables

1. *Comparing decisions in the cases heard in court with those reached in the research situation*

*Introductory Notes*

(a) The matching of cases used in the research with a group of cases heard in court could only be done at a 'crude' level (see Chapter 2, page 35).

(b) In some of the cases given to magistrates there was only one charge; for example, dangerous driving. But in others the offender had been charged with more than one offence; for example, dangerous driving, having no driving licence, and failure to have third-party insurance. When this occurred two decisions were separately analysed; the penalty for the 'research offence' (always the major charge and, in this case, dangerous driving) and the penalty for all the charges added together—the total, or overall, penalty. We only compared the penalties for the *research offence* in the cases sent to magistrates with the penalty for the research offence in the cases heard in court because, of course, in some court cases the list of multiple charges could have varied substantially, thus affecting the total penalty.

(c) Some of the less serious cases included in the study could occur as subsidiary charges to more serious offences. For example, charges of having no insurance occurred in conjunction with driving while disqualified; some offences of failing to stop after an accident were charges subsidiary to careless driving. In these cases the penalty for the subsidiary charge was not analysed separately. Thus the discussion of no insurance, careless driving, failing to stop, etc., centres on cases where these were the *principal* charges.

(d) As the matching of one individual case with some dealt with in court was done on a crude basis, it would have been surprising if the distribution of decisions made by about 100 magistrates in one case was *exactly* the same as the distribution recorded for many benches dealing with a variety of cases—only similar to the research case in three respects. On the other hand, it was hoped that any variation in sentences in the research 'game' would approximate variations found in the courts. Sometimes the range of decisions in one of the cases—for example, one of those of driving while disqualified—differed markedly from the range found for the matched court cases, owing to the peculiar problem of the case. But it was considered that a fair test of the similarities and differences

228

between research and 'real-life' decisions would be a comparison of the distribution of all 500 decisions on the five types of one kind of offence with the distribution for all the decisions in the court cases that matched those five types.

TABLE 1

MEAN FINES AND CO-EFFICIENT OF VARIATION*:
REAL AND RESEARCH OFFENCES COMPARED

| | Mean Fine (£) | Co-efficient (%) | N for Real Cases |
|---|---|---|---|
| **Dangerous driving** | | | |
| Real | 22·5 | 38·6 | 166 |
| Research | 27·2 | 45·4 | |
| **Drunken driving** | | | |
| Real | 30·8 | 45·9 | 277 |
| Research | 33·3 | 40·9 | |
| **Driving while disqualified** | | | |
| Real | 22·9 | 58·1 | 76 |
| Research | 22·2 | 46·4 | |
| **Careless driving** | | | |
| Real | 11·1 | 54·0 | 449 |
| Research | 17·5 | 71·3 | |
| **No insurance** | | | |
| Real | 8·6 | 56·2 | 179 |
| Research | 12·5 | 47·5 | |
| **Failure to stop or report** | | | |
| Real | 8·6 | 69·4 | 149 |
| Research | 8·9 | 56·1 | |
| **Speeding** | | | |
| Real | 6·0 | 46·3 | 1,000 |
| Research | 10·7 | 78·5 | |
| **Pedestrian-crossing offences** | | | |
| Real | 4·6 | 54·8 | 206 |
| Research | 6·9 | 57·0 | |

* The co-efficient of variation is the $\dfrac{\text{Standard Deviation}}{\text{Mean}}$ Expressed as a percentage it is multiplied by 100. The coefficient is a useful measure of the *range* of fines in two different samples because it takes into account the size of the mean. For example, the higher the average fine the greater the range is likely to be. If it is £50 the next amount to be chosen will be £60 or £75, whereas when the average is £10 the next number chosen is only likely to be £15 or, at the outside, £20.

TABLE 2

MEAN PERIODS OF DISQUALIFICATION AND CO-EFFICIENTS
OF VARIATION: REAL AND RESEARCH OFFENCES COMPARED
(excluding those not disqualified)

|  | Mean Period (months) | Co-efficient (%) |
|---|---|---|
| Dangerous driving | | |
| Real | 10·0 | 127·3 |
| Research | 13·8 | 80·6 |
| Drunken driving | | |
| Real | 16·6 | 60·8 |
| Research | 15·0 | 59·2 |
| Driving while disqualified | | |
| Real | 30·0 | 116·0 |
| Research | 22·6 | 60·2 |
| Careless driving | | |
| Real | 6·9 | 124·2 |
| Research | 5·5 | 103·7 |
| No insurance | | |
| Real | 8·9 | 103·9 |
| Research | 6·2 | 68·3 |

NOTE: In the other offences too few were disqualified to make comparisons meaningful.

TABLE 3. NOTE:

These are the fines for the *main* charge only. The range for the total penalties in multiple charge cases was greater (see page 135).

Statutory maximum penalties for serious road traffic offences are shown in the chart on pages 234–235.

[1] The numbers of magistrates who were sentencing cases in each group were: A, 109; B, 105; C, 110; D, 107; E, 107; Total = 538.
As not all answered every case the number actually 'sentenced' varied over cases within each group.
[2] See Col. 3 for the range included.
[3] See Chapter 7, page 128 for a discussion of why these figures were chosen.
[4] There was a wider range for the joint offence of failing to stop *and* report, namely £5–£45.
[5] In this case 31 magistrates ordered a discharge (28 absolute discharge, 3 conditional discharge).

TABLE 3

THE RANGE OF FINES IMPOSED ON THE CASES
SENT TO MAGISTRATES

| Case[1] | Mean Fine (£) Col. 1 | Standard Deviation (£) Col. 2 | Range Imposed (£) Col. 3 | Largest number giving same fine (Fine in parentheses) Col. 4 | Number who fined near the mode[2] Col. 5 | Range near mode[3] (£20 or £25 or £30) Col. 6 |
|---|---|---|---|---|---|---|
| **Dangerous driving** | | | | | | |
| A | 34·6 | 13·4 | 5–100 | 25(£30) | 56 | 20–25–30 |
| B | 21·6 | 9·2 | 5–50 | 32(£20) | 61 | 15–20–25 |
| C | 27·4 | 9·6 | 10–60 | 31(£25) | 80 | 20–25–30 |
| D | 20·0 | 8·7 | 5–50 | 27(£20) | 62 | 15–20–25 |
| E | 32·5 | 13·1 | 0–75 | 24(£30) | 58 | 20–25–30 |
| **Drunken driving** | | | | | | |
| A | 38·6 | 14·0 | 5–100 | 38(£50) | 38 | 45–50–55 |
| B | 34·0 | 13·6 | 10–70 | 29(£50) | 53 | 20–25–30 |
| C | 31·0 | 13·0 | 0–50 | 34(£25) | 55 | 20–25–30 |
| D | 29·0 | 12·9 | 0–70 | 26(£25) | 62 | 20–25–30 |
| E | 33·7 | 12·7 | 10–75 | 27(£50) | 54 | 20–25–30 |
| **Careless driving** | | | | | | |
| A | 16·5 | 5·6 | 3–40 | 39(£15) | 87 | 10–15–20 |
| B | 27·1 | 20·3 | 0–100 | 25(£20) | 53 | 10–15–20 |
| C | 12·8 | 5·2 | 0–30 | 40(£10) | 89 | 5–10–15 |
| D | 11·2 | 5·3 | 3–30 | 42(£10) | 88 | 5–10–15 |
| E | 20·0 | 11·4 | 5–100 | 30(£20) | 76 | 10–15–20 |
| **No insurance** | | | | | | |
| A | 9·7 | 5·0 | 0–25 | 39(£10) | 86 | 5–10–15 |
| B | 13·7 | 7·3 | 3–50 | 35(£10) | 73 | 5–10–15 |
| C | 12·5 | 5·2 | 0–30 | 48(£10) | 84 | 5–10–15 |
| D | 13·0 | 5·7 | 2–40 | 49(£10) | 87 | 5–10–15 |
| E | 13·6 | 5·5 | 3–30 | 37(£10) | 78 | 5–10–15 |
| **Failure to stop or report** | | | | | | |
| A | 8·3 | 4·3 | 3–20 | 38(£5) | 85 | 3– 5–10 |
| B | 9·7 | 5·0 | 1–25 | 42(£10) | 86 | 5–10–15 |
| C[4] | 11·0 | 5·6 | 3–25 | 34(£10) | 86 | 5–10–15 |
| D[5] | 5·5 | 3·9 | 1–30 | 38(£5) | 69 | 3– 5–10 |
| E | 8·6 | 4·1 | 2–25 | 40(£10) | 91 | 5–10–15 |
| **Speeding** | | | | | | |
| A | 20·1 | 11·9 | 7–50 | 25(£10) | 53 | 7–10–15 |
| B | 6·6 | 3·0 | 2–20 | 48(£5) | 72 | 3– 5– 7 |
| C | 6·6 | 2·5 | 2–15 | 38(£5) | 71 | 3– 5– 7 |
| D | 9·0 | 5·1 | 4–50 | 33(£10) | 52 | 8–10–12 |
| E | 11·4 | 6·9 | 4–50 | 31(£10) | 49 | 8–10–12 |
| **Pedestrian-crossing offences** | | | | | | |
| A | 6·1 | 3·4 | 2–15 | 53(£5) | 75 | 3– 5– 7 |
| B | 8·1 | 4·0 | 2–20 | 42(£10) | 48 | 8–10–12 |
| C | 5·3 | 2·8 | 2–20 | 50(£5) | 81 | 3– 5– 7 |
| D | 9·1 | 4·4 | 3–25 | 44(£10) | 50 | 8–10–12 |
| E | 5·8 | 3·5 | 1–20 | 43(£5) | 68 | 3– 5– 7 |

## TABLE 4

### SENTENCES FOR DRIVING WHILE DISQUALIFIED CASES

| | Number Fined | Number Imprisoned | Number committed to Q.S. | Other | Range of fines (£) | Range of Imprisonment (months) | Number giving same fine | Number giving same imprisonment | Total |
|---|---|---|---|---|---|---|---|---|---|
| Case A | 18 | 53 | 23 | 10 | 5–50 | 3–6 | 12 | 40 | 104 |
| B | 77 | 24 | 0 | 0 | 10–50 | 2–6 | 50 | 10 | 103 |
| C | 21 | 73 | 6 | 4 | 10–50 | 1–6 | 13 | 42 | 104 |
| D | 78 | 18 | 0 | 6 | 5–50 | 3–6 | 41 | 14 | 102 |
| E | 6 | 71 | 14 | 7 | 5–50 | 1–6 | 2 | 48 | 98 |

## TABLE 5

### OPTIMUM PERIODS FOR DISQUALIFICATION

|  | Number disqualifying (where at least 10) | Range imposed* (months) | Maximum number giving same length | % | Period largest number gave (months) |
|---|---|---|---|---|---|
| *Dangerous driving* | | | | | |
| A | 61 | 3–24 | 25 | 41 | 12 |
| B | 16 | 1–12 | 7 | 44 | 2 |
| C | 80 | 1–60 | 34 | 43 | 12 |
| D | 74 | 2–36 | 37 | 50 | 12 |
| E | 92 | 2–60 | 28 | 30 | 24 |
| *Drunken driving* | | | | | |
| A | 100 | 6–60 | 39 | 39 | 12 |
| B | 96 | 1–18 | 83 | 86 | 12 |
| C | 82 | 6–24 | 66 | 81 | 12 |
| D | 84 | 6–36 | 64 | 76 | 12 |
| E | 98 | 6–36 | 74 | 76 | 12 |
| *Driving while disqualified* | | | | | |
| A | 66 | 12–72 | 16 | 24 | 12 |
| B | 82 | 6–60 | 30 | 37 | 24 |
| C | 89 | 3–60 | 29 | 33 | 12 |
| D | 93 | 3–60 | 44 | 47 | 12 |
| E | 69 | 6–72 | 25 | 36 | 12 |
| *Careless driving* | | | | | |
| B | 50 | 2–60 | 15 | 30 | 6 & 12 |
| E | 31 | 1–24 | 11 | 36 | Until test |
| *No insurance* | | | | | |
| A | 48 | 2–24 | 22 | 46 | 6 |
| B | 36 | 1–12 | 13 | 36 | 2 |
| C | 51 | 2–12 | 23 | 45 | 6 |
| D | 27 | 2–12 | 12 | 44 | 6 |
| E | 22 | 1–12 | 10 | 46 | 6 |
| *Speeding* | | | | | |
| A | 31 | 1–24 | 10 | 32 | 6 |

* Not including 'until test' or 'life'.

# CHART OF MAXIMUM PENALTIES

From Oyez Table No. 11. *Penalties etc. for the more frequent Road Traffic Offences*, compiled by J. L. Wood, London, Oyez Publns. 1963.

| Offence | Penalty on Summary Conviction | Endorsement R.T.A. 1962 s.7 | Disqualification R.T.A. 1962 s.5 | | Remarks |
|---------|------------------------------|------------------------------|----------------------------------|--|---------|
| | | | First | Second or subsequent | |
| 1. Driving while disqualified | 6 months or £50 or both | Yes, but need not if no disqualification and special reasons | Not less than 12 months unless special reasons | (a) Not less than 12 months unless special reasons and: (b) in any case (unless mitigating circumstances) not less than 6 months additional if, since 9th May, 1963, convicted twice of an endorsed disqualifiable offence within the previous 3 years. Any disqualification must be consecutive to any previous current disqualification | May be disqualified until has passed test. Disqualification cannot be ordered for obtaining a licence whilst disqualified [s.110 (a)] |
| 2. Driving or attempting to drive when unfit through drink or drugs | 1st: £100 or 4 months or both. 2nd or subsequent: £100 or 6 months or both | Yes, but need not if no disqualification and special reasons | Not less than 12 months unless special reasons | Not less than 12 months unless special reasons but not less than 3 years if convicted of same offence within 10 years and as 1(b) above | May be disqualified until has passed test |

| Offence | Penalty | | | | |
|---|---|---|---|---|---|
| 3. Driving recklessly or dangerously | 1st: £100 or 4 months or both. 2nd or subsequent: £100 or 6 months or both | Yes, but need not if no disqualification and special reasons | Discretion | Not less than 12 months if committed within 3 years of previous conviction for same offence, or conviction for causing death by dangerous driving, and as 1(b) above | May be disqualified until has passed test |
| 4. Driving without due care and attention or without reasonable consideration | 1st: £100. 2nd or subsequent: £100 or 3 months or both | Yes, but need not if no disqualification and special reasons | Discretion | (a) Discretion: but (b) in any case (unless mitigating circumstances) not less than 6 months additional, if, since 29th May, 1963, convicted twice of an endorsed disqualifiable offence without previous 3 years | May be disqualified until has passed test |
| 5. Using without Policy of Insurance | £50 or 3 months or both | Yes, but need not if no disqualification and special reasons | Discretion | As 4 above | May be disqualified until has passed test |
| 6. Accident: 1. Failing to report 2. Failing to stop after | £50 or 3 months | Yes, but need not if no disqualification and special reasons | Discretion | As 4 above | May be disqualified until has passed test |
| 7. Pedestrian Crossings: Failure to comply with Regulations as to | £50 | Yes, but need not if no disqualification and special reasons | Discretion | As 4 above | May be disqualified until has passed test |
| 8. Exceeding Speed Limit | £50 | Yes, but need not if no disqualification and special reasons | Discretion | As 4 above | |

TABLE 6
SERIOUSNESS AND 'COMPLEXITY' RATINGS
GIVEN FOR EACH CASE (%)*

| | | Seriousness rating | | | Retire-ment | Need more information | Proportion likely agreement | | |
|---|---|---|---|---|---|---|---|---|---|
| | | Very serious | Serious | Not serious | Would retire | Wants information | All | Most | Some and none |
| Dangerous driving | A | 43·3 | 50·0 | 6·7 | 87·5 | 65·0 | 28·9 | 56·7 | 17·5 |
| | B | 55·9 | 58·4 | 35·6 | 63·7 | 14·4 | 26·0 | 54·0 | 20·0 |
| | C | 37·7 | 55·7 | 6·6 | 78·9 | 46·6 | 27·8 | 61·9 | 14·4 |
| | D | 38·6 | 57·4 | 4·0 | 75·3 | 28·0 | 30·6 | 62·4 | 15·3 |
| | E | 30·0 | 67·0 | 3·0 | 91·0 | 26·8 | 16·9 | 75·3 | 22·1 |
| Drunken driving | A | 52·9 | 46·2 | 0·1 | 74·8 | 24·2 | 26·8 | 57·7 | 18·6 |
| | B | 27·5 | 59·8 | 12·8 | 65·7 | 29·1 | 36·0 | 55·1 | 15·7 |
| | C | 36·9 | 53·4 | 9·7 | 86·8 | 26·3 | 17·8 | 63·3 | 26·7 |
| | D | 23·8 | 55·5 | 20·8 | 87·0 | 53·1 | 18·1 | 78·3 | 13·3 |
| | E | 29·7 | 57·4 | 12·9 | 85·0 | 32·3 | 22·9 | 66·3 | 20·5 |
| Driving while disqualified | A | 61·2 | 36·9 | 2·0 | 94·0 | 16·3 | 28·7 | 56·3 | 23·0 |
| | B | 52·5 | 47·5 | 8·0 | 96·0 | 38·0 | 18·1 | 68·7 | 22·9 |
| | C | 75·0 | 25·0 | 0·0 | 97·1 | 12·4 | 23·0 | 62·1 | 24·1 |
| | D | 41·2 | 52·9 | 5·9 | 77·5 | 49·0 | 26·7 | 61·6 | 19·8 |
| | E | 82·8 | 15·2 | 2·0 | 95·9 | 44·9 | 30·6 | 66·7 | 19·4 |
| Careless driving | A | 2·0 | 54·9 | 43·1 | 51·0 | 46·5 | 35·4 | 55·2 | 10·4 |
| | B | 21·6 | 56·9 | 21·6 | 88·2 | 36·1 | 21·2 | 56·5 | 31·8 |
| | C | 0·1 | 43·9 | 55·1 | 34·0 | 14·6 | 43·9 | 52·0 | 8·2 |
| | D | 0·1 | 27·7 | 71·3 | 64·4 | 42·6 | 35·7 | 54·8 | 19·0 |
| | E | 12·8 | 66·7 | 20·6 | 31·9 | 13·3 | 39·1 | 49·0 | 16·3 |
| No insurance | A | 2·0 | 66·7 | 30·4 | 30·0 | 25·8 | 37·4 | 49·5 | 13·1 |
| | B | 4·9 | 59·8 | 35·3 | 33·3 | 33·7 | 37·6 | 62·4 | 9·4 |
| | C | 14·3 | 62·9 | 22·9 | 66·7 | 21·6 | 27·8 | 58·9 | 21·1 |
| | D | 3·0 | 44·6 | 52·5 | 21·2 | 26·3 | 49·5 | 43·2 | 9·5 |
| | E | 3·0 | 59·0 | 38·0 | 30·0 | 19·6 | 38·9 | 54·4 | 11·1 |
| Failure to stop or report | A | 1·0 | 28·6 | 70·4 | 14·9 | 24·7 | 39·6 | 52·1 | 8·3 |
| | B | 1·0 | 22·5 | 76·5 | 4·0 | 19·2 | 47·4 | 44·3 | 8·2 |
| | C | 4·9 | 56·9 | 38·2 | 32·0 | 43·7 | 31·6 | 55·8 | 15·8 |
| | D | 0·0 | 4·1 | 95·9 | 25·5 | 12·1 | 41·8 | 49·5 | 13·2 |
| | E | 0·0 | 16·2 | 83·8 | 8·2 | 3·3 | 54·4 | 42·2 | 7·8 |
| Speeding | A | 8·8 | 67·7 | 23·5 | 55·5 | 39·0 | 24·2 | 61·5 | 19·8 |
| | B | 0·0 | 8·0 | 92·0 | 3·9 | 12·4 | 65·3 | 32·7 | 2·0 |
| | C | 0·0 | 11·5 | 88·5 | 4·8 | 20·8 | 69·6 | 29·4 | 1·0 |
| | D | 0·0 | 26·5 | 73·5 | 2·0 | 14·0 | 60·0 | 38·0 | 2·0 |
| | E | 1·0 | 43·6 | 55·5 | 6·0 | 8·5 | 49·5 | 43·2 | 9·5 |
| Pedestrian-crossing offences | A | 0·0 | 13·9 | 86·1 | 6·8 | 6·3 | 48·0 | 50·0 | 4·1 |
| | B | 3·0 | 43·4 | 53·5 | 21·2 | 31·6 | 47·4 | 40·0 | 14·7 |
| | C | 0·0 | 18·3 | 81·7 | 3·9 | 4·0 | 62·2 | 37·8 | 3·1 |
| | D | 3·9 | 43·7 | 52·4 | 12·8 | 21·0 | 50·6 | 49·4 | 8·1 |
| | E | 1·0 | 11·3 | 87·6 | 4·2 | 4·3 | 54·4 | 42·2 | 5·6 |

* Of those answering these questions. No Information cases are excluded. N
for every case was approximately 100.

# Bibliography

Major books, articles and reports referred to in the text

APPLETON, G. L. (1969), 'Special reasons', *The Magistrate*, *25*, 54.

BEASHEL, J. F. (1970), 'Disqualification pending test', *The Magistrate*, *26*, 35.

BECKER, H. (1963), *Outsiders*, The Free Press of Glencoe.

BLONDEL, J. (1963), *Voters, parties and leaders*, London, Pelican Books.

BRAYSHAW, A. J. (1967), 'Hard case', *The Magistrate*, *23*, 54.

BRAYSHAW, A. J. (1967), 'Motoring fines and costs: the jigsaw puzzle', *The Magistrate*, *23*, 121.

BROWN, R. (1965), *Social psychology*, New York, Macmillan.

BUTLER, D. E. and KING, R. (1966), *The British general election of 1966*, London, Macmillan.

CARTER, R. M. (1967), 'The pre-sentence report and the decision making process', *J. Research in Cr. and Delinq.*, *4*, 203.

CHAPMAN, D. (1968), *Sociology and the stereotype of the criminal*, London, Tavistock.

COHEN, J. and PRESTON, B. (1968), *Causes and prevention of road accidents*, London, Faber & Faber.

COUNCIL OF THE LAW SOCIETY (1965), Memorandum on *Motoring offences*.

COUNCIL OF THE LAW SOCIETY (1967), Memorandum on *Practice and procedure in magistrates' courts*.

DEVLIN, K. W. (1970), *Sentencing offenders in magistrates' courts*, London, Sweet & Maxwell.

DEVLIN, K. W. (1971), *Sentencing offenders in magistrates' courts* (a study of legal factors affecting the sentencing process), School of Social Sciences, Brunel University, *mimeo*.

ELLIOTT, D. W. and STREET, H. (1968), *Road accidents*, London, Penguin Books.

EYSENCK, H. J. (1954), *The psychology of politics*, London, Routledge.

EYSENCK, H. J. and EYSENCK, S. B. G. (1964), *Manual of the Eysenck personality inventory*, University of London Press.

FITZGERALD, P. J. (1966), Review of *Criminal on the road*, *Law Q. Rev.*, *82*, 121.

FITZGERALD, P. J. (1969), 'Road traffic law as the lawyer sees it', in Leeming, J. J., *Road accidents, prevent or punish?* London, Cassell, 161–75.

GREEN, E. (1961), *Judicial attitudes in sentencing*, London, Macmillan.

HARRIS, B. (1969), *The criminal jurisdiction of magistrates*, London' Butterworth.

HOGARTH, J. (1967), Sentencing research—some problems of design, *Brit. J. Criminol.*, 7, 84.

HOGARTH, J. (1971), *Sentencing as a human process*, University of Toronto Press.

HOME OFFICE (1970), Report of the Advisory Council on the Penal System on *Non-custodial and semi-custodial penalties*, H.M.S.O.

HOME OFFICE, *Offences relating to motor vehicles*, H.M.S.O. (annually).

HOOD, R. G. (1962), *Sentencing in magistrates' courts*, London, Stevens.

HOOD, R. G. (1967), 'Research on the effectiveness of punishments and treatments', in *Collected Studies in Criminological Research*, 1, Strasbourg, Council of Europe.

HOOD, R. G. and SPARKS, R. F. (1970), *Key issues in criminology*. London, World University Library.

JARVIS, F. V. (1965), 'Inquiry before sentence', in Grygier, T. et al. (eds.), *Criminology in transition*, London, Tavistock.

JUSTICE OF THE PEACE (1970), 'Consistency of penalties in traffic cases', *134*, 243.

LEEMING, J. J. (1969), *Road accidents, prevent or punish*? London, Cassell.

LEMMON, N. F. (1971), *The use of information by magistrates in sentencing*, Report to the Nuffield Foundation, *mimeo*.

MAGISTRATES' ASSOCIATION, *Annual reports*.

MANNHEIM, H. (1958), 'Some aspects of judicial sentencing policy', *Yale Law J.*, 67, 961.

MECHAM, G. D. (1968), 'Proceed with caution: which penalties slow down the juvenile traffic violator?' *Crime and delinquency*, 14, 142.

MERTON, R. K. (1957), *Social theory and social structure*. The Free Press of Glencoe.

MIDDENDORF, W. (1968), 'Is there a relationship between traffic offences and common crimes?' *Int. Criminal Police Review*, No. 214 (January 1968), 4.

MORRIS, T. (1966), 'The social toleration of crime', in Klare, H. J. (ed.), *Changing concepts of crime and its treatment*, London, Pergamon.

MORRISH, P. J. (1970), 'Should traffic offences be classed as crime?' *Justice of the Peace*, 134, 361.

MUELLER, G. O. (1960), 'How to increase traffic fatalities: a useful guide for modern legislators and traffic courts', *Columbia Law Review*, 60, 944.

NAGEL, S. S. (1961), 'Political party affiliation and judges' decisions', *Amer. Pol. Sci. Rev.*, 55, 843.

NAGEL, S. S. (1963), 'Off-the-bench judicial attitudes', in Schubert, G. (ed.), *Judicial decision-making*, The Free Press of Glencoe.

NEILSON, G. D. (1964), 'Traffic courts should educate while they adjudicate', *Federal Probation*, 28, No. 1, 18.

OWENS, C. M. (1966), *Interim report on the three year study of the effectiveness of the Anaheim-Fullerton Municipal Court Drivers Improvement School*, mimeo.

PARKER, LORD (1970), 'A team spirit', *The Magistrate*, *26*, 186.

PARRY, M. H. (1968), *Aggression on the road*, London, Tavistock.

PATCHETT, K. W. and MCCLEAN, J. D. (1965), 'The power to order new driving tests', *Crim. L. R.*, 265.

*Report of the Interdepartmental Committee on the Business of the Criminal Courts* (1961), H.M.S.O., Cmnd. 1289.

ROSE, G. (1963), 'Can we train the magistracy?' *New Society*, No. 54, 16.

ROSS, L. (1960), 'Traffic law violation: a folk crime', *Social Problems*, *8*, 231.

*Royal Commission on Justice of the Peace 1946-48*, H.M.S.O., Cmd. 7463 (1948): and *Minutes of Evidence*, Appendix 4, H.M.S.O. (1948).

SAMUELS, A. (1969), 'The motoring offender: what can we do about him?' *Crim. L. R.*, 133.

SHOHAM, S. (1959), 'Sentencing policy of criminal courts in Israel', *J. Crim. Law, Criminol. & Police Sci.*, *50*, 327.

SIEGEL, S. (1958), *Non-parametric statistics for the behavioural sciences*, New York, McGraw Hill.

SPARKS, R. F. (1965), 'Sentencing by magistrates: some facts of life', in Halmos, P. (ed.), *Sociological studies in the British penal services* (Sociological Review Monograph No. 9), University of Keele.

STEER, D. J. and CARR-HILL, R. A. (1967), 'The motoring offender— who is he?' *Crim. L. R.*, 214.

*The Training of Justices of the Peace in England and Wales* (1965), H.M.S.O. Cmnd. 2856.

THOMAS, D. A. (1967), 'Sentencing—the basic principles', *Crim. L.R.*, 523.

THOMAS, D. A. (1970), *Principles of sentencing*, London, Heinemann.

WEEKS, R. (1963), 'A formula for uniformity in penalties', *Justice of the Peace*, *127*, 75.

WILKINS, L. T. and CHANDLER, A. (1965), 'Confidence and competence in decision making', *Brit. J. Criminol.*, *5*, 22.

WILKINSON, G. S. (1963), *Road traffic offences* (4th ed.), London, Oyez Publications.

WILLETT, T. C. (1964), *Criminal on the road*, London, Tavistock.

WILLETT, T. C. (1966), 'The motoring offender as a social problem', *Medico Legal J.*, *34*, 150.

WILLETT, T. C. (1966), *Some aspects of a current research on serious motoring offences and offenders*. Paper to National Conference on Research and Teaching in Criminology, *mimeo*.

WILLIAMS, G. (1967), 'Absolute liability in traffic offences', *Crim. L. R.*, 142.

WOOTTON, B. (1959), *Social science and social pathology*, London, Allen & Unwin.

WOOTTON, B. (1963), *Crime and the criminal law*, London, Stevens.

ZEISEL, H. (1969), 'Methodological problems in studies of sentencing', *Law and Society Rev.*, *3*, 621.

# Index